ENSIGN IN ITALY

A story of the Felix Factor: the nine lives of a young Welsh Guards officer who fought in Italy with his regiment from the ruins of Cassino to the Alps.

by
PHILIP BRUTTON

LEO COOPER

London

First published in Great Britain in 1992 by
LEO COOPER
190 Shaftesbury Avenue, London WC2H 8JL
an imprint of
Pen & Sword Books Ltd,
47 Church Street, Barnsley, South Yorkshire S70 2AS

Copyright © Philip Brutton, 1992

A CIP catalogue record for this book is available
from the British Library

ISBN: 0 85052 324 9

Typeset by Yorkshire Web, Barnsley, S. Yorks.
in Plantin 10 point

Printed by
Redwood Press Limited
Melksham, Wiltshire

IN MEMORY
of
Lieutenant I.P. BANKIER
Lance-Sergeant Frank GOODWIN
Guardsman O.J. JONES 62
and
ALL
THOSE WHO FELL IN BATTLE

May They Rest In Peace

CONTENTS

Acknowledgements

In writing this book, my thanks are due to many for help, encouragement and advice. Sir William Deakin germinated the idea and overcame my initial hesitation. John Keegan introduced me to my publisher, Leo Cooper, who, together with Judy Hayter and Beryl Hill, have been my loyal supporters throughout.

Other than those sources quoted in the text, particularly *Welsh Guards at War* by Major L.F. Ellis, essential background has been provided by *The Grenadier Guards 1939-1945* by Nigel Nicolson and Patrick Forbes; *The Coldstream Guards 1920-1946* by Michael Howard and John Sparrow; John Retallack's *The Welsh Guards*; *Cassino* and *The Monastery* both by Fred Majdalany; *Monte Cassino* by Rudolf Böhmler; *Rome '44* by Raleigh Trevelyan; *Monte Cassino* by David Hapgood and David Richardson; *Alex* by Nigel Nicolson; *Neither Fear Nor Hope* by Colonel-General Frido von Senger und Etterlin; *The Gothic Line* by Douglas Orgill; *The Minister and the Massacres* by Nikolai Tolstoy; *War Diaries* by Harold Macmillan; *Macmillan 1891 - 1956* by Alistair Horne; *The Campaign in Italy* by Eric Linklater and *British Military Planning and Aims in 1944*, an essay by David Hunt.

I am grateful to Brigadier Anthony Cowgill for his help, and the evidence he and his team have produced in the Cowgill Report: the signals exchanged at the time in Italy have provided essential historical evidence and background. I would also like to thank Brigadier John Rickett, Regimental Lieutenant-Colonel commanding Welsh Guards, Regimental Sergeant-Major T.D.J. Thorne, Sergeant M.E. Browne and Mr Meiron Ellis of Regimental Headquarters, Welsh Guards, and Drill Sergeant W. Davies 08, formerly Welsh Guards, for their great help, as well as Major Hugh Toler, Coldstream Guards, the Superintending Clerks and orderly room staff of the Grenadier, Coldstream, Scots and Irish Guards. Major Alastair Tower, formerly Coldstream Guards, provided information and performed many acts of kindness.

I was helped and encouraged by Derek Baty, Captain Sir Frederic Bolton, Colonel David Davies-Scourfield, Elizabeth Déchelette, Captain James

Denny, Colonel Archie Fletcher, General Sir David Fraser, George Gariepy, Lady Glynn, Captain Mark Gilbey, Major Frank Homfray, Anne Lambton, George Lees, Anthony Lejeune, Jane Mitchell, Captain Nigel Nicolson, Captain Bryan Pugh, Colonel George Ramsay, Major Michael Rawlence, Lieutenant-Colonel John Retallack, Kenneth Rose, Brigadier Christopher Thursby-Pelham, Count Nikolai Tolstoy, Auberon Waugh and members of my family.

Finally, I wish to express my gratitude to my mother who kept my letters, my daughter Amanda for finding and guarding them after my mother's death, and to Captain Andrew Gibson-Watt who guided me through the minefield of my own mistakes, placed books before me to read, and invited me to stay at Wyecliff where he, Pammie Gibson-Watt and their daughter Rosalind looked after me impeccably, while Tilly told me tales of old Cymru.

Philip Brutton
Paris 1991

Foreword

by
Brigadier Christopher Thursby-Pelham

This is the record by a young officer of his personal experiences as a platoon commander during the war in Italy and its aftermath in Austria. As such, it will be of great interest to those who were there at the time, as well as to students of the human factor in war and the consequences of war.

The 3rd Battalion Welsh Guards, which the author joined as a nineteen-year-old Ensign in the lunar landscape of the ruins of Cassino, had already fought in North Africa and had won Battle Honours at Fondouk and Hammam Lif. It had just completed a successful series of actions on the heights of Monte Cerasola in the heart of the Arunci Mountains, some 12 miles south of Cassino. The appalling conditions experienced by the Battalion whilst holding that vital defensive position are vividly described. It was, therefore, an experienced, confident and battle-hardened Battalion that he joined. He accepted the situation and learned quickly.

His ability to evoke memories of those days makes this book exceptional. By his lucid description of his surroundings; the relationship between officers, warrant officers, non-commissioned officers and guardsmen; the comradeship between them, based on mutual trust and the acceptance of each other's strengths and weaknesses; the determination of everyone to make the best of every situation in or out of the line, and at the same time endeavour to maintain the highest standards; he brings it all back to life.

His high spirits, exuberance and lack of inhibition served him well during those gruelling times, although there were occasions when they brought him close to getting into trouble with his seniors when out of the line.

His observations on the military and political aspects of the 'repatriation' of the unfortunate Cossacks and Croats who found themselves in Carinthia in May, 1945, are perceptive. Some of his deductions and conclusions may not be wholly acceptable to the more partisan recorders of that unhappy episode. Nevertheless, his account is true as seen by one who was there and used his own eyes and ears.

It is this that makes *Ensign in Italy* so readable and interesting. It has the ring of truth about it.

Prologue

THIS BOOK CONCERNS the experiences of a nineteen-year-old subaltern in Italy in 1944/45. He kept a daily diary and his letters home were preserved. He was slightly wounded, while many around him were killed; his baptism of fire was at Cassino. He served with a battalion of Foot Guards which was seldom out of the line.

It is dedicated to those who fell in battle and to those who were maimed both physically and mentally − so often the unrecognized sufferers of the aftermath of war − as well as to members of their families. Also, the peace which was to follow was not to be of this world for many of the enemy. May all those who fought and fell with honour rest in peace.

The text also covers life out of the line − more bottles than battles − for the occasional rest was essential to counteract what is now called battle fatigue. Rest was simply a preparation for further fighting, because the Italian campaign, which began nearly a year before D-Day, concerned an all-out war which descended upon the length and breadth of a naturally and architecturally beautiful peninsula with the withering incendiarism of man-made destruction.

Out of the line we saw other kinds of service. Whereas campaigns and battles are indeed part of war, so too is serving of any kind, including serving in the NAAFI. Battles, however, are where and when a fighting man receives as good as he gives − otherwise they are a rout − amidst intolerable noise, human anguish and endurance and, too often, either mutilation or physical extinction. Those who have actually fought are in a minority; and the majority of those who have fought would often rather forget it.

In a very junior and minor capacity − as an Ensign or Second-Lieutenant − and, like many of my contemporaries, only a few weeks after my nineteenth birthday, my introduction to battle began at Cassino in what was to prove to be the last fifteen days of that particularly bloody and sometimes criticized contest. Monte Cassino was a strong point which had been considered before the battle by both its defenders and some of its attackers to be impregnable. It was, at 1,700 feet, 300 feet higher than the Rock of

Gibraltar, with some of its approaches just as precipitous. It was surrounded by a range of mountains dominated by Monte Cairo at nearly 5,500 feet and, to the south and east, the position could be defended, and was, by the river barriers which were flooded and icy cold in winter.

Its impregnability was to be proved, for, contrary to popular myth, the monastery position was never captured — nor the remainder of the town held by the enemy — by any one of the formidable number of national formations thrown against it. It was evacuated in good order by its German defenders who had been outflanked and who were, as a result, in danger of being cut off at a time when their undoubted talents were required elsewhere. Indeed, the 3rd Battalion Welsh Guards, in which I was serving, was to meet them further north and nearer Rome a few days after their withdrawal from Cassino.

The problems of the higher command were not exactly in the forefront of my mind as we bumped our way towards the ruins of Cassino, the by now obliterated market town. The black backdrop of the dominating mountains in front of us, which formed the German lines of defence and which were silhouetted against a clear moonlit sky, grew inexorably and menacingly closer. We caught our first sight of the Benedictine abbey.

The stifling effect and pungent smell of exploding smoke shells drifting towards us, together with the omnipresent rumbling of the big guns and the sharper bang of the 25-pounders, now well behind us, were a little reminiscent of Ludwig's words in *The Grand Duke*, 'It's not the ball I mind, it's the bang'. He was, however, referring to a duel with pistols and this was a duel on a larger and louder scale. Some units were marching out in single file, well spread out to reduce casualties in case of shelling or mortaring; others were marching in, including a Polish mule train bound for the mountains.

The jeep driver not only knew the way, he knew the form. We were now in what the Staff College calls the FEBA or Forward Edge of the Battle Area or what my jeep driver called 'This is *it*, sir!' It was the front. He advised, and I promptly accepted his advice, that our jeep convoy should halt, lower windscreens and cover them with sacking to counteract the moon's reflection.

I gave the necessary order just as the first welcoming — and responsive — enemy shells landed where we would have been had we not halted. The mutilated abbey was now occupied by German paratroopers and no longer by monks. The predominant view over the low ground, where we were, naturally remained the same; but the viewpoints and the resultant actions of the current occupants differed considerably from those of their predecessors.

We pressed slowly forward and the advance party, comprising nineteen men and myself, duly arrived in a blackened quarry on the very edge of the town. The quarry had only the night before been savagely and accurately stonked by heavy German mortars. There had, this time, been casualties. I ordered a slight advance beyond the quarry and we de-bussed, or de-jeeped, at the end of the track.

The date was 3 May, 1944. I had been born on 27 February, 1925, and, like all my contemporaries, my childhood and certainly my early youth, had been spent under the shadow of war which was duly and remorselessly replaced by the reality.

I

Joining Up

IT WAS WITH MIXED EMOTIONS that I listened to the Prime
Minister, Neville Chamberlain, announce that we were now at war with
Nazi Germany on 3 September, 1939. I had celebrated my fourteenth
birthday in February of that year.

My father, like most, had seen it coming and my place at Mr George
Lyttelton's establishment at Eton had been cancelled — there could be
zeppelin raids so near to London — and I was entered for Durham School,
much nearer home, physically dominated by another Benedictine abbey, the
finest example of early Norman architecture in England. I went to Durham
in 1938, the year of Munich. War followed a year later. Trenches had been
dug in the summer but all was quiet on our particular front and lessons
proceeded in an orderly and erudite manner. Pythagoras and Sophocles
reigned, while, admittedly, one or two masters were called up, volunteered
or were on the reserve and joined their regiments. One was killed almost
immediately. Altogether eighty Old Dunelmians were to die in battle
(ninety-seven in World War I) after they had left this ancient, public school
of small numbers; re-founded the year preceding Agincourt, in 1414, by
Cardinal Thomas Langley, Prince Bishop of Durham, Chancellor and loyal
servant of Henrys IV, V and VI, who, unafflicted by enfeebling, diabolical
disbelief or debilitating heresy and doubt, was in constant communion with
his God, and tenants whom he occasionally excommunicated when owing
rent, in order to encourage due respect towards his treasury and his person.

I joined the Corps on 1 March, 1940. Puttees were a problem in those
days: they had to be wound in a regular manner, neither too tight nor too
loose. They were wound from the bottom to the top, clockwise for the right
leg and anti-clockwise for the left. The boots, breeches, jacket, cap and
greatcoat were of regular issue, and the badge was that of the Durham Light
Infantry.

The pattern of school holidays changed, perhaps more because I was
getting older than because of the war, and I often stayed with my
grandmother who lived at Shotley Bridge. She was then over eighty, in full

possession of her wits and her property but having difficulty engaging a cook-housekeeper. It had been the housekeeper's job before the war to engage the cook; now there was neither one nor the other. Times were difficult for Granny.

Her maiden name was Margaretta Fanny Forsyth-Forrest and she was the daughter of a buoyant shipowner. At the age of eighteen she married Philip Merlin Brutton, fourth in a family of twelve begat by the good Canon Thomas and Sarah Ann. My grandfather acquired coal mines and ran them. He and Margaretta, or Meg as she was known, had six children, the third of whom was my father – Cuthbert, named after the local saint. The house where they were brought up, near the village of Shotley Bridge on the River Derwent in County Durham, remains in the family.

It was a silver-framed photograph presented to my grandmother that prompted me to join the Welsh Guards. Three of her great-nephews served in the Regiment, Peter Hastings and Pip and Michael Bankier, who were twins. The photograph showed the twins in Welsh Guards uniform. Moreover, their half-brother was at the time the Lieutenant-Colonel Commanding the Welsh Guards, Colonel A. M. 'Bertie' Bankier. One bemused brigadier asked Pip Bankier who exactly commanded the Welsh Guards: 'Is it your uncle or your brother?'

'Neither,' Pip said. 'It's my mother!' Indeed, his mother – another Margaret but known always as Chris – was a woman of considerable Edwardian charm, with a voice that carried loud and clear, and a good strong presence to match.

At sixteen I joined the Home Guard. Originally called Local Defence Volunteers, the Home Guard was never known as 'Dad's Army'; that was a later invention. A more accurate description would be 'Lad's Army' or 'Grandad's Army'. Dad was away at the war or down the mine.

The Home Guard was modern. We wore gaiters and battledress, blancoed belts and fore-and-aft caps. For weapons we had the Lee-Enfield rifle and our high morale. We were the signals company for the area command. We saw much of the area but nothing of the command.

As my eighteenth birthday approached I began to think of the future. I had been entered for Jesus College, Cambridge, but decided to forgo the privilege of university and join the Army instead. The next decision was which branch to join. Other than speaking to the local recruiting officer, I had very little idea of how to set about it. He wore First World War medal ribbons and gave me an intelligence test, which neither of us understood but he said that I had passed. My father having died suddenly in 1942, I wanted my mother to write to Chris Bankier, but she demurred; nor would she write to Charles Brutton, a first cousin of my father's who had served in the Grenadiers – and who had failed to admire her hat at Lords in 1924. I had no idea where to turn next. In the end I simply volunteered, via the local recruiting officer, for the Welsh Guards. He confirmed that at six foot three I should meet the height requirement.

I arrived at the Guards Depot, Caterham, Surrey, on 6 April, 1943, dressed in my Home Guard uniform and armed with my rail pass, washing and shaving kit, underwear and pyjamas. My pyjamas were not required.

According to my first letter home, I found the Depot 'luxurious' by comparison with the Infantry Training Centre at Brancepeth, where a childhood friend of mine had gone (Tony Bailes: he joined the DCLI and was killed, aged nineteen, near Lake Trasimeno, Italy, in 1944). After itemizing my new kit — '3 khaki shirts, 2 v good pairs of pants and vests ...' — I ended on a triumphant note: '*and* £1 a week.'

Nevertheless, it was all a long way from Durham. There was no time for playing games. The barrack room was a hut shared with twenty others, all under the direct command of a guardsman known as a Trained Soldier. One of the earliest lessons we learnt was that under no circumstances was a recruit — we were not yet guardsmen — allowed to speak directly to anyone other than the Trained Soldier. It was also the first regulation that I broke.

I had noticed that there was one group of recruits who were not necessarily Welsh Guardsmen; that is to say, their shoulder flashes indicated that some of them were Grenadiers, Coldstream or Scots Guards. They were the Brigade Squad, I learnt. Providing they survived the training hurdles ahead, they would be commissioned in their regiments.

Early in the war the practice of obtaining a direct commission in any branch of the Forces, except in special cases, had been stopped; all had to serve in the ranks. The idea of the Brigade Squad was that potential officers were chosen *ab initio* by the Regimental Lieutenant-Colonel, who presumably took into account both scholastic qualifications and physical and other abilities, and were then expected to prove themselves in an intensive course lasting nearly nine months. The Brigade Squad was due to spend eight to nine weeks at the Guards Depot, two further months at the Scots Guards' Training Battalion (then at Pirbright), followed by a short leave and then a final four months at Sandhurst.

I learnt this from conversations with two of the Brigade Squad recruits who were in the Welsh Guards: David Stevenson and Sam Hall. What I should have done was to write to Regimental Headquarters, then in Wilton Crescent, but this never occurred to me. I decided to speak to the Company Sergeant-Major. I caught him as he was entering the company office.

'Sergeant-Major ...' I began. He turned round. I said my piece very quickly — and survived. After weathering some banter in the barrack room, I received a summons to the Memoranda being held by the visiting

Regimental Lieutenant-Colonel, who just happened to be A. M. Bankier, or 'Bertie' as I knew him.

There is a story, which I am assured is true, of how Evelyn Waugh applied to join the Foot Guards. His initial interview was at the Irish Guards' Headquarters. He was approaching forty, had been born in London but was of Irish origins and was already well known for his successful writing, particularly his satirical work on the upper strata of British society. This would not have been held against him by the Regimental Lieutenant-Colonels then commanding the Foot Guards. Nor was the age factor necessarily a handicap; there were other 'young' officers in those days who were around forty. The problem was summed up in one damning phrase muttered over the telephone: 'The fella's wearing suede shoes!'

It was the Irish Guards' Regimental Lieutenant-Colonel, Tom Vesey, who turned him down. When he learnt that Waugh had been overheard to say he would now go and see the Welsh Guards, Colonel Tom promptly picked up the telephone to warn Bertie's predecessor, Chico Leatham. The candidate was ushered into Chico's office. Chico raised his eyes from some document. His white moustache twitched. With his 'matchless judgement of officers', as *Welsh Guards at War* puts it, Chico said: 'They tell me you're a shit'.

My reception, luckily, was more friendly. On being fell out, as the military expression goes, after the Memoranda, I was ordered to get my kit and install myself with the Brigade Squad.

II

Training

By THE SPRING OF 1943 the tide of war had turned at last in the Allies' favour. In North Africa, following the Anglo-American landings of November, 1942, the German Army was beaten. Like the Italians before them, the Germans had surrendered. The focus of the War in this theatre moved across the central Mediterranean to Sicily and mainland Italy, where three Guards Brigades were soon dispatched, including 1st Guards Brigade, in which the 3rd Battalion Welsh Guards were serving.

But by this time, too, the war had reached universal proportions, stretching from Europe to the Far East and of course the Pacific — and not forgetting the United Kingdom, still being subjected to German bombing raids. It was with this global background in mind that our military training programmes were fashioned. Wherever we might be sent, to Burma, the Balkans or Berlin, we had to be trained and trustworthy in the face of the enemy, capable of standing by our colleagues, obeying orders and firing in the right direction.

The basic idea at the Guards Depot, and no doubt at Potsdam and other such places, was simple: you learnt discipline on the square, physical fitness in the gymnasium and weapons-handling on the range. You also learnt endurance. This was a question of overcoming assault courses, surviving route marches, wading through or swinging over canals, and anything else that could be invented to test our stamina.

By the time we left Caterham we already understood the basics. Safely passed out, in the parade sense, we were inspected by the Commandant, Lieutenant-Colonel the Earl of Romney, and in a more general sense by Sir Bernard Paget, GOC-in-C. We then embussed and entrained for Pirbright. This is where the Guards Depot is today but at that time it was, as far as we were concerned, a pre-OCTU (pre-Officer Cadet Training Unit). We were now guardsmen and we were to be in Right Flank Company.

We soon grew used to the daily round at Pirbright: drill, weapon training, field exercises, physical training, route marches and assault courses. I remember the joys of the Bren gun, newly introduced into our curriculum.

'*No kick whatsoever,*' I wrote home, '*very smooth to handle.*' The Sten gun I had used in the Home Guard. The ejection of cartridges could damage the fingers of the left hand if the firer became careless. More than that could be damaged if we became careless with 36 hand-grenades, sticky bombs (which we attached to sheets of metal, standing in for tanks) or the PIAT (Projector Infantry Anti-Tank), which some keen instructors fired from the shoulder. I preferred not to fire it at all.

There was, however, some relief to be had in motor-transport instruction. In simple terms, we were taught to ride a motorbike and drive a truck. The instructors deserved a special medal for devotion to duty, but at least none of us was injured, nor did we inflict injury upon others, and most of us learnt to drive with at least passing ability. Where we failed was in matters mechanical; the mysteries of what went on beneath the bonnet of a truck, for instance, remained insoluble.

This lacuna was to prove embarrassing when we left Pirbright on our way to Aldershot, where as a wartime measure the infantry wing of Sandhurst was installed at Mons Barracks, the cavalry or tank wing remaining at Sandhurst. Before going there we were due to take some leave, about two weeks, but first we had to surmount a hurdle: an infantry camp at Wrotham in Kent, run by the 8th Sherwood Foresters. A long way from Nottingham, the Sherwood Foresters were now encamped in the leafy land of the Cantiaci and their job was to test our various capabilities. No bulls' eyes, no leave.

All but five of us passed the tests, but we were kept at Wrotham on the excuse that we were weak on maintenance. The Sherwood Foresters were aghast at our lamentable lack of mechanical knowledge, and disputed our claim that we had more things to concern us than a close understanding of the carburettor. Day followed day and still we were stuck under the spreading chestnut trees of Kent, instead of enjoying our hard-won leave. Signals were exchanged. Eventually we were visited by four Regimental Lieutenant-Colonels (there were no Irish Guardsmen among us), formidable in their blue caps, Atholl grey greatcoats and highly polished boots. Their presence did not improve our knowledge of motor mechanics, but it did have the desired result. We said goodbye at last to Wrotham and went on leave.

At Mons Barracks, Aldershot, I found myself in D Company's No 6 section. D Company was commanded by Paul Makins, ably assisted by Hugh Smiley, Derek Bond — both Grenadiers — and other devoted instructors. Paul Makins was in the Welsh Guards, as was his company sergeant-major, a considerable character called Mineur. There were six others in my section. At twenty, the eldest was Tim Mitchell, who knew my Bankier relations. There was also another Tim, Tim King; George Myrddin-Evans who knew a school friend of mine; Michael Brand; and two

Welsh Guardsmen, David Stevenson and Sam Hall. My bed, the room orderly told me — it was a palliasse on an iron bedstead — had been slept in by Cadet Jean of Luxembourg until he had passed out the week before. I felt as sorry for him as I did for myself.

Mons Barracks at that time was the stamping ground of Regimental Sergeant-Major Brittain, Coldstream Guards. I only fell foul of him once. We were on parade in a thick fog. The man could not see the end of his pace stick, but as though to give himself supernatural powers in our eyes he pretended that he could see through the murk. We heard a bellow that could only have come from him: 'The third man from the right in the rear rank of D Company is idle, Company Sergeant-Major Mineur. Take his name.'

It happened to be me. I was duly marched before the Company Commander and on the invitation to speak, 'Yes please', I explained that I was not idle and that in any case the fog was so dense I had been unable to see the front rank let alone the man in the distance who said I was idle. I received the classic reply: 'If the Regimental Sergeant-Major says you are idle — you are idle. Two extra drills.'

The great watershed of our training was Wales. There are warmer places on earth than Bettws-y-Coed in September, but at least it did not rain. We climbed mountains, even Snowdon; we were left in the wild to find our way back to base. Jerome Trehearne hitched a lift and came in suspiciously first. No marks were given for initiative, but several were deducted for cheating. He had to lead the assault on the next mountain the following day. Somehow he led us up the wrong one, and was heard to say that he wished he was trying for a commission in the Wrens. He was killed on D-Day +6.

One of the pleasures of Wales was the availability of that miracle of nature, the humble hen's egg. Although eggs were rationed during the war, at any rate up to the borders of Snowdonia, Llewelyn's spirit of independence led him to defy regulations. The eggs were not given away, unless you spoke Welsh, but you were asked how many you could eat. A four-scrambled-egg supper was a very welcome supplement to Army fare, and well worth the minimal cost.

On our return from Wales we spent two weeks on night exercises, which at least had the advantage of removing parades, assault courses and gymnastics from our curriculum and must have been efficacious as it gave me a certain confidence in being able to see better in the dark than hitherto. This new confidence led me to walk home, as the saying goes, an attractive member of the Canadian Women's Army Corps who was providentially stationed within the same barrack compound at Aldershot. I invited her to have dinner with me after I was commissioned, but she stood me up, alas.

It was nearly the end of our time at Sandhurst. All that remained was the passing-out parade. This great event has long been noted for the chance it affords one man to display the full power of his stentorian tones, and the command 'Eyes front' from Sergeant-Major Brittain could move birds from the trees and arouse involuntary exclamations from the onlooking ladies. We had now been trained by Brigade of Guards instructors in the intricacies of drill for more than thirty-two weeks, but caution rather than confidence was the predominant feeling within the ranks of D Company. I was placed as the right-hand man of the second rank, which did not provoke any particular sense of joy, as this meant that when we turned to our right for the march past, together with the cadets on my right and left, I would be the first to be observed. In fact the parade went off well. On my right was Mickey Brand, on my left Tim Mitchell. Both were going into the Coldstream, with whom Mickey Brand would be wounded, Tim Mitchell killed.

After leave which I spent with my mother, I had to report to the Training Battalion, Welsh Guards, then at Sandown Park, Esher. The Regimental tailors, shirtmakers and hatters had been down to Sandhurst to take our orders and we went up to London for our second fittings. The shopping list for an ensign in 1943 was as follows:

Service dress uniform at Johns and Pegg, Clifford Street, W.1	£15	0s.	0d.
British warm	£15	0s.	0d.
Blue	£20	0s.	0d.
	£50	0s.	0d.
Sam Browne belt at John Peal & Co, Oxford Street, W.1	£3	10s.	0d.
Pair of boots	£3	2s.	0d.
Pair of shoes	£2	13s.	0d.
	£9	5s.	0d.
Blue forage cap ⎱			
Service dress cap ⎰ from Edward Smith of Cork Street, W.1	£7	9s.	0d.
6 shirts made at Meyer and Mortimer	£10	0s.	0d.
1 mackintosh	£5	0s.	0d.
1 ash walking stick from Briggs		5s.	0d.
	£22	14s.	0d.
Grand total:	£81	19s.	0d.

The Army allowance for an officer's uniform was £45, so there was a shortfall of £36.19s.0d. Blue had been officially discouraged since August, 1943, as a matter of economy, but if it had been ordered before that date or had been inherited or simply ordered afterwards anyway, it was unofficially encouraged to be worn. I still have the trousers and use them for gardening. I have, however, removed the red stripe.

After the passing out parade, Sam Hall and I arranged to go and see *Strike a New Note*. The seats were to cost 12 shillings each (60p). We went to the theatre in our new uniforms and then on to the Bagatelle. All this was organized by Sam whom I considered to be an experienced man in these operations. On Friday night, our plans were to go to the Queen Charlotte's Ball at Grosvenor House — very much 'carry on London' — and take a couple of girls: Clayre Paton, a Wren aged twenty and Susan Rhys-Williams, a Predictor Officer on the Hyde Park gunsite, the daughter of Sir Rhys Rhys-Williams (Sam's Godfather). Susan, also twenty, was to have a busy winter, thanks to the Luftwaffe. Susan's mother was on the board of the hospital and had organized the table where another friend, Rosemary Cator, who was doing war work, joined us. This was my first outing with older women. My outlay was four guineas for two tickets.

After leave spent with my mother, I reported to the Training Battalion, Welsh Guards, which was then stationed at Sandown Park, Esher. Any idea that drill stopped at Sandhurst was quickly dispelled. There was, and remains, a ritual known as asking the officer's permission to drill him: the drill sergeant approaches the senior officer present, salutes and asks 'Permission to drill the officers, sir, please?' to which the reply is, 'Yes, please.' This is followed by 'Right, gentlemen. Fall in here. Sharply now, gentlemen.'

We had become gentlemen at Sandhurst but it made no difference on the square. I was the senior of the three Welsh Guards cadets for no better reason than my surname began with B, David Stevenson and Sam Hall being the others. We had all been given Cs when we passed out 'in order that our Training Battalion would not expect too much of us', as Derek Bond explained with considerable acumen. The sword had gone to a cadet called Jack Hosegood who had the pleonastic sobriquet of Rogerwell. The belt had gone to Gerald Farrar; both were Grenadiers.

The Training Battalion at that time was commanded by Tom Oakshott. He was undermined constantly by his company commanders who were far senior to him in terms of service but had resigned their regular commissions and returned at the beginning of the war. Colonel Tom had been a reservist, presumably. In any case he had been appointed by Colonel Bertie. One of these company commanders was Cecil Wigan who was considered very *mondain* by the subalterns. His housekeeper was said to be French, but had the strange name of Fafka Lupeekin.

If Cecil's housekeeper was dubiously French, there was no doubt that the Master Cook was Welsh. During one of his many inspections – 'Kitchenhouse, shun!' – Colonel Tom observed shortly before Christmas, 1943, that the turkeys were all present and correct but that, given he was due to entertain Colonel Bertie, could the Master Cook kindly arrange that a bird be sent round to his billet. This was done. It happened, too, that others had guests of considerable importance and eventually all the turkeys ordered by the Training Battalion, Welsh Guards – about sixty in number – had to be re-indented. The Quartermaster died, it is believed, from pneumonia brought on by shock. I went to his funeral on 23 December, 1943, the only military funeral I ever attended. (In battle the fallen were buried simply.) I was sent to learn all about it. I wore khaki service dress, a black arm band, leather gloves and a blue cap.

The Quartermaster's successor died. I did not go to his funeral. Then either the third or the fourth one died as well. We lost count. The court of inquiry, however, that had been set up to inquire into the loss of sixty turkeys was postponed *sine die* and the men's Christmas dinners were amply supplied with fowl from the second indent which the officers, by tradition, served. Colonel Tom made a short speech in Welsh, which was a mistake. A guardsman got up to thank him for granting the Battalion a week's leave which was not what he said, or thought he said, at all.

Welsh speakers were exclusively recruited by Walter Thursby-Pelham into the signals company. In Cassino I later heard them speak in clear and the Germans shelled us with leaflets in every known language of the Indian sub-continent except English. The Commanding Officer's soldier servant was a Welsh speaker. He always received a credit for the presentation of his bed: blankets folded in the correct manner, boots highly polished and so on. The point, however, was that he never slept in this bed but had arranged his own private quarters next door in a part of the racecourse buildings which were locked and barred to the soldiery. In a moment of boredom or curiosity, Colonel Tom asked for the keys. The Quartermaster – the first to die – was sent for and so were the keys. On unlocking this Alhambra, the secret was out and the servant was in close arrest.

The order of dress which I wore for the Quartermaster's funeral was the same, less the black armband, as I was told to wear just after Christmas for a court martial. David Llewellyn, later a Member of Parliament, was the Assistant Adjutant who instructed me, 'You say nothing except that you agree with the presiding officer.'

On the day before the funeral of the poor Quartermaster, Pip and Michael Bankier arrived at the Training Battalion on their way to Italy. I spoke to

13

one of them and rather gathered that their half-brother commanding had felt that their ardour for London life and the fact that the future Queen of Yugoslavia had also fallen in love with Michael was likely to be more efficaciously exorcised in Italy than in further training with the 1st Battalion in Yorkshire. It was to lead, for one of them, to a gallant death in Italy.

Together with Cecil Wigan as the Captain and Sandy Paget as the Subaltern, I as the Ensign reported to Wellington Barracks on 24 January, 1944. We had joined the Westminster Garrison Battalion, then commanded by Eddie Hay — Lieutenant-Colonel Lord Edward Hay who had served in the Grenadiers before the First World War. He was to be killed within a few months when the V-bomb fell on the Guards Chapel.

Cecil, Sandy and I were accompanied by a half-company of Welsh Guardsmen — the other half comprising a detachment from the Irish Guards — and our duties were those of the West End, in particular guarding Buckingham Palace and St James's. The Regiment had not mounted guard since 1940 and we had been well rehearsed at Esher under the observant eye of Drill Sergeant Fitzgerald, a rotund figure whose dress had received particular attention from the Regimental tailor, whose puttees were impeccably rolled and whose boots were highly polished by a privileged, if unofficial, guardsman.

Wellington Barracks was not short of officers who had seen parades; but the parade of Drill Sergeant Fitzgerald and his opposite number in the Irish Guards, who was virtually his twin, was a remarkable sight to see. They were inevitably known as Tweedledum and Tweedledee and their role was paramount before the arrival on parade of the officers, among whom the Captain would take over command from the Subaltern during the mounting of the Guard. We practised for two weeks before we mounted Guard on 3 February watched by Colonel Bertie, Tom Oakshott and his second-in-command, Howell Moore-Gwyn, together with Paul Makins and the critical but satisfied Regimental Sergeant-Major of the Training Battalion.

Cecil was wondering what he was going to be given by the outgoing commander of the Old Guard. Normally keys were handed over but Cecil recalled that he had once been given a dead mouse. In the event he received keys. After the ceremony in the forecourt of Buckingham Palace, the New Guard, less those left behind at Buckingham Palace under the command of the Subaltern, marched to St James's Palace. The Captain fell out and it was the Ensign's job to give the order: 'To the guardroom, dismiss'. This I duly did and went to the first floor of the Palace where the Officers' Mess was situated. At that time during the war no colours were carried and steel helmets and small packs were worn.

The mess itself comprised a few armchairs, a fender in front of the fire, a writing desk, a sideboard and a large dining-room table which could sit about twelve or fourteen people. The question of guests and how many had to be approved by the Captain of the Guard. Dinner was a men-only affair; lunch could be mixed and also tea. It was a rather liverish existence and the only place we were allowed to go to outside our Palace rounds was the Turkish baths at the Royal Automobile Club. I went once and found them not to my liking. The food in the mess was excellent and the guardsmen ate well too, in their own mess on the ground floor. The second floor contained bedrooms.

On 14 February I walked around Buckingham Palace garden in the morning and climbed on to the roof. The garden was most disappointing and reminded me of a neglected park. Of course it was February and gardeners were scarce.

It was a good moment to entertain friends. John Grigg, who had been at Sandhurst, came to dinner; also Kenneth Kendall who became well known on television in later life; Tim Mitchell, mentioned earlier; George Myrddin-Evans, a former fellow cadet and others, as well as my mother, cousin Chris, Bertie and Squiff Ellis who later wrote *Welsh Guards at War*. It was a forty-eight hour guard and we dismounted on the third day.

Interspersed with Public Duties were private sorties which included the Guards Club, which I joined when it was in Upper Brook Street. At my first dinner I ordered half a bottle of Algerian wine which cost five shillings (twenty-five pence in today's terminology) and was barely drinkable, but it was all I could afford, having divested myself of too much cash at such exalted places as Ciro's, the Berkeley and lesser known haunts. All Brigade officers were strictly forbidden to use the downstairs bar at the Ritz. It had a bad reputation. Public houses were never used, nor public transport, there being plenty of taxis, and under no circumstances were we to be seen carrying luggage. These rules or guidelines were not followed too literally, but it was better not to be seen. We hardly ever wore civilian clothes.

Air raids were fairly constant but the worst raid as far as the Guard was concerned took place on 23 February. Paul Makins had taken over from Cecil Wigan but had fallen sick and Cecil returned to mount Guard on this day. David Stevenson came to dinner and also David Llewellyn, the Assistant Adjutant. The air-raid sirens sounded and we had finished dinner and were sitting on, or standing near, the fender when we heard the very ominous whoosh of a bomb cluster − a whistling noise indicated that the bomb was further away − which meant that the bombs were falling on top of us. I dived for the floor, Cecil remained imperturbable on the fender and the noise of the explosions was execrable, but we were alive.

The pictures remained hanging. No glass on the table was broken. There was silence. The screen, a montage of *fin-de-siecle* ladies in daring petticoats which had been assembled by officers in the 1890s, was usually locked, but the key, inadvertently left in the lock before dinner, must not have been properly turned and the door to the screen incongruously swung open. Much more to the point, however, the curtains covering the huge windows were lined and interlined and also impregnated with the dust of ages. It was these curtains which took the full force of the shattered window panes, blasted inwards by the exploding bombs. Otherwise we would all have been severely cut and maybe worse. None of us was hurt. Our first concern was the Guard, particularly the sentries and also everyone living in the Palace.

As far as both the sentries and the Palace were concerned we were lucky in two respects. First, it was a standing order that the sentries under the clocktower were to be withdrawn immediately the siren sounded and were to fire-watch in the tower itself. Their lives were saved as a result. Indeed, there were many dead immediately in front of where they had been on guard. The sentries would certainly have been killed. One of the civilian dead – such is the village life of city centres – was recognized as the black-market gin distributor to many of the West End night clubs. He had been decapitated. His bottles had been smashed and their remnants lay strewn around his corpse, while the scrap of metal which moments earlier had been his motorcar lay crushed like some black coleoptera underfoot. Swirling around this macabre scene was a mass of water from a ruptured main, flowing past the Palace, then on towards the Mall, undulating the broken bottles and the bodies of the dead whose blood pinked the water like angostura bitters.

The second piece of luck was that damage to the Palace was not substantial. A stick of bombs had fallen, destroying, among other property, St James's Theatre and damaging the King's Secretary's residence near the clocktower and also a corner structure of Clarence House which adjoins the Palace. In order to assess the situation, Cecil did his Captain's rounds immediately – we all did rounds and the Ensign's were at two o'clock in the morning – and reported that all could have been worse but that the Chapel Royal was damaged. He then ordered me to escort David Llewellyn to the nearest available form of transport as he had been slightly concussed by the blast, and, having done that, I was to stay by the telephone 'in case the King should ring'. He did not. In fact no one telephoned WHI 2079.

Feeling, therefore, that I could safely hand over to the mess sergeant, I went on my own tour of inspection. There were about twenty-six dead in the immediate area. In Crown Passage, opposite the Palace, there was an unforgettable sight. Seven people who had been sheltering there had been truncated by the blast, including a lieutenant-colonel who was doubled up, lying on his back, still wearing his cap. This gruesome scene was not untypical of the effects of blast. On the level of tragi-comedy, an American major and his girlfriend had been blown out of bed and were wandering the street, dazed, nude and wrapped only in blankets given to them by the ARP.

On returning to the mess, after an absence of about a quarter of an hour spent outside the Palace, I found Cecil, his nerves understandably taut, not best pleased that I had handed over the telephone vigil to the mess sergeant. There had been no calls. Nevertheless, he put me in close arrest, then, a minute later, in open arrest and, then, in the next minute after due reflection and in more practical mood, 'Philip, you can offer us all a drink.' I was more than happy.

It was not the only drink to be placed on my account. The daughter of the King's Secretary, Winifred, had to be dug out. Her father, Sir Alexander (Alec) Hardinge, had been in White's at the top of St James's Street, but his wife, Helen, had been with her daughter, but not buried under the débris. The whole family arrived in the Officers' Mess, the first time, at any rate overtly, any women had been there after six o'clock. 'The Ensign,' said Cecil, 'will offer you a drink.' This phrase was not without its nuance, as the mess sergeant was there to serve it. In fact, the girl and her mother refused but the Secretary, who was very shocked, drank most of the bottle. I paid before we dismounted. It was a memorable Guard which could well have been worse and I was not complaining. Indeed, there was another raid the following night and this period became known as the 'mini-blitz'. It preceded the V-1 and V-2 rockets, one of which was to destroy my mother's flat, which she had taken in Maida Vale, and very nearly killed her.

The tragedy of the V-1 striking the Guards Chapel is well known. I was certainly relieved to be drafted to Italy a few weeks hence. It might be safer.

We dismounted guard on Friday, 25 February, and I returned to the Training Battalion at Esher, Sandy Paget and I having been replaced respectively by Norris Kennard and Cyril Daniels, a rather elderly Ensign who was later to become the subject matter of a Regimental Order following an indiscretion in southern India. The 26th saw a rehearsal for St David's Day and the 27th was my nineteenth birthday which I seem to have celebrated fondly with Wendy, the elder sister of a young boy called Christopher Brasher who was to become well known as an Olympic runner.

There is a diary entry for Friday, 3 March: *See picture on Russian Army and VD.*' Presumably there were two unrelated pictures. Also: *St David's Day Ball. Brian Kent* [a company commander] *'well away' kicks Bernard in the pants.*' The entry ends: *'Rather drunk myself. To bed at 0230 hours.*' At least I knew what time it was.

Bernard Greer, the Adjutant at Esher, had chosen me to accompany him on the draft to Italy to join the 3rd Battalion, Welsh Guards. David Stevenson had been sent on a course to Barnard Castle and was shortly to join the 1st Battalion. Sam Hall had fallen asleep on the train from London and had, most gallantly, thrown himself out of the moving carriage as it drew out of Esher station on to the grass verge between the railway line and the racecourse in order to avoid being late for parade. His efforts were in vain. He received a week's picquets and was not to join us in Italy for several months.

Preparation for the draft involved drawing tropical kit which had to be obtained at the London District Transit Camp. I also attended a course given at East Grinstead by Colonel Guy Rasch in the Grenadiers. It was an umpire's course, no doubt valuable training for Italy.

III

Advance To Battle

ON 9 APRIL, 1944, I arrived in Naples. I was nineteen years old, below which age, officially, a man or woman could not be posted abroad. We had sailed from Liverpool on the *Cape Town Castle*, not just Welsh Guards but Grenadiers, Coldstream and Scots Guards, as well as Canadians, sailors and I forget who else. As my diary records: '*Ship packed like sardines.*' After an eleven-day voyage, mercifully without incident, we were approaching our destination. 'See Naples and die': however banal, the thought was much on our minds. Indeed, the scene that met us, that misty Sunday, was depressing, for Naples had been subjected to heavy Allied bombing; ships had been sunk in the harbour and the docks were in a shambles. However, Naples itself was not my destination.

The 3rd Battalion, Welsh Guards, had arrived in Italy with 1st Guards Brigade, now part of 6th Armoured Division, from North Africa. (The 1st Battalion, motorized infantry like the 3rd, and the 2nd Battalion, trained as an armoured force, were in the Guards Armoured Division, then stationed in Yorkshire.) They had landed at Naples on 5 February, two months before us, to join the Italian campaign.

Italy had surrendered in September, 1943. Mussolini had been forced to resign in July that year and was imprisoned; but he was rescued by the Germans, who still occupied northern Italy. It was thus the German Army that the Allies now faced in Italy, and they continued to be a formidable force. Equally formidable was the terrain. High mountain ranges extend the length of the Italian peninsula, crossed by few roads but divided by many rivers – a constant obstacle to an advancing army, particularly in winter. Allied air domination became more or less absolute; yet such were the natural defences offered to the Germans that they were able to withstand extraordinary punishment from air bombardment as well as artillery. Time and again, it was only the infantry on the ground who could drive the German from his position.

The concept of the Italian campaign had evolved very gradually.

Following the success of Eighth Army at El Alamein and the Anglo-American landings in North Africa, the south littoral of the Mediterranean had been cleared of Axis forces. This would provide the springboard for an Allied attack on 'the soft underbelly of Europe', as Churchill put it. The firm decision was now taken to invade north-west France in 1944, and all other operations were to be ancillary – but here the Italian campaign played its crucial part in overall strategy, by tying down German forces who would otherwise be used against the Allies in northern France or in Russia.

Ironically, had the enemy decided to withdraw to the Pisa-Rimini line and hold a front at the neck of the Italian peninsula, the containment roles would have been reversed; the Germans would have needed far fewer troops. In the event, however, Hitler ordered Field-Marshal Kesselring to stand and fight. The Allies were already advancing up the peninsula, and in November, 1943, Kesselring decided to make his stand behind a line of fortifications, the Gustav Line. Part of this line stretched across the valley of the River Liri, taking in the small town of Cassino.

Some fifty miles north-west of Naples, standing low in the valley but dominated by tall mountain ranges, Cassino was considered to be the pivotal point of the German defence. It was here, on 17 January, 1944, that the Allies launched their heavy direct assault on the Gustav Line: the French to the north, in the mountains; the British X Corps to the south, across the River Garigliano; and the gallant II US Corps across the River Rapido. The French and the British gained a little ground but the Americans suffered grievously, taking 10,000 casualties in what was to become known as the first battle of Cassino.

Meanwhile, on 22-23 January, the Anzio landings had achieved remarkable initial success. A total of 50,000 troops had landed to the rear of the German defences, only thirty-five miles from Rome. While the Allies were consolidating their Anzio bridgehead, however, the defenders rushed in reinforcements. It would be four months before the Allied breakout was finally achieved.

In February the 3rd Battalion Welsh Guards arrived to take up positions on the shoulder of Monte Furlito, 1,000 feet above the Garigliano at a point some twelve miles south of Cassino, where the British had won a vital salient. The 2nd Battalion, Coldstream Guards, under Lieutenant-Colonel Hugh Norman, held positions on the reverse slope of a steep ridge which comprised Points 751, 718 and Monte Ornito. Monte Cerasola, 2,463 feet, was on their right. Ahead rose the menacing grey mass of Monte Maio, the principal enemy artillery OP – when anything could be seen through the mist and rain – and the main base for their desperate but determined counter-attacks to regain the ground they had lost two weeks earlier. It was on this desolate

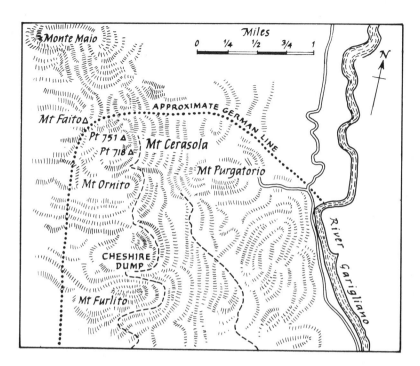

spot that the 3rd Battalion, Welsh Guards, would relieve the 2nd/4th Hampshires.

10 February: The morning was cold and sunny, the evening snow and icy sleet. This was the day the Welsh Guards were heaving themselves and their equipment towards the Hampshire lines. At the same time Ian Skimming, commanding No 2 Company of the Coldstream on Point 718, observed Germans clambering up the forward slope of Point 751 to his left, defended by No 3 Company, which was promptly shelled just before the German attack came in. Hugh Norman immediately ordered a platoon under Tom Jackson to attack the enemy right flank, while Henry Green, commanding 3 Company, called for an immediate artillery barrage which blunted the attack. The enemy were finally cleared by a bayonet charge led by Michael Hollings, who took seven prisoners. The attack had cost the Coldstream Battalion forty-five wounded. Tom Jackson and six men were killed.

10 February: The Hampshire/Welsh Guards relief was done in darkness. The sleet and snow, driven by a biting wind, masked any light from the near full moon. There was little cover, and to reach mulehead from where the jeeps unloaded at 'Cheshire Dump' involved a three-hour climb. At mulehead there was a further three-quarters of an hour's journey over jagged grey rock to rear Battalion headquarters, whither supplies were carried by Basuto and Indian porters. The narrow path to Cerasola had not existed

21

previously. The edges were unsafe, slippery and crumbling from the sleet or rain and there was constant shelling and mortaring, when the ricocheted rock was as dangerous as the shells and mortars themselves. In addition, a 100-foot-deep ravine had to be crossed by a rope bridge. The approach and crossing of this swaying and vertiginous barrier took at least half an hour.

The dead were left on the verges until time and men could be found for their burial. Four men, sometimes six, were allotted to each stretcher and many of the wounded did not survive the twenty-hour descent. It took thirty-six hours to carry David Duckham and lift him to the other side of the river and thence to a base hospital, after he had been badly wounded.

The lines facing the enemy could only be fortified by erecting sangars constructed from local rock, and as the Hampshires who were being relieved were under strength, this meant that more of these shallow butt-like structures had to be built immediately. This was, nevertheless, a better situation than that which faced the Commandos when they won the ground in the first place. The incessant rain soaked the one blanket per man which was, in any case, frozen in the morning when the first German counter-attack was launched and repulsed. The enemy were in some cases only fifty yards away and snipers on both sides were active. No fires could be lit. Each man had a small cooker which contained solidified methylated spirit, a twenty-four-hour food ration, plus chocolate, biscuits and bully beef. Frostbite was prevalent and Lieutenant-Colonel Willy Makins was one of its victims. He was ordered by the new Brigade Commander, Charles Haydon, to hand over to the second-in-command, David Davies-Scourfield, who was himself suffering from a poisoned foot.

11 February: The first German attack against the Welsh Guards' lines came in at dawn and was repulsed by a bayonet charge led by the company commander, David Elliot, who was killed. His place was taken by Robin Barbour who faced, once more, an enemy onslaught, and once again led a bayonet charge. He, too, was killed. Only thirty-eight men were now left in No 2 Company; in the few hours' fighting, twenty-two had been killed and forty-nine wounded. Night patrols into no-man's-land were constant. In one Anthony Schuster was killed, and a member of his platoon, Guardsman Walter Jones, took over. He himself was later killed. Christopher Williams-Ellis then took out a patrol. He, too, was killed. Bryan Pugh, No 3 Company, with whom I was to serve, then patrolled behind enemy lines, broke through them and returned safely with much useful information.

Throughout the whole engagement signals communications had to be kept open and the signals officers – in the Welsh Guards' case, Mike Chinnery – worked incessantly with their teams, often under heavy fire, to do so.

17 February: The Coldstream lines were again attacked. No 2 Company on Point 718 warned Bob Palmer, No 4 Company on Point 751, of an imminent

German attack. The enemy were immediately mortared and subjected to searing crossfire from No 2 Company. The German attack was halted but the enemy could not be thrown back: they were in dead ground in terms of small-arms fire and too close to be pounded by artillery. In consequence a smokescreen was laid down and Hugh Whitwell led a bayonet charge which dispersed the enemy and netted twenty-six prisoners.

The Germans, however, with considerable daring, returned the same evening, and both Ian Skimming's and Bob Palmer's companies were involved in bitter fighting. Reinforcements were called for and a company each from 3rd Grenadiers and 1st/4th Hampshires, which had been sent up by the Brigadier, were moved into position after heavy casualties had been inflicted on Coldstream reinforcements by enemy mortaring and shelling. The Grenadiers were held ready to counter-attack, and the Hampshires took over the Ornito position from No 4 Company. Nos 1 and 3 Coldstream companies were merged under Henry Green, such had been the casualties.

18 February: The morning once again found the Germans in dead ground only fifty yards away, just over the ridge. Once more Hugh Norman ordered smoke, and the bayonet charge over the crest was led by David Toler leading No 4 Company. This time there were only ten prisoners but more enemy dead. In the evening the Grenadier company relieved No 4 Company on Point 751. The Coldstream battalion had suffered forty-three casualties in the twenty-four hours' fighting. Enemy casualties were considered to be well above that figure.

Meanwhile, in the Welsh Guards' lines, casualties, following those suffered on 11 February, included five killed and twenty-one wounded, before the final German attack came in.

19 February: After heavy enemy mortaring and shelling, a frontal attack materialized at dawn against the Welsh Guards on Cerasola, which was held by 3-inch mortar fire and small arms, but the enemy came round the northern flank of the salient up an easier approach and round to the rear of the Battalion lines. The Adjutant, David Gibson-Watt, led a counter-attack with Drill Sergeant David Davies who was badly wounded by a grenade, thrown by a would-be surrendering German who was not given a second chance and died on the way down. The enemy, however, were now caught on three sides and when daylight came they were sitting targets.

Another enemy attack had, meanwhile, been put in on the southern slopes of Cerasola along the saddle which joined it to Ornito where No 2 Coldstream Company were placed, as well as a company of 1st/4th Hampshires who finished the battle with a bayonet charge. Many of the enemy were killed and wounded by crossfire. One hundred and twelve Germans were taken prisoner. There were also casualties on our side. Richard Pattinson, the Welsh Guards Company Commander who had opened fire on the enemy at the commanding officer's 'O' Group and killed the leading German, was himself killed under heavy shellfire. At 'Cheshire Dump', in Battalion Headquarters, Company Sergeant-Major F.G. Baker and the Master Cook Sergeant A. Evans were killed, and so were fourteen others during the course of the battle. Johnny Wolfers and nineteen guardsmen were wounded. In the nine days on Cerasola the Welsh Guards lost some forty-four killed and ninety wounded. The Coldstream casualties were thirty-three killed with 157 missing and wounded. Also, fifty men were sent to hospital suffering from frostbite or severe exposure. In all, the Coldstream losses amounted to twenty-five per cent of their strength. The two battalions and the Hampshires had undertaken six sorties.

There were also casualties among the supply units. One of these units was led by a British Pioneer officer of sixty-one, whose use of a hunting horn apparently soothed the mules but alarmed the Algerian muleteers. Perhaps the most extraordinary case treated by Dai Morris, the Welsh Guards' Medical Officer, was the guardsman who suffered from concussion after a German mortar bomb landed on his helmet but failed to explode. Another unique encounter occurred when a German came face to face with his Welsh Guards opponent: both men raised their weapons and fired — but both mechanisms jammed. The German beat a hasty retreat.

19 February: The Battalion withdrew from Cerasola after it was relieved. The last out was David Davies-Scourfield.

20 February: The Coldstream were relieved and withdrew.

1 March: After ten days' rest the Welsh Guards returned to the line within the same salient but to the right of Cerasola on a mountain called Purgatory — Monte Purgatorio. In practice, the hell of the first was incomparably worse than the temporary suffering of the second where there were fewer casualties. Maybe St David kept an eye on matters, given the date of the Battalion's return to the line. After two weeks the Welsh Guards were relieved by the Coldstream. Then, after a short rest, the Welsh Guards relieved the New Zealanders in ground recently taken just to the south of the railway station at Cassino. There was neither much railway nor much station by that time. Nor, for that matter, was there much of a town; this, however, was my destination in April.

On disembarking in Naples, the Adjutant, Bernard Greer, told us to march against the traffic as usual. In Britain that means on the right of the road. In Naples I marched my men on the left. 'Mr. Brutton!' Bernard shouted, 'You are marching your men on the wrong side of the road!' 'Not in Italy!' I shouted back. We then embussed and drove the forty miles to the 1st Battalion (Guards) Infantry Reinforcement Training Depot.

At the Depot I shared a tent with Jim Jerman and John Nichol-Carne; a few weeks later John would be dead. My Army pay was increased by 4s.6d

(22½p) a day to £20 per month, of which we could draw only £13. My cousins Pip and Michael Bankier came down to the Depot and were able to collect two parcels I had brought from their mother. Two former fellow cadets were also at the Depot, Christopher Carlisle and Tim King, both in the Coldstream. We were also visited by Francis Egerton and Tim Hayley who had come down from the 3rd Battalion. Francis was to become adjutant in succession to Bernard and after the war for many years ran Mallett's, the antique dealers in Bond Street. Tim Hayley was killed within a few weeks.

On 21 April I wrote to my mother: '*Since our arrival we have been training in the mountains. Do not picture the mountains like those of Scotland, the Lake District or Wales, nor the weather which one usually associates with those areas. On the contrary, the weather here is hotter than that of an English summer; the mountains are terraced and cultivated by the Italians, although still covered with trees in many parts. The valleys below are not marshy and desolate but very dry and dusty and covered with agricultural development in the form of vineyards and cereals. ... I have just returned from an expedition to Mount Taberna* [probably Mount Taburno, 4,573 feet, near Benevento].... *We climbed to the summit and there was cultivation all the way up. We met peasant boys in rugged green-grey capes which are characteristic of this part of the world, usually driving a flock of goats and some undernourished cattle to more lowland pastures. All the animals had bells round their necks. The women carried heavy loads of brushwood on their heads.*' The views from the mountain top were spectacular. We could see Vesuvius in the distance, aeroplanes below us like dragonflies. '*Everything is looking very beautiful,*' I concluded.

Down below, meanwhile, there had been problems. Some Italians had assaulted one of our police patrols and a corporal had died. Three Italians were arrested; one was shot and the other two got long prison sentences. I resolved to keep my revolver with me at all times.

Jim Jerman left to join the Battalion as assistant mortar officer. Bernard and John Nichol-Carne left too, on temporary attachment, as did Tom Dubuisson with whom I had shared a cabin on board ship. The Battalion's former Commanding Officer, Lieutenant-Colonel Sir William Makins, Bart, arrived at the Depot from hospital.

After much training, including more mountain-climbing − most of these exercises under the direction of Joe Gurney, later known as 'Muley' Joe in acknowledgement of his skill with the animals − on 22 April I too left to join the Battalion.

It seemed a long journey, no doubt because I was in the back of a 15-cwt truck, but at last I arrived. I was posted to No 3 Company commanded by Bruce Goff, with Tim Bolton as second-in-command and Bryan Pugh and Christopher Maude as the other subaltern officers. '*No 8 platoon,*' I wrote to my mother, '*is extraordinarily good, the majority having been in action all the time. This is a great help because they are all reliable and this gives one confidence. I only hope I'll inspire them in the same way.'* The food was excellent, I noted, and my soldier servant, 35 Lewis, was *'a first-class man and an invaluable help. He was at the Army and Navy and Constitutional clubs before the war as a waiter and then on King's Guard. I believe I am his first 'employer' in his present occupation. I am very lucky.'* Lewis, however, did not feel so lucky. He maintained that Bernard had got hold of the wrong Lewis. As there were many in the Regiment, this is possible. He had been blown off the jetty at Boulogne when serving with the 2nd Battalion in 1940. His health was later to let him down, but not before he had shown the most conspicuous courage. He was twenty-four.

Lewis accompanied me into Cassino on Wednesday, 3 May. My diary reads *'Company advance guard to Cassino. Leave 1945 hrs with 19 Other Ranks. Meet Recce Regiment in quarry. Place men in sangars. Recce all patrol positions in Cassino, both Castle Hill and Gully. In charge of administration and local protection as well. Sleep rear company headquarters. Heavy mortaring by Jerry.'*

In fact the mortaring the night before we arrived had been devastating. A ration party had just arrived in the quarry and they and those whom they had come to meet were all assembled in this small area to the north of the town. There were many casualties and not many rations after the event. When we arrived it was a blackened and depressing scene which met us. However, so confined was the space that any vehicles which had been brewed up had now been removed. The approach, as far as I was concerned, would have been infinitely more difficult had the jeep driver not known the way. Maps existed but they were not much use when the roads themselves had ceased to exist and features could not be seen clearly. The immediate approach to Cassino was a wilderness.

We had long ago passed the gun lines, the heavies, the mediums and 25 pounders, in descending order, as we bumped our way forward over the ruts and rubble, more and more slowly as the surface deteriorated, sometimes making way for outgoing vehicles, their tasks completed and returning to base, maybe to repeat their journey again before it was light. Always there was movement, men in vehicles, men on foot, and those who were marching peered through the dust at our shoulder flashes or observed the 63, the blue-red-blue logo and that of the 6th Armoured Division, the mailed fist, painted on the vehicles.

It was the land of the foot soldier, whether he were transported or whether he marched, and his supporting arms. In other words, it was the front line and the noise of our guns behind us was now rivalled by those in front. There were other noises, too, as we drove closer, those of the mortars and heavy machine guns. It was altogether quite some noise.

26

It was the second excursion of the Welsh Guards into Cassino itself. The first had been from 7 to 24 April. In both cases they were stationed in the northern section of the ruins, after the last assault had captured half the town. The other half was still occupied by the enemy. 'Tons of bombs and uncountable shells had shattered every building, obliterated every road, let loose the waters of the Rapido and sown the ruins with undiscovered death,' wrote Squiff Ellis in *Welsh Guards at War*. [In fact, the Germans had dammed the Rapido and then blown up the dam.] Most live a "troglodyte existence in the gloom of half-underground ruins never left in daylight; partly [the strain] was due to the impression on the mind made by this stagnant pool of death. In the country around, the sun might shine; it never reached them in the depths of this inferno. In the country around men went about their lawful occasions by day; here they left their cellars only when it was dark. 'Only the bullfrogs revelled in this scene of horror, croaking and chuckling with delight.... The very atmosphere made one's flesh creep'."

The jeep driver made no mistakes. There were, of course, military signposts, but none of them were of much help to an advance party. As the great mountain range behind Cassino loomed above the cover of our incessant smokescreen, the peak of Monte Cairo, 5,475 feet, was clearly in view and, shortly afterwards, the ruins of the monastery. It was at this point that the driver said we should lower the windscreens and cover them with sacking, just thirty seconds before the welcoming salvo fell fifty yards in front of us. Before this interruption, I had ordered a halt and given the command: 'Lower windscreens. Cover with sacking.' We proceeded.

In fact, we ourselves were covered with the creamy dust of the dry Italian earth, and our shoulder flashes, the object of curiosity of the troops we passed, were hardly legible. Our way to the quarry led us past a crossroads where the lives of the military policemen directing traffic, always without helmets and wearing their red caps, were inclined to be at high risk, as the Germans had pinpointed the spot and their shells or mortar bombs, given the noise and grind of the traffic, were impossible to hear. All this activity, of course, took place at night, and the difference between a split second's warning of oncoming danger and being able to hear it and that of having no warning and not being able to hear anything but the whine of vehicles in low gear often meant death – and there was plenty of death in Cassino, on both sides.

IV

Cassino

THERE HAD BEEN THREE allied assaults hurled against the Gustav Line and the great bastion of Cassino up to this date. The first began on 17 January, as mentioned above, and the second on 15 February after General Bernard Freyberg had assumed command of the Cassino front when his II New Zealand Corps — 4th Indian Division (two-thirds Indian with British officers and one-third British), the 2nd New Zealand Division, the British 78th Division and a combat group of 1st US Armoured Division — was given the job of taking the town and the monastery which the Germans claimed was unfortified (and they said that they had placed three military policemen outside to keep the rough soldiery at bay), but the immediate surrounding ground *was* fortified, indeed up to the walls. It was not a distinction likely to be appreciated or even believed by an assaulting Allied soldier. In military terms the monastery and the adjoining land were indistinguishable and inseparable and it was exactly for this reason that St Benedict had chosen the site for his abbey, and the Italian and German Commands had complimented him on his choice. The monastery was now not only plumb in the middle of a defensive line, it was also the pivot. No Allied soldier could be expected to attack the position while the monastery stood. It was necessary, as General Freyberg put it, to soften it up.

The building covered, and covers since its restoration, seven acres. Its walls were and are fifteen feet thick, a point that General Tuker, commanding 4th Indian Division which was ordered to attack the place, discovered from a book acquired at a Naples bookshop. He also discovered that the building had been reinforced as a *military* bastion by the Italian Government in the 1890s and, thanks to the decision of an Italian Government in 1940 to enter the war on the side of Hitler, was about to be destroyed. The monks were duly informed and the first bombs were dropped on 15 February by a bomber which carried the appropriate apocalyptic number of 666. The Germans then occupied the ruins which made an excellent defensive position and held Point 593, which was not bombed, known as Mount Calvary, the key to the monastery and the immediate objective. The Allied attack was a very brave, very bloody and very close run thing. It failed.

Meanwhile the 2nd New Zealand Division attacked south of Cassino town over land which had been deliberately flooded by the Germans, mined and barbed-wired. The town had also been fortified and tunnels had been constructed between cellars which, in turn, had been reinforced by concrete. The station was captured and lost. It then poured with rain for three weeks.

15 March: The third battle of Cassino began, again directed by General Freyberg. As a preliminary step, the town itself was obliterated by bombing and a massive artillery barrage (600,000 rounds of artillery shells, fired by 800 guns) was to follow. Needless to say, the German paratroopers under Colonel Heilmann, who were virtually entombed in the town, suffered grievous losses, but those who survived this cataclysmic bombardment stayed to fight and retained half the objective while the New Zealanders captured the other half, including the railway station and the castle. They lost one thousand men in so doing. Meanwhile the Gurkhas, despite extraordinary gallantry, captured but could not hold Point 435, Hangman's Hill. Five days later, having made repeated use of the Red Cross as their casualties mounted, they were pulled out at night from a hopeless position.

In the town the huge craters caused by the bombing became flooded. Tanks could not advance; many were put out of action by the Germans and the line was stabilized, in many places only a few yards from the enemy. Any raised voice could clearly be overheard. In the rubble and ruins of the town both sides whispered and it was obvious that the endurance of the German defenders in the town against all odds of personal survival, and their losses were horrendous, was a reflection of the highest degree of courage and the esprit de corps of the 3rd Parachute Regiment who were in the town at the time of the bombardment and the New Zealand Division assault.

The German order of battle in Cassino town, the monastery and its surroundings was then changed; at the time of the Welsh Guards presence it included the 4th Parachute Regiment, with 1st machine-gun Parachute Battalion under command, all serving in the 1st Parachute Division under the direction of General Heidrich. To the north-west was now 3rd Parachute Regiment, moved from the town, under the command of Colonel, later General, Heilmann, with the 1st Battalion on Mount Calvary, which was the key to the monastery. The 2nd Battalion was placed north-west of Colle Sant Angelo on the flank of the von Ruffin Battle Group (4th Mountain Battalion and 2nd Battalion, 100th Mountain Regiment) which was also under command of 1st Parachute Division. In reserve was the 1st Parachute Regiment, to which were attached 721 Grenadier Regiment and 2nd Battalion 741 Grenadier Regiment. The Corps Commander of LI Mountain Corps in which these groups served was General Feuerstein. General von

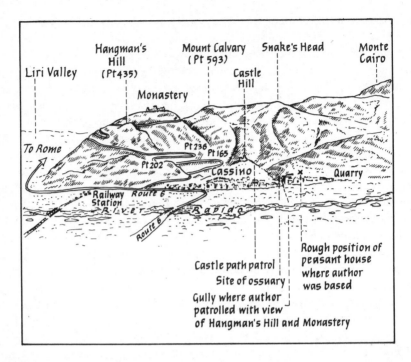

Hangman's Hill (Pt435)   Mount Calvary (Pt 593)   Snake's Head   Monte Cairo — Liri Valley — Monastery — Castle Hill — To Rome — Pt 236 — Pt 165 — Pt 202 — Cassino — Quarry — Railway Station — Route 6 — River — Rapido — Route 6 — ×

Rough position of peasant house where author was based

Castle path patrol
Site of ossuary
Gully where author patrolled with view of Hangman's Hill and Monastery

Senger und Etterlin's XIV Panzer Corps was now concentrated in the Liri Valley and along the Garigliano Valley. It was his mischance to be on leave when the great assault began on 11 May and his corps was smashed.

Descending precipitously from the exalted level of General von Senger und Etterlin to that of 2nd Lieutenant or Ensign, it may be assumed quite correctly that I knew nothing about the German order of battle at that time. I left that sort of thing to the staff. My precise concern was that the German order of battle, particularly its parachutists in my immediate neighbourhood, should be unaware of my exact whereabouts and those of my men at any given moment. A known spot of use or occupation, like the quarry, was a risk which had to be taken. Any extenuating risk beyond that was to be avoided or reduced to its minimum. Sometimes this was difficult, such as during patrols, going to and from the castle. In fact any form of swanning or walking about during the night was better reduced to a minimum. In an attack, of course, or defensive action the emphasis lay on firepower and adequate cover. That was a different story.

My immediate job was to unload our equipment and I thought it prudent to do so a little beyond the quarry which was clearly a priority target for the Germans. The road, such as it was, continued for a few yards and, the jeeps being easily manoeuvrable, this presented no problem. The vehicles then returned to the Battalion and, with the help of my opposite number in the

Recce Regiment whose men we were relieving, I placed the guardsmen in their sangars both as a matter of protection and also for the local defence of the immediate area for which we were responsible.

The quarry was north of the town, near the Rapido Valley and at the foot of the mountain range which began its steep climb immediately above Cassino and its environments. The castle and, much higher up, the monastery lay in a westerly direction.

We had eaten before leaving the Battalion and had brought one day's rations. Thus, after seeing that the men were in position and that food and ammunition were correctly stored, I set off with the Recce Regiment officer to see the ground, accompanied by 35 Lewis. The road had been bulldozed just beyond the quarry but it quickly dwindled into a narrow dirt track with rubble and ruins on both sides of the white tape, beyond which lay mines and booby traps and, further on, Germans. To the left was the gaol in which Battalion headquarters would be situated in two days' time and had been in the first involvement here. To the right was the gully which was fully exposed in daytime but was patrolled by both sides at night. At this point the stink of the town hit one forcibly — the sickly sweet smell of putrefying bodies which were left unburied half under or in the rubble of the rocks and ruined buildings, too dangerous to approach and dig out for decent burial; the stench of urine and human faeces, the first pungent because of lack of recent rain, the second diminishing because of the daytime heat and fairly well controlled by latrine discipline; the acrid smell of our smoke shells and the nasty drifting waftage of cordite emanating from the armaments and explosions on both sides within the perimeter of battle.

Our outposts were fifty yards from the point we had reached and from now on our lives depended on being silent and remembering the passwords. There were two passwords, changed nightly: one which was given by those in the sangars which followed the barely audible 'Halt! Who goes there?' and the other was the reply. The reason: the posts might have been overrun and we could have walked into a trap; conversely, instead of our patrol arriving, it could have been the enemy. There was nothing, in fact, on the ground to prevent either occurrence except prudence on the part of the Germans and vigilant concealment on ours. There were, however, mines, but these could be dismantled.

We were challenged at the first post, very quietly, and equally quietly gave the correct response and passed on to the furthermost half-section which was installed about thirty yards beyond. These outposts were in sangars, camouflaged with sacking, which were abandoned during the day as they were overlooked, their occupants withdrawing to an adjoining ruin with peepholes as observation posts. No movement of any kind was permitted. In their direct line of sight was Hangman's Hill, so called because the wrecked cable-car pylon looked exactly like a gallows, and beyond that the monastery.

We then returned to the point whence we had started and began our approach to the foot of Castle Hill. Overhead was the incessant whistling of our smoke shells which mingled with the mist rising from the valley and the stagnant pools which had formed within the craters after the bombing and torrential rain. If this was hell for humans, it was heaven for mosquitoes, bullfrogs and fireflies at night and every kind of fly by day. This scene of total desolation – not having yet observed anything by day – could only be imagined beyond the immediate vision provided by the moon, but obscured by the mist and smoke, and imagined without too much difficulty.

It was important, indeed a matter of survival, to have markers; disorientation could mean death. I have never lost this habit of noting exactly where I am, either in cities or in the country. In Cassino we turned right on our first reconnaissance of the gully outposts, just after the dead soldier lying beyond the tapes. He was face-down, wore khaki and was half-buried. There were many like him of all nationalities and his, at this moment, was unknown. He was considered to be booby-trapped. No one, as yet, had got around to asking the Sappers to have a look. They were very busy on other, more urgent, matters than the common decency of burying the dead, and sometimes when they did so the body would blow up in front of them and create the need for more crosses. This one was to kill a journalist, after the fall of Cassino, on 19 May when the Press were allowed to see the place.

On retracing our steps, we noted the dead soldier carefully and turned right towards what had once been a square or open space at the mouth of the gully. The fifty yards between the body and the beginning of this open ground was covered by a track between the rubble of the buildings which at this time of year was bone dry and powdery. We made no noise. Our helmets were covered with sacking held in place by camouflage nets and we were wearing battledress. Denims, the uniform of battle in the spring and summer months, were to be worn two weeks later. Lewis carried his rifle and I my Tommy gun or Thompson Machine Carbine (TMC) with which I had been issued before leaving. It used .45mm ammunition. At that moment I also carried a .38 in my holster. All weapons were covered to avoid any possibility of reflecting moonlight.

As we moved forward there was suddenly a considerable amount of shelling and mortaring on both sides. The German 8.2cm mortars were becoming too heavy and too close for comfort. Heavy and medium machine guns could also be heard above the crash and noise of this dead-of-night exchange of compliments, also the low-pitched bursts of Spandaus and the screeching high note of the Schmeissers; and, no less deadly, the swallow-like, tremulous, twittering noise of the long-range heavy machine-gun bullets which indicated that they were pelting down from their high trajectory through the smokescreen. This was cover from view, but not exactly from fire and Colonel Guy Rasch's rules for umpiring were inapplicable. We had to be careful, but without protection there was not much we could do. We padded on. Suddenly there was silence, like the pause between thunderclaps in a midsummer storm; then the gaol, a little to our left, was again stonked. However, its protective covering of rubble, masonry and any other reinforcement which man could devise was sufficient to guard those incarcerated below from anything other than extreme discomfort – with luck. Once outside, however, it was distinctly more dangerous both for the occupants and their visitors, such as ration parties, the brigade commander or his staff.

As for ourselves, our next marker on the edge of the open ground was the ossuary. It was on our right and had been virtually destroyed. Gaps were in the walls and we were now privileged to gaze on a pile of skeletons, the bones of which were scattered in the most grotesque positions. One skull actually rested on the wall nearest us, like a sentinel at the gates of Hell, mist swirling and eddying through its eye sockets and its teeth, with a skeletal left arm, near enough to touch, dangling in a bizarre and casual manner over the broken stonework, the finger bones languidly pointing towards the ground. I almost looked for the cigarette. We sprinted across the open ground.

We were now at the bottom of the steep castle approach route, on one side of which were the enemy and the other were our friends, except that it was very obvious that the Germans presumed we were there in strength whereas I knew we were not. From the dozen or so reconnaissance patrols I was to make in Cassino, it was apparent that the German lines were much closer to the castle track than were our own. To the best of my belief then and knowledge now, the German lines were within a few yards of the track to the left, whereas we were at least, in terms of fixed positions, a hundred yards further away on the other side of the gully, in the outposts we had just visited, where there were no more than eight men. In the event, the enemy never attacked in strength but he patrolled and so did we. It was imperative to keep the lines of communication to the castle open. My task was to let them know that we were there, but not to reveal our exact positions nor that there were only two of us. Equally, our orders were to capture, kill or simply discourage any enemy we met in this nightly game of hide and seek.

The path up to the castle was steep and the noise of pebbles rattling down on either side of this hog's back track would certainly have informed the Germans that we were there. It was also most unnerving, certainly for us and probably for them. Grenades were occasionally thrown, but never when I was there was there any rifle or machine-gun fire, presumably in order not to give away the German positions and invite retribution. Another reason for this mysterious inactivity from a resolute and intelligent enemy was probably the belief that we were far stronger on the ground than, in fact, we were.

It took nearly half an hour to reach the castle, sometimes with the aid of a rope. It was hard going, even without heavy equipment, wireless tack and, of course, weapons. The castle was not large and the German positions were virtually adjoining; no movement of any kind was possible, as the place was completely overlooked by the German lines and dominated by the monastery. My company commander, Bruce Goff, was to occupy the castle position this time, a position he shared with the Coldstream Guards on alternate tours of duty. Bryan Pugh accompanied him with two platoons of No 3 company, 3rd Battalion Welsh Guards.

Bruce Goff's description appears in *Welsh Guards at War*: 'The worst part was getting up to the position; it was a good twenty-five minutes' hard climb with the aid of ropes in several places and you were in a muck sweat when you reached the top. It was a case of single file all the way as there was only one track; luckily the Germans never attacked us on the way up. Our own smoke shells often fell near us and made it hard to breathe, and rifle grenades were fired at us from the German positions further down the slopes; but in the castle itself life was quiet and eerie. There was a steep drop all around the position, of which the diagram gives a pretty clear idea. 'A' was a cellar in which one platoon lived; 'B' was a sangar only occupied at night; the rest of the company lived in sangars shown in and around the Keep.

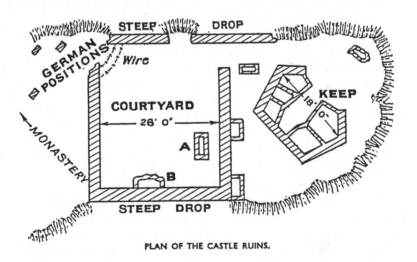

PLAN OF THE CASTLE RUINS.

'Communication with Battalion headquarters was by wireless only and there was no movement by day as we were completely overlooked by the Monastery. We lived in our sangars all day, rations being given out each night. And we took turns with a company of Coldstream Guards each holding the place for two days at a time. The smell of dead bodies was particularly bad both in the Castle and on the way up, and after Cassino fell and we were finally relieved we counted seventy-four bodies of different regiments and nationalities, all unburied.'

While pondering the difficulties of climbing the castle track, I also bore in mind, when we eventually retraced our steps, the difficulties of attacking it and the fortitude of the New Zealanders who captured it. These thoughts were fleeting as there was a break in the smokescreen just as we arrived at the bottom of the track and were about to cross the open ground. The monastery, with its gaunt smashed walls still standing forty feet high and its ruins dominating the whole area, was clearly visible; and if the monastery was visible, so were we. Only we were smaller and anything that we carried which could glint was covered. There could, however, be Germans on patrol behind us. We decided to take the risk. We sped across the open space to land, thankfully, in the arms of the ossuary skeletons, then past the dead soldier on our left and back to base. I returned to place eight Welsh Guardsmen in the two outposts, thus relieving the Recce Regiment, and then retraced my steps to prepare for the Company's arrival. I slept for a short while on the stone floor of a house tucked into the side of the hill and out of sight of the enemy by day; but if you moved in daylight, you had to move sharply when crossing certain spots of the approach route which was nothing more than the beginning of a mountain track. I reflected that to move at all by day was a luxury in this place.

Small mercies meant much and there was even a flower growing near the doorway, a honeysuckle, the roots of which had survived the holocaust. There were no birds, however, only flies, mosquitoes and desolation − and what desolation we beheld in the morning.

Our room with a view was, quite literally, out of this world. First, the room itself was something of a miracle in a town which had received the attention on 15 March of 775 aircraft, including 142 Flying Fortresses dropping their 2,500-ton bombload, complemented by the 600,000 shells of the artillery. In addition, there were mortar bombs and tank shells. This had taken place exactly seven weeks earlier. The monastery, it will be recalled, was destroyed on 15 February.

The bombing of the town, while decimating the defenders, provided the survivors with tank traps and terrain from which they could not be completely dislodged. In fact, no one was more surprised than the New Zealanders to discover that there were still Germans in Cassino and, furthermore, Germans who were prepared to fight. However, as mentioned earlier, the castle was taken. It had been built in the ninth century and was known to the Romans as Rocca Janula and to the current adversaries as Point

193. That is to say, it was 193 metres or 633 feet of precipitous slope above the town, or perhaps more accurately above sea-level. It was not a point of too close consideration at the time of its taking by the New Zealanders.

At the time of this third assault (15 March) on the Cassino positions, the communications and conditions were so bad in the mountains — severe weather, mud, sleet and snow, telephone lines cut, wireless battery replacements often being blown up on the backs of mules or human porters — that Mount Calvary, Point 593, to the north of the monastery, which was the essential point from which to attack the by now ruined and occupied structure, was not in Allied hands at that moment, as it was thought further back, but in those of the German 2nd Battalion, 4th Parachute Regiment. The New Zealand Corps Headquarters had, it was learnt after the event, got it wrong, so Point 593 and the monastery ruins which should have been bombed were not. This third attack was intended to be a pincer movement with one arm attacking the town directly and the other attacking the monastery via the castle, the hairpin bends on the road to the monastery, and Hangman's Hill (Point 435). The castle, half the town and the railway station were the consolation prizes.

In fact, luckily for the morale of all concerned, we were totally unaware that the whole concept of frontal attack and close outflanking movements meant that, fighting against troops of the calibre which were opposing us, Monte Cassino itself was not going to be taken. The true military objective was never the monastery, which seemed to attract the inexhaustible weaponry of Allied arms like a giant magnet, but the six-mile-wide Liri Valley situated between the Aurunci Mountains to the south and south-west and the Abruzzi lying north and north-east. Through the Liri Valley ran the Via Casilina or Route Six — and Route Six ran to Rome. To have outflanked the monastery, as Juin advocated, would have involved the most difficult and bitterest of fighting, but he had the right troops to do it; so, too, had the 4th Indian Division; and 1st Guards Brigade had proved it could also fight in the mountains. The resultant fighting would not have been worse than that which took place in the four battles which preceded the evacuation of Cassino and its mount.

The problem, however, was not only the determined defence which was now obvious, but also the equally evident terrain, the weather in winter, the seven-hour trek to the front and bad communications between the front and headquarters who were sometimes unsure, as in the case of Point 593, whether strongpoints were held or not. Nevertheless, once details of both sides became known long afterwards, it was apparent that opportunities had been presented on more than one occasion of achieving the objective of the Liri Valley if a final push had been made by the Allies; but in all major assaults there were not enough immediate reserves to exploit the

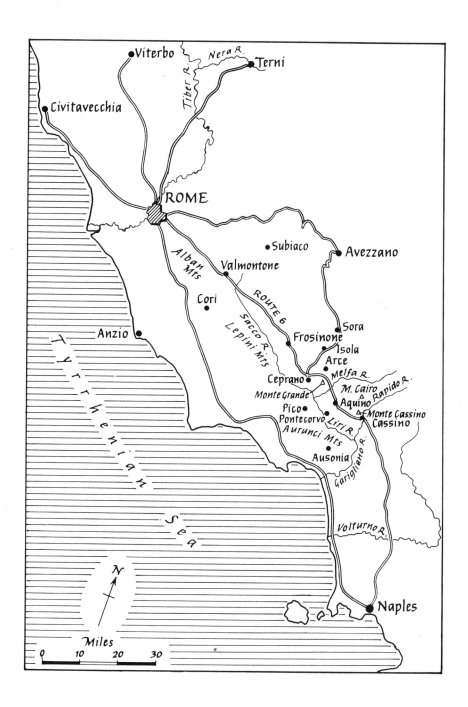

Viterbo
Nera R.
Terni
Tiber R.
Civitavecchia
ROME
Subiaco
Avezzano
Alban Mts
Valmontone
Cori
ROUTE 6
Sacco R.
Sora
Anzio
Lepini Mts
Frosinone
Isola
Arce
Tyrrhenian Sea
Ceprano
Melfa R.
M. Cairo
Rapido R.
Monte Grande
Aquino
Pico
Monte Cassino
Pontecorvo
Liri R.
Cassino
Aurunci Mts
Ausonia
Garigliano R.
Volturno R.
N
Naples
Miles
0   10   20   30

37

achievements and the gallantry of the vanguard. It is, equally, not perhaps wholly irrelevant that, before the Allied invasion of Italy, a joint staff exercise involving the German and Italian High Commands resulted in the conclusion that the position, per se, was impregnable. In other words, Monte Cassino and its monastery were always considered to be a prime *military* position by its *defenders*.

Thus, the confusion, the casualties, the countryside, the appalling weather until the spring and the difficulties of communications when batteries were low, rations not arriving and the mule teams being decimated during a fourteen-hour return trip from their base in the valley, all contributed to a successful as well as a gallant defence of the position by the Germans, for whom conditions were equally difficult. In addition, the bombardment had turned the monastery into a first-class defensive position – ruins are better than buildings, not least because they do not collapse – and the town into a tank trap. I would not, nevertheless, have liked to have been a German during the bombardment.

It was this last thought that was in my mind as I looked at the scene. What had, until recently, been a recognizable Italian country town was now nothing but rubble. The trunks of a few trees, totally defoliated, stood out, together with some buildings, like pieces of high relief created by some deranged artist. Also, interspersed with the desolate remains of stone walls and knocked-out tanks which protruded from the stinking, by now ·drying, mud, were bomb craters filled with stagnant greenish-yellow pools of filth, plagued with mosquitoes and ebullient bullfrogs. Furthermore, there was smoke: our smokeshells and canisters saw to that. There was a perpetual pall of dust from exploding shells and mortars as well as smoke; but the smokeshells were more or less constant with varying effect depending on the wind and the state of battle; and the state of battle also affected the number of mortars and high-explosive shells which were rained down upon the ruins and their hidden inhabitants. At night these estimated 1,500 denizens, Germans and Allies, of this destroyed town – the Cassinati had, of course, long fled, were expelled, or were dead – would emerge on both sides of the line from their burrows like four-legged mammalia in the forest to forage and perform natural functions. In fact, in the case of forage, the rations were brought up at night, together with mail, ammunition, batteries and anything else which was required.

The pro and con of my own position was that I could move within a restricted area by day but had the duty of patrolling the gully, the exposed dangerous gap beyond the ossuary, and Castle Hill by night. On balance it could be described as a more pleasant existence by day than at night. At any rate by day it would have meant certain death, so by night I felt more secure, by comparison, until one night I neglected to notice a break in the smokescreen and we were promptly mortared while crossing the open space beyond the ossuary and before Castle Hill.

This was our weak point: no cover from anything and, effectively, running towards the enemy lines just over the ridge of the track. As we raced for the dubious safety of the start of this track, with our own static patrol positions a hundred yards behind us and the Germans a few yards in front, both Lewis and I thought that 'this was it'. But it was not. Neither the grenades, automatic fire nor any of the enemy in person followed up this opportune piece of observation from the heights and its rapid result. We completed our patrol further up the track and returned whence we came. The ossuary welcomed us as before. We named our skull sentinel 'Musso' or 'the night porter'.

Our room with a view was one of the few peasant houses to have survived the bombing. It was built into the side of a hill which could not be seen from the German positions. Also, the trajectory was too steep for them to hit us with their shells or mortars. We thus had a view of most of the town, Castle Hill and the monastery, but we had to be quick and run across those parts of the track which were under enemy observation when we went further down towards the recently mortared quarry and the point where we had arrived on the night of 3 May. At one point along the track, to our right, in what had been the narrow back area of a bombed cottage, built into the side of the hill which rolled in its upper reaches into the Abruzzi mountains beyond, was the body of a young German. He was lying on his back, his head separated from his body by an inch or so; his finger nails were growing and so, too, his red stubble. He had blue, sightless, eyes. He was the victim of bomb blast, I reflected, as I remembered the havoc near St James's Palace in February. His was a difficult position to approach in order to afford the man a decent burial, and he was probably booby-trapped. So he was left where he lay.

My diary entry for Thursday, 4 May reads: '*Extensive preparation for company's arrival. Liaise with Poles in Half-Way House. Polish Cadet speaks English. Arrange guides. Jerry mortars gaol and hospital. A échelon neglects to send water. Ring up and make a fuss at Brigade. Water arrives; also Bruce and Bryan and 42 Coldstream who are completely unexpected. Muddle through.*' This was the first time I had been told about the Coldstream. They were fitted in. I then accompanied Bruce and Bryan to the foot of Castle Hill.

Friday, 5 May: 'Other officers are Bob Palmer and Ronnie Callander in the Coldstream and Johnnie Egerton, machine-gun officer, Welsh Guards. Reorganize after last night's muddle satisfactorily in the day. Johnnie Egerton causes confusion with Ronnie Furse about supplies. Rations arrive in quarry OK. Shortage of water. Send back for more. Mail arrives but unsorted. More mortaring and shelling.' Also more patrolling which involved the relief of the outposts by those engaged in local protection further back.

Saturday, 6 May: '*Daily dose of both sides mortaring and shelling. Rations arrive 2130. Christopher Maude there. Also papers and mail. Comparatively quiet night. Sleeping on stretcher. Patrol.*' I also wrote home on this date: '*Up to the moment of writing, I have still not received more than one letter but am expecting many in a short while. I cannot tell you where this one is written from, but it's been in the news a great deal and you may be able to guess. I am lucky enough to be sleeping on a stretcher! The first night was on a stone floor. I have found the sleeping bag I bought at Harrods invaluable. It is only two blankets sewn together, but very warm and keeps everything intact. I get on very well with the Quartermaster* [Kenneth Grant] *and find all my brother officers easy to get along with, particularly those in my company. I am very fond of them all.*' I could have added that the whole company and, indeed, Battalion esprit de corps, was excellent. We were particularly lucky in our senior non-commissioned officers and warrant officers. Our own Company Sergeant-Major John was particularly helpful to me and I remember how he and Bruce Goff roared with laughter when I ran for cover, mistaking the noise of a shell splinter ricochet for the whistle of an oncoming shell. It was this example of light-hearted comradeship which held us all together in more serious situations.

Sunday, 7 May: I recall talking during the day to Bob Palmer, Ronnie Callander and their Company Sergeant-Major, CSM Manders, who wanted to be a municipal gardener after the war. They were going up to the castle that evening. I accompanied them with Lewis some of the way. There was a considerable amount of smoke as there was nearly a full moon which was due the next day. '*Usual routine. Bob and Bruce exchange Company Headquarters for castle. Everything goes without a hitch. Sergeant Hinton recces reserve company headquarters where we are to rest for a few days. It's a quarter of a mile outside Cassino and called Pasquale. Some Sunday this!*'

Monday, 8 May: '*Explosion in castle keep kills platoon sergeant, medical sergeant and CSM Manders who died on way down. Three wounded including Ronnie Callander. Boche respected Red Cross flag. Tragedy caused by upset of grenades during stonk. Relieved by John Bowker. My party (48) arrive Pasquale via gaol and checkpoint. Shells overhead.*'

The explosions which had occurred in the castle were caused by a chance mortar shot which dislodged the grenades which were kept in the keep, the outcome being that both the mortar bomb and the exploding grenades resulted in casualties. There had been no exchange of fire in the town at the time and the explosions, from where we were placed in our headquarters, indeed appeared to emanate from the castle. After a few minutes a Red Cross flag was seen being waved at the entrance and a stretcher party of four bearers appeared and made its way precariously and very slowly down the precipitous path leading to the gully. It was an eerie sight. Any movement at all by day in Cassino was unique and the drama of the explosion added to the tension, together with the fact that every Allied and German eye was watching intently. An ambulance had been blown for and its driver also made his way in daylight into the north of the town, past the quarry and to a point out of sight of enemy lines.

I went down to this point and was saddened to see the pallid and expressionless face of Company Sergeant-Major Manders on the stretcher. The walking wounded or those able to wait until nightfall (including Ronnie Callander who came down on a stretcher and recalled years later being rushed across the open space at the mouth of the gully by his stretcher-bearers) were all brought down later. That night I was relieved by John Bowker in the Coldstream. My party of forty-eight and myself marched past the gaol and along a straight stretch of road, the Pasquale Road, which was the target of a fixed German line of heavy machine-gun fire on the right of the road coming out of the town, but was inactive during our move. We were well spread out because the road was also invariably stonked and I believe either it or Route 6 was named by the Press as the 'Mad Mile' or 'Spandau Alley'. What ever it was called then, it was certainly no lovers' lane.

Tuesday, 9 May: 'Breakfast 0900. Sunbathe. Recce water supply. Have bath in well in view of monastery. Decide this is asking for a stonk. So don't do it again.'
In fact the well was stonked. So keen were the field glasses of the enemy they did not take pot shots at the peasantry who were still trying to go about their business, risking their lives where there might be mines. Our house was shared with the occupiers who used the front of the house in sight of the Germans. Apart from the slit trenches which had been dug, they were our best protection.

'Play first [and last] *game of housey-housey. Lose sixty lire.'* I believe the playing of housey-housey was discouraged by the military. However, with stakes at not much more than the value of matchsticks, any card game occupied the time in a rest area where only one side of the house, a two-floored building, was sheltered from enemy view, and the well, only fifty yards away for example, was in full view.

'Rations arrive all right. Rumours about big attack. Bottle of rum arrives. Write David Stevenson.'
Wednesday, 10 May: 'Usual routine. Little shelling. 48 Evans nearly shoots Bailey. Accident with TMC whilst on guard, for which I deliver rocket.' I also remember that a cottage a few yards away had a loft with an open window through which I began to imagine we might be watched by an incumbent German! We investigated. There was no one. This feeling of being watched, however, was one of, if not the only, reason for the decision to bomb the monastery. There were a thousand windows in this building, a great number of which overlooked the attacking troops.

That night, 10 May: 'Letters 2, 3 & 4 arrive with rations. *Christopher* [Maude] *tells me about big push. Am sleeping on bed* [with three legs]. *Civilians living in part of the house!'*

There were two Orders of the Day issued by General Alexander about this time. Neither of them reached the nether regions of my half-company at Pasquale: no dispatch rider arrived, braked, revved and then choked his motorcycle engine, in the traditional manner, outside the peasant house during the night. However, with good grace, some extracts are repeated here:

'Operation Order No 1. Headquarters, Allied Armies in Italy.
From Army Group Commander to Commanders 8th and 5th Armies:
(a) Eighth Army
(1) To break through the enemy positions in the Liri Valley in the general direction of Highway No 6 and reach the area east of Rome.
(2) To pursue the enemy in the general direction Terni-Perugia.
(3) Thence to advance on Ancona and Florence.
(b) Fifth Army
(1) To take the Ausonia defile and thence advance on an axis parallel to that of the Eighth Army, but south of the Rivers Liri and Sacco.
(2) To launch an attack from the Anzio beachhead via Cori on Valmontone with the object of cutting Highway No 6 in the vicinity of Valmontone and thus preventing the reinforcement and retirement of those German forces opposing the Eighth Army.
(3) To pursue the enemy north of Rome and capture the Viterbo airfields and the port of Civitavecchia.
(4) To advance on Leghorn.
The second Order of the Day was more familiar in tone, intended for all ranks and was supposed to be read out loud and clear, but it never reached us:
'Throughout the past winter you have fought hard and valiantly and killed many Germans.
'Perhaps you are disappointed that we have been unable to advance faster and farther, but I, and those who know, realize full well how magnificently you fought among these almost insurmountable obstacles of rocky, trackless mountains, deep snow and in valleys blocked by rivers and mud against a stubborn foe.

'The results of these past months may not appear spectacular, but you have drawn into Italy and mauled many of the enemy's best divisions which he badly needed to stem the advance of the Russian armies in the east.

'Hitler has admitted that his defeats in the east were largely due to the bitterness of the fighting and his losses in Italy. This is in itself a great achievement, and you may well be as proud of yourselves as I am of you.

'You have gained the admiration of the world and the gratitude of our Russian allies.

'Today the bad times are behind us, and tomorrow we can see victory ahead. Under the ever-increasing blows of the Air Forces of the United Nations, which are mounting every day in intensity, the German war machine is beginning to crumble.

'The Allied armed forces are now assembling for the final battles on sea, on land and in the air, to crush the enemy once and for all.

'From east and west, from north and south, blows are about to fall which will result in the final destruction of the Nazis and bring freedom once again to Europe and hasten peace for us all.

'To us in Italy has been given the honour to strike the first blow. We are going to destroy the German armies in Italy.

'Fighting will be hard and bitter and perhaps long, but you are warriors and soldiers of the highest order who for more than a year have known only victory. You have courage, determination and skill.

'You will be supported by overwhelming air forces, and in guns and tanks we far outnumber the Germans. No armies have entered battle before with a more just and righteous cause. So, with God's help and blessing, we take the field − confident of victory.'

Thursday, 11 May: 'Distribute comforts by drawing lots. I draw a pair of socks and talcum powder. See Geoffrey Evans [Intelligence Officer]. *Write home letter 7. At 2300 attack starts. Deafening row from mortars and 900 guns. No sleep. Very little back from Boche.'*

The flashing, grumbling, rumbling roar of 900 guns, which continued for twenty-four hours with the barrels becoming so hot that they could hardly be approached, let alone touched, looked and sounded like the fires of Hell. At the given second, indicated on all synchronized watches, monitored by a secret signal from the BBC, the sky was instantly illuminated along the whole length of the Allied lines facing and to the flanks of the Cassino front, when the barrage and roar of these 900 Promethean starting pistols opened up simultaneously against the German lines to begin the lethal race for Rome. They continued throughout that night and during the following day, without cease.

The Germans called this the Third Battle of Cassino, the Allies named it the Fourth. It was, however, for many to be their last, as the cemeteries which surround the town bear witness. It took a full week for the enemy defences to be pierced and at no time did the German-held part of the town or the monastery ever succumb to direct assault. Three days after the great barrage and the massive assault on the German lines we left Pasquale and went back into Cassino.

V

Cassino II

THE MASSIVE BOMBARDMENT had stunned the Germans. My entry for 11 May continued: '*[enemy is] caught out of cover during relief on Monastery Hill.*' This last piece of information, which will have been disseminated the following day, amounted in fact to the Poles on the right flank encountering double the numbers anticipated, but there were, in counterpoint, enemy casualties caused by the limited cover available within the German sangars which resembled rock-constructed butts, only the occupants were not shooting grouse and their guns were, unsportingly, Spandaus, Schmeissers and Mausers with no noticeable shortage of ammunition. These weapons were backed up by mortars, grenades, heavy machine guns and artillery, although virtually no air support, and the initial attack of the Poles was heavily mauled despite German losses. The relief of the occupying parachutists, by other units within their Division, was normally carried out at maximum speed, since within the sangars there was adequate room for two or three but not for four or six, and the approach was over stony ground and thin soil without cover. This meant that rock splinters became as lethal as the exploding shells and their ricochets.

The following day, 12 May: 'Misty morning. Probably partly due to barrage which has been kept up all day. Poles reported doing OK. River crossed [on left flank] *but behind schedule. Monastery shelled and mortared all day. Spandau machine gun and* [enemy] *air activity. Poles later repulsed. 8th Division tanks to rescue of 4th Division.'*

13 May: 'Battle progresses favourably. Weather, as always lately, good. Report that Germans evacuating Cassino proves to be false. Poles now surrounded. French OK.'

Two events not recorded either in my diary or in my letters home have remained in my mind over the years. They must have both occurred during the early part of the battle, as we returned to Cassino on the night of the 14th. The first concerned radio communications. We had in my company office-cum-sleeping quarters a battery-operated wireless set which we tuned to the network of one of the assault Divisions of the left flank now across the

Rapido River. The wireless operator was Guardsman Jones 62 and after some deft fiddling of the tuning knob we could hear quite clearly and visualize vividly the shunting and turning of our tanks in battle, during those moments that the network was open or switched on for speaking, as they stalked — and were counter-stalked — by the enemy, waiting and manoeuvring to position themselves in order to fire the single armour-piercing shot which would knock out the enemy tank, the dreaded Tiger, and in all probability kill the crew and thus avoid the same fate befalling them.

It was close, fairly flat country, once the river had been crossed, but it was also heavily cultivated, which afforded camouflage for both sides, and there were trees. The trees concealed a particularly lethal weapon for the tank commanders, whose field of vision was immeasurably improved by sticking their heads and necks outside their turrets. Heads and necks provided targets for German snipers who had been left behind — courageously, as far as they were concerned — after the withdrawal of their comrades. They concealed themselves in the branches of the oaks, sycamores and other trees, all in leaf, which offered a sufficient height and field of vision for them to fire the single, mortal shot or, perhaps, burst of fire. Casualties from snipers had been heavy and, in some cases, after carrying out their orders and unable to withdraw, the snipers would attempt to surrender.

'Able One to Sunray. Able One to Sunray.'

'Come in Able One. Hearing you loud and clear.'

'Able One to Sunray. Permission to shoot snipers.'

'Sunray to Able One. Permission granted.'

'Wilco. Out.'

The second episode which I remember so clearly concerned a tall Polish officer cadet of about my age or younger and the mule train he was leading to the Polish sector on the right of Cassino town. He had missed his turning further back and had taken the road through Pasquale, winding past green fields, oak and olive trees and scattered peasant houses to the threshold of Hell which was Cassino. He was at the Pasquale end of the road which led directly into the ruined town, along which we had marched some five or six days earlier. He was the second Polish cadet I had met, but in this case his second language was French. He wore no helmet and his black beret with the Polish eagle emblem pinned upon it was perched upon the back of his head, revealing a high intelligent forehead and a very determined expression in his eyes.

'Je suis un peu perdu. Puis-je vous demander si je suis sur la bonne route pour rejoindre mon régiment?'

I advised him that he was not. He should have turned right further back. This road led to Cassino and were he to take it he might well end up in the inhospitable embrace of the Germans. On the other hand, with luck, he would pass our Battalion headquarters in the ruins of the gaol and someone might guide him through the jungle of débris, mines and booby traps to the path which led to the recently mortared quarry and thence to the Polish lines.

'*Je pense qu'il vaut mieux retourner au croisement pour retrouver la route.*'

'*Je ne veux pas revenir en arrière. Je vais continuer.*'

To turn round was out of the question. He gave the necessary order. Twenty mules and ten muleteers passed me in single file, the backs of the animals stacked with ammunition, food, wireless batteries and, it is to be hoped, some alcoholic sustenance for those brave men and boys. When we returned to Cassino on 14 May I found no trace of him or his mules and muleteers, so it would seem that his will had paved the way where others might have faltered.

14 May, a Sunday: 'Change over with John Bowker [Coldstream Guards]. *Walk past checkpoint to gaol. Lose way after gaol. Very dark. Regain road eventually that leads to quarry. Visit both patrols* [gully and Castle Hill] *with Lewis* [soldier servant and runner]. *Very little mortaring but* [German] *flares a nuisance. Very tired and very hot.*'

Losing the way in Cassino was not the best way to relieve John Bowker nor, for that matter, to remain alive. In fact, leaving the town was easier than entering. This may have been because there had been more moonlight six days earlier or because the ruins of the gaol were silhouetted against the skyline, whereas entering the place, once past the gaol on the left, every feature immediately ahead was a blurred mass of rubble and bomb-blasted blocks of stone. Ironically, it was at this very spot earlier, when I was on my own without Lewis, that I had unnecessarily deviated from my accustomed path in an early effort to find the track to Battalion headquarters by climbing over some large blocks of masonry that I reckoned could not conceal any mines.

The word '*eventually*' in the diary entry meant within thirty seconds or a minute, but the fact that I had entered it at all and remember the incident now underlines how dangerous such a situation could be and how important it was to know not only the general direction, which I did, but every inch, which at that particular point I did not; and there were forty-eight men behind me. Had we made any noise? The Germans were within thirty to fifty yards. They were firing flares. Only that day Coldstream Drill Sergeant Walker had cautiously pulled aside some sacking covering a slit in the wall of a forward position to take a quick peek at the enemy lines and had been shot dead by a sniper. On my part, however inadvertent, to invite a mortar stonk or grenades being thrown at us by my not recognizing the route was irresponsible. Maybe, however, the route had been ruptured by shell and mortar fire and, in any case, other than flares revealing our position, it would have been the leading man who would have gone up on a mine and that would have been me.

The Coldstream were relieved, as I was in a different sense, to have found the path. There followed the well-drilled routine of exchanging passwords, placing the outposts in the gully and patrolling across the open space beyond the ossuary and up the Castle Hill track, all without incident.

After some sleep I was able to read various letters received the day before. We could send three air letters a fortnight but there was no limit to the number received. My mail included a letter from David Stevenson, an English cheque book from one of my trustees (Lloyd's Bank branch in Cassino was temporarily closed), a pack of cards from my godmother who considered both temporal and spiritual matters important for she had given me her late husband's pocket bible, carried in the Great War, which I still possess and then wore in my left-hand battledress pocket over my heart, having read how snipers' bullets in the First World War had been diverted by such effective bullet-proofing. Well, it was thicker than a packet of cigarettes and I was a non-smoker, a fact which led to a certain degree of popularity as the addicted received my ration. There was also a letter from Owen Lloyd-George who had replaced Cyril Daniels as the Welsh Guards Ensign at Wellington Barracks.

That evening I received a visit from the Brigade Commander, Charles Haydon, a former Irish Guardsman, accompanied by his Staff Captain Q who was also a Mick, Jim Egan. The Brigadier slipped on his return and nearly joined the German with the severed head and growing finger nails at the back of the cottage adjoining the path between the quarry and the house on the hillside, which was company rear headquarters. We grabbed him and perhaps more than dignity was saved.

16 May, Tuesday, the following day: 'Beginning to get very tired of Cassino. Take out Castle Hill patrol. Bruce Goff [Company Commander] *changes over with Bob Palmer* [Coldstream]. *In the castle.'*

Not everything had gone according to plan and the plans for the fourth and final battle of Cassino had been laid as early as the third week in March when it was evident that the third battle had failed. The intended breakthrough and at the same time the intended breakout from the Anzio beachhead was preceded by Operation Strangle. This was the strategic bombing of the German lines of communication from the Alps and beyond to a few miles behind the front.

On 20 March Churchill had cabled Alexander: 'I wish you could explain to me why this passage by Cassino, Monastery Hill etc., all on a front of two or three miles, is the only place you keep butting at. About five or six divisions have been worn out going into these jaws. Of course I do not know the ground or the battle conditions, but, looking at it from afar, it is puzzling why, if the enemy can be held and dominated at this point, no attacks can be made on the flanks.'

Alexander replied that the flanks in the current appalling weather were out of the question, that the direct assault had depended upon surprise and the concentration of firepower, plus the massive bombing, but 'the destruction caused in Cassino to roads and movement by bombing was so terrific that the employment of tanks or any other fighting vehicles has been seriously impeded. The tenacity of these German paratroopers is quite remarkable considering that they were subjected to the whole of the Mediterranean Air Force plus the better part of 800 guns under the greatest concentration of firepower which has ever been put down and lasting six hours. I doubt if there are any other troops in the world who could have stood up to it and then gone on fighting with the ferocity they have.' He concluded by saying that the plan must envisage an attack on a wider front 'and with greater forces than Freyberg has been able to have for this operation'.

Alexander put into practice what he had envisaged and with the approach of spring he ordered the transfer of Eighth Army now under a former Coldstreamer, General Oliver Leese, from the Adriatic front to take up positions alongside Fifth Army. A whole Army Group was being massed for the great attack and this was a considerably larger force than the American platoon which had reached the monastery walls on 5 February.

17 May: The Germans received their orders to evacuate the now encircled and outflanked positions in the town, the monastery and Mount Calvary where No 1 Company of the 1st Battalion, 3rd Parachute Regiment now numbered one officer, one non-commissioned officer and one soldier. There had been 700 German paratroopers at the beginning of this fourth Battle of Cassino and half that number would fight no more. Polish losses were nearly 4,000 officers and men. 1st Parachute Division, considered to be the elite of the German Army, had lost half its strength. More than 118,000 officers and men were lost on the Allied side between 17 January, the date of the first Cassino battle, and the entry into Rome.

17 May: '*Attack going OK. Poles reported to be near rear of monastery. Heavy mortaring and shelling. Air raid by Jerry.*' This was covering fire for the evacuation but we were not to know it at the time.

18 May, Thursday: [my platoon sergeant] *Lance Sergeant Lewenden, was wounded by shrapnel in the early hours whilst on the Castle Hill patrol.*' It was to be the last patrol. The German paratroopers were slipping away in silence to reach first the monastery and then take a line of withdrawal along mountain tracks, leaving the wounded, too sick to carry, in the care of medical orderlies who were found by the Poles when they entered the monastery.

The first sign any of us in Cassino saw that the Germans had evacuated the town was the sight of two Poles leaping over the ruined monastery and hoisting the Union Jack and the Polish national flag of white and red. On the monks' return, the renowned bronze doors, cast in Constantinople in 1066 for Abbot Desiderius, later Pope Victor III, were discovered among the ruins and restored. Meanwhile, the monastery 'seemed to have regained almost something of peacefulness; at least it was quiet,' wrote *The Times'* correspondent, Philip Ure. 'British troops looked down on us from the lesser height of Castle Hill and waved cheerfully. They are irrepressibly cheerful, these men who have endured so much with stolid, simple courage.' These men were Welsh Guardsmen of No 3 Company, led by Bruce Goff, Bryan Pugh and Company Sergeant-Major John. They were to descend the Castle Hill slope for the last time and for the first time in daylight, other than the stretcher party, and reached the bottom just before another journalist blew himself up on the dead man who had been our marker. He had indeed been booby-trapped. Now there were two bodies to bury – or, at any rate, the pieces.

'For first time in months movement seen in daylight. Such lack of movement was eerie, Battalion moves back to Pasquale. Get very tight [on new wine] *and fall down slit trench.'*

On the way out, along the Pasquale road, we marched in single file past Battalion headquarters in the gaol. Standing outside was our new Commanding Officer, David Davies-Scourfield, whom we saluted. He had been acting Commanding Officer following the hospitalization of Willy Makins at Cerasola.

The upper room of the two-storeyed peasant house at Pasquale was long enough to seat all the Battalion officers who sought this opportunity to meet. Battalions, being often divided into companies not only operationally but also physically, always tried to make the best of such chances. If practical, the sergeants' mess would also foregather.

As the only ensign and most junior officer, I sat at the end of the table. The former Commanding Officer and his successor sat side by side at the far end, opposite me, their neighbours being the Company Commanders, David Gibson Watt (1 Company), Robert Cobbold, David's brother-in-law (No 2), Bruce Goff (No 3) and Julian Martin-Smith (No 4). Nearby was the new Adjutant, Bernard Greer, Tim Bolton, Bruce Goff's second-in-command, Dick Kingzett who was to become Signals Officer, the Intelligence Officer, Geoffrey 'Glob' Evans, Tom Dubuisson, Michael and Pip Bankier, Christopher Maude and so on. On my right, facing the colonels at the far end, was Hugh FitzGerald Arbuthnot, the officer in charge of 3-inch mortars; as Hilaire Belloc put it:

'Like many of the upper class
He liked the sound of broken glass.'

The Mortar Officer, on consuming quantities of new wine to which he was wholly unaccustomed, had developed a sudden antipathy towards Colonel Sir William Makins, third baronet, whose motto was 'Shine thou in the light' and whose target area, as it were, was fully revealed by the light of the candles flickering in front of him. The Mortar Officer felt that his antipathy should now be made manifest, which he expressed by throwing another form of missile, namely a full bottle of wine. Thus, with complete disdain for both the contents of the bottle and the intended target, Captain, shortly to be Sir Hugh, seventh baronet, motto 'Innocent and true', propelled with considerable dexterity and flick of the wrist this unusual form of missile in the direction of his former Commanding Officer and, ipso facto, also in that of his successor. Luckily both Colonels were talking to their neighbours and the missile whistled between them and smashed against the wall behind. No one paid any attention. In the candlelight it may not even have been observed. Everyone continued their conversation. The mess waiters remained expressionless and imperturbable. Thirty-nine years later, Hugh's brother officer, Owen Lloyd-George, who was not present, wrote his obituary notice in *The Times*: 'Hugh showed great courage and zest for the battle at all times and was adored by his men ... a person with an enormous sense of fun ... and for the uninitiated a spontaneous excursion could prove an alarming experience. But he was at heart a gentle compassionate man.'

It was on leaving the cottage that the new wine went both to my head and my knees with the result that I fell into a slit trench. Even so, I thought it better that I should be there than that, perhaps, it might have been the fate of poor Willy to be laid to rest without shine or light except that from heaven. I thought of another rhyme:

'Billy in one of his nice new sashes,
Fell in the fire and was burnt to ashes;
Now, although the room grows chilly,
I haven't the heart to poke poor Billy.'

In the ashes and ruins of the monastery, on 18 May, 1944, the Poles who had placed the flags of the British Empire and Poland on its crumbled ramparts said that they could literally not take a step without treading on a dead German. The badly wounded who had been left behind stated that they had not eaten for three days. In just over a week's time the paratroopers who had withdrawn from their positions in Cassino were again in battle and this time in direct and bloody opposition to the Grenadiers, Coldstream and

Welsh Guards in a battle which was to last three whole days on the road to Rome.

Meanwhile Army Group headquarters announced the fall of Cassino with a half truth: 'Cassino and the monastery have been conquered. The last attack against the town was delivered by British troops, while the Poles took the abbey ... after the unique feat of the Fifth Army in penetrating the Gustav Line on 14 May, and, thanks to the swift advance of French and American troops into the mountains, the enemy has been completely out-manoeuvred by the Allied armies in Italy .... 1 Parachute Division, the best fighting unit in the German Army, is estimated to have lost half its strength.'

A German source was to write: 'The salient feature of this hard fight had been the chivalry displayed by both sides. When the German attack on Rocca Janula [the castle] failed, the British Commander at once agreed to a two-hour truce, and the Indians and Germans worked side by side, gathering the dead and tending the wounded ... exactly the same decency was shown by both sides when the second German attack on 22 March also failed. The garrison of the castle handed over the German wounded, and the British medical officer even gave the Germans four stretchers to help with their evacuation. The Gurkhas gave their opponents − and not only the wounded − cigarettes and chocolates, offered them a swig from their water bottles and in many other small ways demonstrated the esteem in which they held a worthy foe. But the moment the truce ended, the fighting continued as bitterly as ever. The next day, however, when the German medical orderlies returned the stretchers they had borrowed, the Gurkhas received them with all the courtesy of their race' (*Monte Cassino*, Rudolf Böhmler).

Alexander cabled Churchill that the capture 'of Cassino means a great deal to me and both my armies'. The Poles had a special medal struck with 'Monte Cassino' inscribed on it. As far as I was concerned, I was extremely grateful that the last attack against the town, contrary to the announcement made by Army Group headquarters, had not been delivered by British troops or any troops. It had simply been evacuated. That fact meant a great deal to me.

VI

The Battle Before Arce

THE HOLDING POSITION of 1st Guards Brigade in Cassino, where the Battalion had spent twenty-nine days in all, was immediately exchanged for a more aggressive role. My entry for Friday, May 19 reads: *'Leave with advance party to new harbour area, three miles away as crow flies — sixteen the way we went. Took us 7½ hours and then we arrived after the Battalion. I was in [Bren] carrier. Most uncomfortable. First [assembly] area cancelled. Arrive very tired and dusty* [despite some rain]. *Traffic congestion was considerable'*.

The traffic congestion was an Army on the move — some 20,000 vehicles, 2,000 tanks and artillery — along one Roman road, the Via Casilina or Route 6, which had been built for the legions in their marching columns and latterly for two-way single traffic some thirty years earlier with the advent of the motor car. Inevitably other traffic lanes had been created across the fields of the fertile Liri Valley, including the former railway track methodically destroyed by the Germans and, with equal devotion, later restored by the Royal Engineers.

The bulk of the traffic — that is to say the armoured divisions and infantry divisions plus their supporting artillery and forward echelons — was ahead of us or even amongst us, having just fought for seven days to smash their way through the German lines of defence. In fact, the whole front was now advancing. In the mountains to our right, Polish troops, Indian and other units of the British Dominions were capturing height after height, and on our left the French were pressing through the Aurunci Mountains, while the American II Corps were pushing up the coast towards Anzio with considerable help from the Royal Navy and other Allied naval units who were bombarding the retreating Germans.

Meanwhile, I was thankful that it was not I who was in charge of this advance party because no one, not even the jeep driver, could possibly have known the way. Tim Bolton and his dust-covered advance party arrived after the Battalion, guided more by determination than directions given. Rome, eighty miles away, was the political objective, its airfields further north and the entrapment of the German army further south were the military prizes.

The latter objective was to be achieved, it was intended, by trapping the German Tenth Army between Eighth Army and Fifth Army forces advancing from the south and Fifth Army's VI Corps breaking out of the Anzio beachhead, which Churchill described as the 'cop'. Initially, fifty miles separated the two fronts of the Allied Armies.

The general momentum of the advance was, however, slowest in the Liri Valley. British and Dominion formations were fighting their way northwards in an increasingly bloody battle to break through the Senger Barrier (formerly Adolf Hitler Line) between Pontecorvo and Aquino just to the left of Route 6. General von Senger und Etterlin had returned from leave, but even his undoubted gifts of generalship were unable to stem the advance and the line was broken by the Canadians after bitter fighting on 23 May. German artillery had also been trained upon the Canadians by the paratroopers who were still on the Monte Cairo massif and were not dislodged by the Poles until 25 May.

It was also on 23 May that Truscott's VI Corps broke out of the beachhead with written instructions from 15th Army Group to take Valmontone and trap the retreating German Tenth Army, the western flank of which was XIV Panzer Corps commanded by von Senger.

22 May: 'Enemy aircraft overhead [during the night]. *Very cold, so get up. Rumours about move. Bruce* [Goff] *and Bryan* [Pugh] *L.O.B. Tim* [Bolton] *i/c Company* [aged twenty-three].' Enemy aircraft, luckily for us, only flew at night. Allied domination of the sky was absolute, which meant that the Germans' principal movements were made after dark, including their withdrawal from the battles later on and their escape from the traps being set for them.

23 May: 'Run, walk and baths.' Bruce Goff's idea of leadership was what would now be called laid-back, but Tim Bolton's was definitely based upon physical jerks and cold showers. We were on *'four hours' notice to move'*. I wrote more letters and received some. *'Germans reported withdrawing'*, which was not unlikely, given the current situation. Yet there was also something which was not given world coverage at the time: *'See Sergeant Monroe about second star.'* This referred to my automatic — let there be no false modesty — promotion from Ensign to Lieutenant, namely two stars on each shoulder, after six months of commissioned service, an increase of pay to £292.12s, less £22 income tax but plus £100 overseas allowance, which was due to take place in a few days' time. It very nearly did not take place, however.

We had followed the battle after leaving Cassino, weaving our way through fields, vineyards, olive groves, orchards and copses all ripped apart by shell fire, mortaring and bombing, not to mention minefields. Dust on our faces, uniforms and vehicles looked as if a bag of cream-coloured flour had exploded above us. The fields were ploughed anew by the wheels and tracks of a fully armoured and motorized army; some of them would move no more, nor their occupants. Enemy tanks and vehicles were also strewn around. Improvised graves were everywhere, marked by no more than a rifle stuck into the ground and the helmet of the dead man placed on its butt. Shell cases, ammunition dumps abandoned in the German withdrawal, stores and equipment, broken artillery pieces, their crews dead and, when not yet buried, spread-eagled around their guns. It was St Benedict's monks who always referred to the Liri as *Campana felix*, joyous countryside or perhaps, more loosely, Happy Valley.

Our convoy was sometimes overtaken by other units and occasionally by senior commanders, their red flags flying from the masts on the front of their jeeps and their dust-coated red insignia adding a muted dash of colour, while their ADCs and wireless operators were stuck in the back or following close behind. There was more dust as they passed us.

On 24 May reveille was at 0400 hours. We awoke in the midst of the cornfields and poppies where we had harboured. Fireflies and crickets were everywhere and the inevitable croaking of the bullfrogs in some nearby patch of water was still in full throat, but of birds and of peasants there was none. *'Breakfast at 0500 hours. All cock. Do not move off in early morning as Canadians have taken up all road space during advance. Write airgraphs. Do not move off as expected. 31 Roberts has spider in rifle barrel.'* (Not surprising in Italy. A hoary joke in England, hence it being mentioned.)

Thursday, 25 May: *'Spend whole day travelling in jeep* [in the back. Tim was in the front].' We travelled, I believe, thirteen miles in eighteen hours. *'Convoy takes very long time to reach new harbour area. Dive-bombed during the night. Very light casualties considering.'*

Tim Bolton wished to hold an 'O' group. My attention was, however, distracted by the German aircraft overhead, engine noise being something to which all of us were attuned. Either on the Chinese principle that if you pay no attention the nuisance will go away, or on the British that nuisance is to be ignored with disdain, the 'O' group, like the plane overhead, droned on. I had noted that the carrier platoon, a short distance from us, had incautiously started to brew up and the flames from their petrol cookers were, presumably, engaging the attention of the lone ranger above. Furthermore, our 'O' group was being held in a signals vehicle.

I thought it better to say nothing and do nothing. I was attending this important conference about the state of 8th Army as it affected 3 Company, 3rd Battalion, Welsh Guards, and there was someone in charge of the carrier platoon who had, it appeared, thought fit to allow petrol cookers to be lit. I was, however, after five minutes, dismissed and, on emerging, sought the safety of a slit trench and awaited the whistle of bombs, or the whoosh. I was wrong. It was a Stuka and its pilot, having taken note of the light from the petrol cookers, improved his view by dropping flares and then dive-bombed with an increasingly menacing whine while preparing to release both incendiary and high-explosive bombs. He returned for several encores. If dive-bombing at night was a tricky business for the pilot, it was a singularly unpleasant one for the target. The unit harbouring next to us was also hit, some of their ammunition trucks went up; two 17-pounder anti-tank guns were destroyed as well as some Welsh Guards vehicles. Three guardsmen were killed and twenty wounded.

Needless to say, the 'O' group was abruptly adjourned and the participants hurled themselves out of the vehicle and piled on top of me in the slit trench. The 'O' group then reassembled, the dead were buried and the wounded were tended. The incident was closed with the Battalion minus twenty-three men and letters would be written to the bereaved. The wounded would write that they had had a narrow escape and, presumably, no one mentioned the petrol cookers.

The Allied lines had, meanwhile, moved forward.

22 May: Despite some setbacks, the French Expeditionary Force, under Fifth Army Command, had continued their great advance through the trackless mass of the Lepini Mountains between US II Corps and the Liri Valley, with 12,000 goumiers in the vanguard. On this day they took Pico and were on a line to take Ceprano, a town four or five miles south-west of Arce, had Alexander acceded to the request of Mark Clark who had observed the comparatively slow progress of Eighth Army. The River Sacco, however, was the boundary between the two armies and Alexander refused, saying that Route 6, on which lay both Arce and Ceprano, could only cope with those columns currently using it. In fact, Eighth Army had been held up in the valley while the heights on either side were being cleared.

23 May: The Canadians broke through at Aquino and, on the Anzio front, General Truscott's VI Corps broke out of the beachhead with orders issued by Alexander to trap the German Tenth Army at Valmontone. Truscott had been joined by the US II Corps advancing from the south.

24 May: After the Canadians had begun their advance on the 23rd, General Burns' 5th Armoured Division reached the Melfa River.

25 May: The Poles captured Monte Cairo. The Derbyshire Yeomanry (6th Armoured Division) had reached the Melfa River during the afternoon on the Canadian right flank. Three troops of Stuarts and Shermans crossed the river but were ordered to withdraw under heavy fire. Motorized infantry were also unable to cross. The Germans withdrew on the Canadian front – on the left flank of 6th Armoured Division – and the Canadians advanced five miles to the Liri (on 26 May) opposite Ceprano. However, through a misunderstanding, or possibly as a result of a technical infringement of crossing corps boundaries or misappreciation of enemy intentions which was

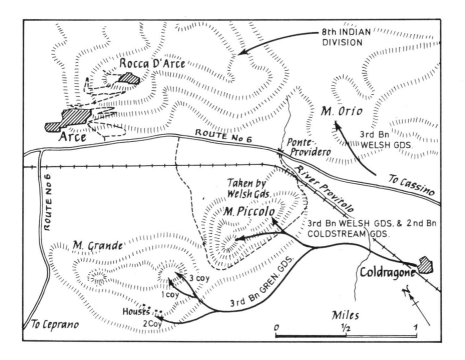

prevalent in this sector, the Canadians withdrew from Monte Grande on 25 May. On the same day General Richard Heidrich ordered 1st Parachute Regiment, commanded by Colonel Karl Schultz, to take up defensive positions on high ground a mile and a half south of Arce, comprising three features – Orio, Piccolo and Grande – which blocked the approach to the town and lay on either side of the road. The 1st Battalion was commanded by Major Werner Graf von der Schulenberg, the 2nd by Major Gröschke and the 3rd by Major Becker. All three majors had a mountain each.

25 May: With the Canadians approaching Ceprano, both XIII Corps and Eighth Army headquarters considered it important that 6th Armoured Division on the Canadians' right should reach the hills beyond Arce and push on to Isola. These plans and subsequent orders were based on the presumption of a German withdrawal – current on most sectors of the front at this moment – and Higher Command's tactical appreciation that the enemy were not going to defend Arce or occupy its protective line of hills facing the thrust of 6th Armoured Division's drive northwards. The importance of Arce to the retreating Germans must have been realized by Corps and Army Commands. However, the information they are said to have received – for the alternative is that their plan was based upon wishful thinking – was precisely that 'Arce was now being evacuated and the hills flanking the pass were not being held' (*Welsh Guards at War*). The enemy were in difficult straits, but after defeat they were making an orderly and carefully calculated withdrawal. At this moment, however, the attention of Higher Command was mainly focused on Frosinone which was the penultimate objective before the Fifth and Eighth Army trap was sprung at Valmontone — the trap, in fact, which was never sprung.

The enemy, on the other hand, regarded the holding of the forward defences of Arce as vital. The town not only lay on the route to Rome, but it was also a pivotal point for the German LI Mountain Corps' withdrawal towards Subiaco and Isola, Sora and Avezzano. Not surprisingly, General Fuerstein put in his best troops to defend it. In consequence, LI Mountain Corps' escaped the trap that was, in this case, never laid. On the contrary, thanks to faulty intelligence or its interpretation — either way, always a grave risk in war — it was we who marched into a trap, albeit an obvious one, for the evidence was before the eyes and ears — it was very noisy — of both Brigadier Charles Haydon, a much respected and cautious man, and General V. Evelegh who may well have tried to dissuade Corps Headquarters; but 'Press on!' or 'Push on!' was the order and pushed we were in more than one sense of the word.

26 May: The 'Derby Yeo' recrossed the Melfa at 1030 hours and were followed by the 3rd Battalion Grenadier Guards on Shermans of the 16th/5th Lancers at 1100 without opposition. They advanced rapidly in close country to the village of Coldragone and the hamlet of Le Cese, just beyond, three miles north of the River Melfa which they reached at 1500. On their front, due north, was the 1,600-foot-high Monte Orio, at the foot of which lay the hamlet of Providero. North-north-west were two sharp and long hills called Piccolo, 600 feet, and Grande, 720 feet, divided by a valley with steep slopes on either side, 250 yards wide, a mile and a half south of Arce. Route 6 and the destroyed railway line ran through the defile between Orio and Piccolo. This was the first natural barrier which lay astride the Liri Valley, and the 1st Parachute Regiment was now in position to act as a determined rearguard, while von Vietinghoff's German Tenth Army withdrew from the hills and valleys towards the north.

The miscalculation of XIII Corps Intelligence — or Eighth Army or 15th Army Group — was to confuse an enemy evacuation through or of the town with a withdrawal from the heights before and beyond it. The negative side of air domination was that the enemy were well practised in effective camouflage and movement by night. On the other hand, movement through Arce might have been risked as Allied air forces would not have wished to bomb Italian civilians unnecessarily, when the escape routes north were receiving all due attention. Civilians could also have been a source of intelligence, likewise prisoners of war, agents or SOE behind the lines and enemy radio communications. It could well be that what was received was misinformation – the confusion between town movement and the occupation of the heights – or deliberate disinformation either directly or by radio.

26 May: Meanwhile, after an hour spent in regrouping, the Grenadiers at Coldragone/Le Cese moved forward behind the tanks of the 16th/5th Lancers. It was the divisional and brigade intention that Arce should be taken this day. The Grenadiers were ordered to occupy the high ground on either side of the pass between Orio and Piccolo in order to create a safe, or safer, passage for the tanks to pass through. This was a basic military necessity and required no particular knowledge in higher echelons of the events at Thermopylae, Roncesvalles or the Khyber. As the Grenadiers approached the high ground on both sides the 1st Parachute Regiment opened up with machine-gun fire which killed five men and wounded seventeen. The road running between the two points was impassable, pounded by heavy shellfire and mortaring. Meanwhile the tanks of the 16th/5th Lancers tried to move away from the road along the parched and dusty farm tracks where visibility was limited to about 100 yards. This attempt was also stopped by shellfire directed from the German OPs traditionally placed on the forward slopes of the hills ahead. Another obstacle to the tanks was the fact that the bridge across the dried-up River Provitolo, the Ponte Providero, was blown and the site was assumed to be covered by enemy guns.

The Grenadier rear companies, meanwhile, dug in behind the low hill beyond Coldragone near the hamlet of Le Cese. It must now have become clear to Brigade and Divisional headquarters that not only was Arce not going to fall on this day but that this forward position was being defended with vigour and in some strength. Nevertheless, the initial mistake, of appreciating the importance of Arce to the enemy but discarding prudence on receipt of erroneous intelligence, was compounded by the orders which were now given to the 3rd Battalion, Welsh Guards, namely to pass through the Grenadier lines and advance towards Arce. It did not require second sight to know the outcome: the opposition which had halted the Grenadier advance to and beyond Arce *on the hills flanking the pass* in the afternoon made it clear that the Germans were not only occupying the heights and thus controlled the pass, but had under command an effective amount of artillery to block Route 6. In fact, the information given to Lieutenant-Colonel David Davies-Scourfield in the early evening that the enemy were believed to be withdrawing and that the heights were not occupied was palpably false. Whether or not disinformation was being disseminated by radio and picked up by Intelligence (correct information of the enemy withdrawal three days later was intercepted and their lines of withdrawal were duly bombarded), evidence of the enemy presence *on the ground* was clearly set before all those in command, whose 'O' Group was hardly held under circumstances of relief and relaxation.

David Davies-Scourfield, nonetheless, was given orders to pass through the Grenadiers — who were known by Brigade and Division headquarters *not* to be occupying the heights whatever else might have been momentarily imprecise about their forward companies' positions, due to a form of breakdown in their communications — and, as stated, advance through the pass towards Arce. This was pure fantasy.

The use of mechanized infantry in an armoured division when the tanks are held up is a classic exercise and was duly carried out when the Grenadiers were sent forward. They proved, not least by their casualties, the presence of the enemy on the hills overlooking both sides of the pass and, thus, the German capability of blocking the road to Arce.

Instead, therefore, of accepting the facts and taking the necessary action, the worst decision was made at divisional level (when divisional artillery was still in the column at the rear) to repeat an exercise which had already proved the futility of a repetition, and which had revealed the necessary intelligence upon which to act: the enemy were there. Ergo, dig in, bombard, attack and outflank (the last mentioned eventually being done by 8th Indian Division) all of which, *force majeure*, were executed in the course of the next three days — 300 casualties later.

The Welsh Guards were a long way back in the column when they were ordered to cross the Melfa. They were separated from their transport — as motorized infantry — which meant that the wireless batteries could not be recharged and communications were consequently gravely affected, as we were brought forward on the tanks of the Lothian and Border Horse from which elevated position we had a commander's view of the battlefield. To left and right were at least five Canadian tanks which had been knocked out. The smell of rotting corpses was pungent. We then passed the wreck of the dug-in and well-camouflaged 88mm anti-tank gun which had caused most if not all of the damage. Its crew were scattered lifeless around their weapon. While we were observing all this, scores of German prisoners were trudging wearily past us.

Bird life was not very evident, but there must have been some doves remaining in no-man's-land as four of their white downy underfeathers fell on my lap. Memories of the book of that name came to mind, then the irony of the symbol of peace; but the dove was also the symbol of the Holy Spirit. Then the tank swivelled suddenly on its tracks as the driver changed direction and the attention of all of us was concentrated upon clinging for dear life to anything that could be clutched. Anything included pots and pans roped to the superstructure. It was called 'marrying'. We were, however, a little uncertain about its legitimacy, let alone the location of the honeymoon. The date of the 'wedding' was Friday, 26 May, the feast of St Philip Neri, the Florentine founder of the Oratory, who was once heard to declare that 'for one who truly loves God, there is nothing more difficult and painful than to remain alive'. The next three days were to prove, for those who were in both 1st Guards Brigade and 1st Parachute Regiment, not only difficult but sometimes singularly painful.

26 May: 'Prepare for battle. 'O' group spend whole day swanning. See first Jerry prisoners. March up Route 6. Mortared. Church bells ringing in no-man's-land. Letter from Mother.'

26 May: We jumped off the tanks in an assembly area behind the Grenadier positions and I attended an 'O' group underneath a vehicle – not a particularly safe haven – where I found my cousins Pip and Michael Bankier. Then, towards the end of daylight, at 2130, Colonel David Davies-Scourfield received his orders to advance.

At the same time both Brigade and Grenadier headquarters were uncertain of the precise position of their left-hand forward company, facing Piccolo, and John Retallack, Welsh Guards, a Liaison Officer at Brigade Headquarters (and, much later, commander of the Guards Parachute Battalion) was sent forward to find out what was happening. This was difficult to determine, although what was clear was that the Grenadiers were *not* occupying the hills on either side of the pass. The Welsh Guards were then ordered 'to push forward during the night, ahead of 3rd Grenadier Guards and make their way as far as possible towards Arce' (1st Guards Brigade War Diary). At Arce, or beyond, the Grenadiers would pass through and the Coldstream, with 17th/21st Lancers under command, were to advance towards Isola. Not surprisingly, none of this happened. We moved into battle at 2300 hours.

We marched up Route 6 in the direction of Arce. The fact that we were being mortared meant that we were beginning to enter into battle. Helmets were worn. Only small packs, weapons, ammunition and trenching tools were carried, plus wireless sets, if they worked, and stretchers. In the trouser pockets of the battledress or denims were inner pockets for an emergency ration of concentrated chocolate and a field dressing. In the small pack were mess tins, mug, washing and shaving kit. In the pouches attached to the webbing in front was ammunition, in my case .45mm for my Tommy gun, and also grenades. Diaries were left behind, although paper and pencil could be fitted into the small pack or battledress. I had also brought a paperback, *I Claudius* by Robert Graves. Boots with gaiters were our footwear.

The platoon and company wireless operators had to lug their heavy sets on their backs. The PIAT and Bren operators might also have to carry their Lee-Enfield rifles in addition. Battalion headquarter communications were, as far as possible, conducted from an armoured White scout car equipped with wireless. Glued more or less constantly to this set for the next three days, with only the barest moments of snatched sleep, was the adjutant, Bernard Greer, doing a very different job to that which he had fulfilled at the Training Battalion with equal competence and devotion to duty.

The first sign of trouble as far as we were concerned was the sight of the Grenadiers sitting by the side of the road, some wearing their peaked caps as they would when out of the battle area. We were advancing in single file along Route 6, platoon by platoon, on alternate sides of the road to minimize casualties against the shelling and mortars. It was obvious that the Grenadiers were nowhere other than on the road.

The local church bells were ringing loudly in the middle of the night, either to warn the parishioners or the 1st Parachute Regiment who were 'believed to be withdrawing' north of Arce, in spite of the shelling which wounded two men in the leading company, not far from David Davies-Scourfield, who was at the head of the column.

The black silhouette of the hills grew closer and more menacing. It was pitch dark, only four days after the new moon, and the Commanding Officer decided that, given the nature of his orders and his assessment of the current situation, the two stood a good chance of being incompatible. To advance through the gap in accordance with his orders could indeed be into the valley of death – all 600 of us. He called a halt and ordered the companies to take up positions on either side of the road and dig in. At dawn, David Davies-Scourfield ordered patrols to establish whether or not the enemy were on the hills in strength or had simply left a thin rearguard, or had positioned an artillery OP or were, as Higher Command would have it, not even there at all.

The Germans began their field day at dawn. The sun was shining and they had an excellent view with an equally good field of fire. No smoke shells impeded them. In fact the OPs were quite close, for as General von Senger und Etterlin was to write – and was not so very far away himself at that moment – in his book *Neither Fear nor Hope*: 'It was German practice to place the artillery observers half-way up the hills in a concealed position with a camouflaged background'. The German OPs must have wondered at the folly of their enemy and their luck in not being pounded to pieces.

Not only was the Battalion halted in the valley below, but so too were the supporting arms and tanks, all queuing in column or scattered at the side of the road. We were sitting targets, subject to constant and accurate shelling and mortaring.

27 May: '[Continue] *move up Route 6.* [Now being] *shelled. Eerie church bells* [still] *ringing in no-man's land. Companies make recce in force on Monte Piccolo and Orio. No supporting fire* [or smoke]. *7 men killed* [next to me]. *Several wounded. Myself very slightly in leg with shrapnel. Christopher Maude killed in slit trench next to self. Shell hit tree and burst down* [wards]. *Mick Bankier wounded. Pip Bankier missing. Tim Hayley and Robert Cobbold killed.'*

Calmly and quietly Colonel David Davies-Scourfield ordered two companies to reconnoitre the hills on either side of the road and, if possible, to occupy them. On the right Julian Martin-Smith (4 Company) sent Tim Hayley with a twelve-man fighting patrol to the crest of Monte Orio and we watched as they crossed a number of spurs and reentrants. Suddenly we heard shots. Only three of this patrol returned. The rest were either killed or wounded and then taken prisoner. Julian Martin-Smith then moved his whole company in a right-flanking movement which was shelled and sniped at, wounding Mick Bankier and several others. This movement was supported by Sherman tanks but not artillery and No. 4 Company established itself near the peak of Monte Orio.

On the left, Robert Cobbold's company was to probe and, if possible, occupy Piccolo, to the right of Monte Grande and next to the pass which led to Arce. Standing at right-angles to the road, long, rocky and steep in terms of No 2 Company's approach, which began by crossing a thick wood, Piccolo was terraced with two to three-foot-high walls for olive cultivation and strewn with rocks and boulders. Twelve tanks and a Gunner OP accompanied them, but the enemy had not yet been located. When he was, it was impracticable to fire.

The leading platoon, pressing through the wood, went too far to the left. Batteries not being able to be renewed because of separation from our transport on Divisional orders, wireless communication could not be made and Robert Cobbold tried to bring this platoon back in the right direction by going himself. He and several members of the platoon were killed.

Two other platoons were meanwhile making their way in increasing heat and enemy fire, clambering over the terraced olive groves, sweating their way to the top. They had suffered casualties but their ascent had, in fact, been a trap. From the flanks and summit, the 1st Parachute Regiment opened a withering fire. Pip Bankier, now in command, was able to silence some of the German posts, but he was outnumbered and suffered casualties from every burst of Schmeisser and Spandau fire which ripped into his much-reduced company. Unable to take the summit, he with five men covered the withdrawal under Johnny Davies who was wounded.

This withdrawal was done with calmness and skill. Pip Bankier and his five gallant companions were all killed. One guardsman, 30 Jones H.R., was badly wounded and dragged himself back towards our lines. He was found, on the third morning, alive, having fired all his ammunition. A final count of No 2 Company revealed a strength of forty-six men under Company Sergeant-Major Hillier.

Meanwhile, No 3 Company, under Tim Bolton, with Christopher Maude and myself as the officers, was stationed in reserve near the White scout car of Battalion battle headquarters. We were on the left-hand side of the road, in a green field behind a hill and near a dried-up stream, the banks of which were covered with trees. Beyond the hill, immediately in front of us, was open ground and then the slopes of Monte Piccolo. The moment we had received orders in the early hours of the morning to remain where we were, we had dug in. At dawn, shells — high explosive (HE) and armour piercing (AP) — began to come down on us as well as mortar bombs, directed no doubt by enemy OPs almost within hailing distance.

As I did my rounds, I had to call several times for stretcher-bearers. Their hands were full and some of them were wounded. Likewise, the medical centre under Dai Morris, a most calm, loveable and competent medical officer with a quiet, lilting Welsh voice, had more than enough to keep them busy. Lewis had dug us a double-breadth slit trench. It was not deep but enough to save our lives.

The first targets were the infantry. Despite efforts at camouflage they could clearly be seen by the enemy, for we could see them too on the heights of Orio. Next in line were the command vehicles — the White scout car, the Battalion wireless truck, carriers, jeeps and any other transport. Then there were the tanks of the 2nd Lothian and Border Horse who were under command. In what was by now full daylight in blazing sunlight, and no cover provided by smoke canisters or artillery counter-barrage, the cranking, grinding and whining engine noise of tanks was now amongst us as they took up position in the dried-up bed of the Provitolo to our left, under cover of the trees, and in the field just beyond.

The enemy began to concentrate his fire upon us, not least because the tank fire was beginning, in its turn, to concentrate on his own forward positions. I moved momentarily from the small open field to see if there was any better cover for the company in the banks of the stream bed which was about a foot or so deep. In so doing I was within ten feet of the nearest tanks, and after several enemy shells had sliced through the leaves and exploded very near to me, luckily not hitting the branches, I decided that it was a pointless manoeuvre. Had the tanks not been there, it would have made sense.

Lewis, meanwhile, had divided his time between digging and helping with casualties and our hole in the ground was six inches deep. We then heard the whoosh of a salvo descending upon us. It was, in all probability, a short-fall aimed at the tanks. We dived into our shallow refuge but all around us was carnage. The casualties this time were considerable. Two guardsmen next to me were killed outright, their clothes and bodies on fire, and no amount of earth heaped upon them by their comrades could save them from dying on the field of honour. Others lay around dead or wounded. A stretcher-bearer had a piece of shrapnel lodged in his buttocks. He had been a sergeant, reduced to the ranks for, in all probability, a comparatively minor offence and it was almost a tradition that the dangerous and humanitarian job of stretcher-bearer would be offered to someone of his courage and initiative.

Tim Bolton during this time had been attending a Battalion 'O' group. The Company was moved forward to a small hill in front of us where there were two peasant houses. One was on the crest of the hill which we avoided at all costs as an inevitable target, the other was hidden from view and was smaller. Outside the smaller building and within a few yards of the larger, some slit trenches had been dug and the Company 'O' group, comprising Christopher Maude, some senior NCOs and myself, were gathered to hear our orders from Tim who was to join us.

I then remembered *I Claudius*. I had reached page 65. I disliked, then and now, turning down pages, even of paperbacks, and had memorized the page number in case the marker should slip out. I began to read on the top of one of the slit trenches when, instead of becoming absorbed in what I was reading, I felt prompted to get inside the trench. A professionally-dug job, luckily in soft earth, it was long enough to sit in and stretch out and deep enough to come up to my chest had I stood. I settled down and began to read.

Next to me, standing in an adjoining slit trench, was Christopher Maude, wearing his steel helmet, and with him was one of the platoon sergeants. They were chatting to the others. Shells were passing overhead, their trajectory taking them over our small hill to their targets beyond, namely the tank squadron. Air-burst shells were not then in use. We were not the target, although we were only a very short distance in front and our attitude was an unconscious collective tribute to the accuracy of the German gunnery.

Guns, however, fired from a mile or two away can, in terms of their trajectory, be an inch or two out. The explosion and the dust which momentarily blinded me, plus a short stabbing pain in my left leg, indicated that a shell had landed next to us. In fact, in passing overhead, it had hit the branch or trunk of an olive tree and blasted its shrapnel in all directions. I heard one of those next to me cry out, 'Oh, my God. Oh, my God. Oh, my God.' It is not something I am going to forget. The shrapnel had mercifully killed him immediately, piercing his helmet and penetrating his skull. Some others in the 'O' group were badly wounded. Tim and I buried Christopher and helped to bury the others. The wounded were evacuated to the caring hands of Dai Morris. My leg wound was trivial and a surgical dressing was applied.

Throughout the day we stayed in the same area, while No 4 Company made its way to the summit of Monte Orio and the remnants of No 2 Company withdrew or lay low until nightfall. At Division headquarters the reality of the situation had certainly dawned and, together with 26th Armoured Brigade, 1st Guards Brigade was now preparing this time to attack the enemy positions on Piccolo and Grande in strength with full supporting fire, the guns having now been placed in positions where they could fire.

During the night, however, there were moments of silence and shortly before midnight on the 27th we heard the phut-phutting of a diesel-driven enemy motorbicycle and sidecar coming slowly towards us. They had obviously lost their way. Suddenly we heard three dull thumps, followed by our 3-inch mortars exploding in front of us. Hugh Arbuthnot and/or his boys were wide awake. The phut-phutting ceased.

27 May: Corps headquarters, acknowledging the facts, sent the 17th Brigade of 8th Indian Division on a right-hook operation through the mountains towards Arce. On the left some of the Irish Regiment of 11th Brigade in the 5th Canadian Armoured Division swam the Liri and entered Ceprano against opposition and established a bridgehead. On the same day tanks of 26th Armoured Brigade failed to climb the approaches and reach the summits of Piccolo and Grande and also to discover a route to Arce from the south-west, around the left flank of Grande.

27 May: The 2nd Battalion, Coldstream Guards were ordered to undertake a night attack against Piccolo, while the Grenadiers were ordered to attack Grande, further to the left. As the Coldstream moved off they passed the church, the bells of which again tolled their mysterious warning. The 3rd Battalion, Grenadiers, under Lieutenant-Colonel John Goschen, also supported by a creeping barrage of heavy artillery, followed behind the Coldstream and then moved in the dark towards Grande.

28 May: The Grenadiers suffered casualties on the left flank during the initial approach but occupied the right-hand promontories of Grande. At dawn a German counterattack, preceded by intense mortar and shell-fire, then forced a Grenadier withdrawal, one Company commander, Tony Way, being badly wounded. There was also a shortage of ammunition which was compounded when one of the relief carriers bearing the much-needed boxes containing bullets, mortar bombs and grenades received a direct hit. The enemy had, in addition, infiltrated between Piccolo and Grande as well as round the left flank of the Grenadier position, which had been weakened by the casualties inflicted on No 2 Company commanded by Mervyn Sandys whose survivors were rallied by Tony Denny, the second-in-command.

28 May: At the same time most of Piccolo was taken by the Coldstream and the attached Scots Guards company (all the officers of which were casualties) against a thin line of machine-gun posts which were heavily shelled and mortared by Corps artillery and Battalion supporting fire. Several wounded Welsh Guardsmen were found and evacuated. Then, at 0430, the first German counterattack was launched, principally against Grande. This was followed by a further attack at 0800 against the Coldstream company under Desmond Chichester and the Scots Guards company under Andrew Neilson who was badly wounded but stayed at his post and refused to be evacuated. Humphrey Bridgeman, Scots Guards, was killed. The forward slopes were lost, and the Grenadier withdrawal exposed the left flank, but the situation remained under control. Water and ammunition finally reached the companies in what was by now full daylight on a blazing hot day. At 1500 the Germans formed up to launch a further attack and were heavily shot up by the Ayrshire Yeomanry and the guns of the 17th/21st Lancers who were firing hull-down only a few yards behind where we were placed, and 1000 yards (900 metres) from the enemy.

28 May, Whit Sunday: 'Still in this bloody hole. No one has had any sleep. Move back to hill to defend BHQ.' A late entry for the day: *'Am only subaltern in battle unwounded or alive. John Davies wounded also John Nichol-Carne and Ossie Smythe.'*

In the early hours of the morning we moved back slightly to escape the heavy shelling – and incidentally to defend Battalion headquarters – but by now our own firepower had been organized. The German positions on Piccolo and Grande to the west were being pounded by 26th Armoured Brigade together with the divisional artillery and 4-inch mortars.

The Germans withdrew to avoid the bombardment, but returned when the barrage ceased and fought hard to dislodge the Coldstream and Scots Guards. In the course of the night and during most of the following day, very sharp and continuous fighting took place with the Germans still holding a vital part of the summit, a spur which protruded from the main part of Piccolo and which commanded the road through the pass.

The Welsh Guards were then called upon to finish the job. David Davies-Scourfield ordered No 1 Company to take and hold the position. An intense artillery barrage was put down – all the Divisional artillery, plus an AGRA (Army Group, Royal Artillery), tank guns and Battalion mortars. The Germans, however, replied with a very heavy stonk which caused casualties, and the attack was made with only two platoons. Thus, at 1800, David Gibson-Watt, leading a depleted No 1 Company, moved through the lines of the Coldstream. At this moment No 1 Company sergeants, among them Elfred Morgan, John Meredith Powell and Frank Goodwin, showed outstanding courage and initiative, the last-named attacking and silencing a post initially at eighty yards' distance with small-arms fire, grenades and finally his own body which was found riddled with bullets and the barrel of the Spandau stuck in his chest. He was twenty-five years old. The German gunner was also dead.

Guardsman T. J. L. Arnold twice took command of a section when his superiors were killed or wounded and Guardsman C. J. Keogh twice had his Bren gun blown out of his hands while firing from the hip; although twice wounded he took the nearest post. The whole company pressed on to capture the last outpost on Piccolo. During the night the Germans withdrew from the whole position and also from Monte Grande. Twenty-two men were killed or wounded in this last attack and among the wounded were Ossie Smythe, John Nichol-Carne and Company Sergeant-Major W. Davies.

28 May: At 0730 the bridge established by the Canadian Division across the Liri collapsed and, when restored ten hours later at 1730, Army headquarters gave priority to units of XIII Corps.

28 May: The 1st Parachute Regiment defended Rocca d'Arce against the 17th Indian Brigade which had passed the Welsh Guards' right flank on Orio. It entered Rocca d'Arce at dawn on 29 May.

29 May: Charles Haydon, commanding 1st Guards Brigade, made wireless contact with David Gibson-Watt. Would he send a patrol into Arce to see if the Germans had withdrawn? He explained that he was the only officer left; his NCOs and men were exhausted but he would go himself if ordered. 'Go and have a look through your glasses and tell me what you think'. What David Gibson-Watt thought was that the enemy had withdrawn. On the strength of this observation, No 3 Company passed through the defile towards Arce.

29 May, Whit Monday: 'No sleep as usual. (No 3) Company moves off up Route 6 on Lothian [and Border Horse] *tanks. My platoon detailed to see if Rocca d'Arce is clear. Climb mountain* [road] *in two 'Honeys'* (half-track armoured vehicles) *under my command.'*

As we passed through the gap and crossed the dried-up Provitolo river bed where the Providero bridge had been blown, the familiar pungent smell of death hit our nostrils. There on our left as we trundled down the river bank were the remains of the German motorcycle combine, its sidecar twisted, pointing skywards and its two occupants lying dead beside it. The noise of their engine would have drowned the whistling shriek of the falling mortar bombs and they would have died instantly.

Rocca d'Arce at 1,800 feet dominated Arce but luckily the road was not mined and the enemy had duly withdrawn. There was a magnificent view from the castle ramparts. After our descent, our mission accomplished, we were ordered to rejoin the company. In a few minutes the peace of Rocca d'Arce was turned into the by now familiar carnage of battle. I wrote: *'Next harbour area with tanks (is) shelled, NEVER harbour infantry and armour together; casualties. Return for rest.'*

The Lothian and Border Horse tanks entered Arce around 0900, whereas we did not enter the town ourselves. In the hills beyond Arce the German rearguard was shelling any target they could pick out. We were in open country and very tired. Tom Dubuisson's soldier servant was so exhausted that he lay down during a moment's pause and fell asleep resting on his right elbow. In that position he was killed. On my own initiative, I withdrew my platoon about twenty yards further back under the shelter of an overhanging escarpment and in so doing left my small pack in the middle of what had become the enemy killing ground. My senses were numbed through lack of sleep − and that sixth sense was important, if not vital − and I did not feel like going to get it, but knew that I must do so because it was an obvious example to the men.

It was then that Lewis volunteered to retrieve it − at very definite risk to his life as enemy shells were falling in fairly regular salvoes. He moved into the open immediately following one of these salvoes and returned to our position just ahead of the next, with my small pack. Shortly afterwards we were ordered to retire. On emerging from our dubious shelter we again came under fire and I gave the order to double march. We had just reached the junction of the road where we were to meet the Sherman tanks of the 2nd Lothian and Border Horse, which were to take us out of the battle, when Tim Bolton sprinted after me and questioned the wisdom of running out of battle. I replied that double march was a legitimate and recognized military command. I felt, but did not say so, that under the circumstances it was more appropriate than ordering a slow march, or changing arms while on the march, or even marking time. The point was taken with good grace.

Mounting our tanks, we returned to the rest area which overlooked Christopher Maude's grave and we went to sleep in the untouched house which we had earlier considered as being the obvious target for enemy fire. In the three days and nights of this battle, 1st Guards Brigade alone suffered 283 casualties of whom 112 were Welsh Guardsmen. The Coldstream casualties amounted to 73 and the Grenadiers 71. There were 27 casualties among the personnel attached to the Brigade. Nearly 100 German dead were counted on Piccolo alone and 30 on Grande. Ten prisoners, mostly wounded, were taken after the German withdrawal and their casualties, which were evacuated, are not included. Rudolf Böhmler wrote: 'The holding of Arce had been of paramount importance, since it was vital to keep open the road to Avezzano, LI Mountain Corps' only line of retreat. The 1st Parachute Regiment accomplished this task, holding on grimly until the evening of 29 May when they abandoned the town to the advancing Indians, 6th Armoured Division having captured Monte Grande [Piccolo and Orio] south of Arce which had been tenaciously defended by 1st Parachute Regiment.'

30 May: 'Rest area overlooks Chris' [Christopher Maude's] grave. Artillery behind us!' In the low ground behind, seventy yards away, where we had been shelled and mortared three days earlier there was now a battery of field artillery. We were so exhausted that we slept for twelve hours through a series of barrages which were fired with the gun crews holding their hands

against their ears. Luckily, the enemy was too busy retiring northwards towards Avezzano to lay down a counter-barrage which, given our exposed position, could well have disturbed our sleep.

'Have first night's sleep in about a week. 35 Lewis not in very good shape. Will try and leave him out of battle permanently. Write to poor Chris [Bankier] *about Pip. Parcel from Gibney (my dentist!)'.* What the dentist sent me I cannot imagine. Due to some exceedingly neglectful dentistry during my childhood, I had to wear a band round my teeth from about eighteen to twenty. Maybe he sent me some lead soldiers.

I also wrote to my mother on 30 May: *'I received your 12th letter on the 27th* (on the first day of the battle) *and was so pleased to hear you were so well and enjoying life. It was the second anniversary of Daddy's passing two days ago and I only prayed that I should be spared ... As you know, I am now a full lieutenant and no longer an Ensign ... My new standard of pay* **whilst overseas** *is £292. 12s. per year. With allowances this means nearly £400 which isn't too bad. Of course, there is income tax which will reduce my army pay to about £270 (plus the allowance). Since my last letter to you, we've had an extremely rough time, but we are resting for a day or two and I am very happy and perfectly well. Mick Bankier was wounded and Pip unfortunately is missing. His body has not been found and therefore it is hoped that he may be a prisoner of war; we don't know. I have written an airgraph to Chris which may arrive after this, so ring her up and tell her it's coming. Mick is not seriously wounded, some shrapnel entered his back but it's not serious ... You can tell Chris quietly that I'd definitely like to stay in the Regiment afterwards. So she can mention it to Bertie. Yes, Cassino was an experience and I often slept on the stone floor of my cellar when the stretchers were not available but I'd rather not have (had) the experience ... I was very slightly wounded in the leg but only a matter of sticky plaster. The same shell killed Christopher Maude. I was lying in my slit trench. He had his head out. Slit trenches are very safe. Am genuinely happy and well. All my love. Philip.'*

In their usual kind and humorously dry way, Bruce Goff and Bryan Pugh had congratulated me on my reaching the heights of being a lieutenant. So, too, did Tim Bolton. We were standing within a few feet from the graves of the fallen just before breakfast. Throughout the battle, the rations and mail had always come up and somehow the company cooks had managed to prepare a meal. Thanks to the Quartermaster, Kenneth Grant, the Regimental Quartermaster-Sergeant, H. P. N. Dunn, and the Company Quartermaster-Sergeants, a hot meal was always served up whenever possible. In addition to food and mail, ammunition, wireless batteries and other vital necessities were brought up to the line and also whenever possible that dangerous but vital role of laying and repairing telephone lines linking field telephones to Battalion and Brigade was carried out under the calm and competent leadership of the signals officer, Dick Kingzett, together with his signals platoon.

Meanwhile a joint religious service was held in which our own padre, Malcolm Richards, had a leading role. The press attended the service on Piccolo and wrote moving accounts, cuttings of which reached us later. Also, as always, it was the duty of all company commanders and the commanding officer, and others if the need had arisen, to write to the bereaved. My mother received a copy of the letter written by Colonel David Davies-Scourfield to Colonel Bertie which he wrote on 1 June and which was one of many which he will have written, let alone others who did so, and which summarizes the sacrifices made by all the fallen. I have his concurrence to quote it:

My Dear Colonel,

I fear it will come as a very terrible shock to you and Mrs. Bankier to know that Pip has been killed in action and Mick has been wounded ... We had a very unlucky three days which started with being dive-bombed at night in our harbour area which caused [casualties] ... followed by a night operation which we were rushed into, resulting in us not getting our objective and having to consolidate in a bad piece of ground surrounded by our own tanks which drew a lot of shelling and caused 4 deaths including Christopher Maude and 3 O.R.s and we were ordered to patrol to, and seize if possible, two big features astride the axis of advance in daylight. Julian sent a recce patrol, strong enough to fight if need be against small resistance, to see if the feature was held and if not to hold it. This was led by Tim Hayley. They found it held and Tim Hayley was killed. Robert's task was rather different, being further and closer country. I sent him with his whole company, with the fine support of 12 tanks and a Gunner O.P., so that he could establish a firm base nearer the ground his recce platoon was working on. Unfortunately Robert lost contact with his leading platoon, went off to try and find it as wireless had failed and never regained contact with his other two platoons. Pip and John Davies then decided to go for this feature and led their platoons well up nearly to the top of the ridge when the Bosche, who had let them get right up, opened up on them.

A very confused fight took place and it was then that Pip was killed. It was learned afterwards that Robert had been killed too. Pip was killed how his mother and you Mick would have liked him to go – fighting gallantly at close quarters with the enemy, refusing to be overcome by the odds. How wonderful those two have been out here and so loved by their men. Pip and 5 others we buried where they were found. Thank goodness it was quite obvious that Pip was killed outright.

We had a simple and very moving ceremony on the hill which his Coy. and the officers and Brigadier Charles attended. The Guardsmen had collected wild flowers and wild broom and the graves looked lovely. Pip could not be laid to rest in a more lovely spot. Please tell Mrs Bankier how very much I feel for her and how the Bn. has lost one of the best and most gallant of officers. Personally, I feel it too and was so glad Pip had had a happy week's leave near Ravello or Sorrento before he came back to the line. I will try and let you know how Mick is going on as soon as I hear. I am so very sorry and will write Mrs Bankier a line later, if operations give me a chance. Yours ever, David.

Operations were not to give him a chance. He was wounded a week later.

Meanwhile, both sides were having trouble about orders being carried out. The Commander of Fourteenth Army, General von Mackensen, disagreed with Kesselring over the positioning of some of his divisions, Kesselring rightly interpreting Alexander's intentions to trap his forces in a pincer movement, von Mackensen being apprehensive of a seaborne landing further up the coast (but unaware that there were hardly any landing craft, which had all been removed for the French coast operations). More important, on the Allied side, was Mark Clark's decision on 25 May to switch the main thrust of US VI Corps from Valmontone, which would certainly have fallen the following day, to the Alban Hills and Rome. Truscott stated later that he was dumbfounded. As a result Valmontone was held long enough by the Germans for Tenth Army to escape the trap and Rome fell ten days later.

On the German side, von Mackensen was sacked. On the Allied side both political and military matters were involved. Clark maintained that his flank had become dangerously exposed to enemy positions in the Alban Hills (Truscott did not agree); also there were other escape routes for the Germans, a fact proved by Kesselring's skilful withdrawal, which von Senger and von Vietinghoff put into practice; thirdly, knowing the date of the Normandy invasion, everyone hoped that Rome would fall before this date − but following the 'cop' − in order to receive maximum political impact. At the same time, he slid out of his agreement, formalized by Army Group orders, gave the necessary orders, which became irreversible when Alexander heard the facts, then momentarily became incommunicado.

Mark Clark did not want a discussion with Truscott, his Corps Commander, nor with Alexander, his Army Group Commander, whose written orders he was about to disobey. In consequence, a token force was sent to Valmontone and a communications smokescreen was laid down for what he considered to be the greater and certainly his greater glory. He had an obsession about entering Rome first. He may, of course, have had political encouragement from Roosevelt's caucus established in the area, but the balance of the argument is that vanity replaced military obedience and loyalty. Politics, however, prevented his suffering the same fate as von Mackensen.

General Truscott wrote: 'There has never been any doubt in my mind that had General Clark held loyally to General Alexander's instructions, had he not changed the direction of my attack to the north-west 26 May, the strategic object of Anzio would have been accomplished in full. To be first in Rome was poor compensation for this lost opportunity.'

31 May: 'Leave on recce party to near Strangolagalli [five miles north-west of Arce]. *German advance reported. Retire in good order under Elydir Williams and Miles Gulland.'*

1 June: 'Leave on recce at 0330. Scare about S mines proved false; only plot of Italians to save their crops.' I had arrived either ahead of or with the recce party at the designated spot, a field lying between the road and a quietly flowing stream. No particular skills of castrametation were required of me. The basic question evolved: was the field mined or was it not?

Beyond the stream, standing in a group on some higher ground, some peasant farmers were watching us. By the side of the road they had put up notices in rather crude English which indicated that the field had been sown with S mines. They were returned Italian immigrants from the United States and spoke some English. Despite the notices, I walked across the field and asked them if they had put up the notices, receiving a rather noncommittal reply. Since the Germans did not as a rule inform us about minefields, I assumed (correctly and happily for me) that it was just a worthy ploy to save their crops.

Raymond Buckeridge, a brother officer, took the opposite view, namely that the notices were genuine. To prove the point I walked all over the field. Eventually and with considerable caution, the first vehicles of the Battalion began to move into the area. Suppose I had been wrong? Well, my instinct told me that I was right and my instinct was to guide me on more than one occasion in the future.

VII

Perugia to Florence

ROME FELL ON 4 JUNE. Following a hasty withdrawal by the Germans, Fifth Army had entered the Eternal City.

German losses since 11 May were heavy, around 10,000 dead and as many wounded. They were exceeded, however, by Allied losses. Eighth Army had suffered 14,000 casualties (nearly three per cent being in 1st Guards Brigade), Fifth Army 18,000 and the French Expeditionary Corps 10,000 — a total of 42,000. Excluding the 20,000 German prisoners of war, enemy losses were thus about half those of the Allies. And as I wrote home, there was 'still plenty of sting left in Jerry'.

On 3 June my diary entry read: *'Coy* [and Battalion] *moves off to battle.'* On the 5th they passed Rome in the distance on their left, the dome of St Peter's being clearly visible. The following day saw the launch of the great Allied invasion of German-occupied France.

The day before the Battalion left, 2 June: *'Very pleasant day. No guns. Just peace and quiet ... finish I Claudius. Concert party for guardsmen.'* I wrote home: *'Pip's body has now been found. He is buried in the most beautiful country on the summit of a hill. ... Mick is not seriously wounded. ... The Battalion has been resting for two days and it is hoped that it will do so for another couple of days. I am LOB for the next fray, so that gives me even longer to rest. ... I don't want anything except a long pair of khaki stockings to wear with my short (KD) trousers.'* 3 June, I added: *'David Howard-Lowe has rejoined company. Tim and I are LOB. 'A' echelon moves late at night to point north of Frosinone* [which the Canadians took on 31 May].

4 June: *'John Nichol-Carne returns from hospital. Rome falls to Allies. A very hot day indeed. 35 Lewis leaves for IRTD.'*

5 June: *'Move in morning to new area. Spend most of day on road travelling. Very dusty in TCV. Climb hill to Trivigliano* [on minor road about twenty miles north of Frosinone]. *Received most hospitably by local population.'*

6 June: *'Move in morning. All day on dusty roads. There is no rest. Learn that 2nd Front has opened by news bulletin from RASC truck wireless. Arrive 'A' echelon at dusk. Am missing Lewis.'*

7 June: 'A' echelon moves again. Transport very packed. This time sitting in PU. Travelling 20 miles or more. Drive to[-wards] Rome on Roman road. Rather bumpy in PU. Country changes from mountains [Monti Premestini] *to undulating plains* [the flat country of the Campagna di Roma]. *Evidence of very hurried* [German] *retreat.'*

On 8 June I wrote home: *'The German retreat at the moment is so fast that we only remain one night in our camping area and travel about 20 miles the whole day. Going is slow because of traffic and bad roads; but I've certainly covered some miles since Cassino. Our present site is only 3 miles from Rome. I'm LOB but we can't go there. Lewis has gone back to the IRTD. He was invaluable.'*

On the same day, 8 June: *'A echelon 3 miles east of Rome.'* Then news reached us by dispatch rider: *'Battalion shelled and mortared. David Howard-Lowe killed and his servant. Commanding officer* [David Davies-Scourfield], *Bryan Pugh and James Pugh wounded. Lance-Sergeant Wetheral* [my platoon sergeant] *killed. Blown for. Jocelyn Gurney acting commanding officer* [who succeeded officially].'*

The war diary of XIV Panzer Corps read: 'June 8: 26 Panzer Div. occupies Tiber crossings and to the south and holds them against attacks by weaker forces. 334 Inf. Div. is arriving from 10th Army. 90 Panzer Gren. Div. on the march to Orvieto. June 9: attacks on the Tiber bridgehead repulsed. Advanced units of 90 Pz. Gren. Div. reach Orvieto.'

The engagement which resulted in casualties for the Battalion occurred some fifteen miles north of Rome when the leading tanks of 6th Armoured came under shellfire and were held up. The Battalion was ordered to make a night advance up the left bank of the Tiber as it winds its way alongside Route 4. The Germans, as they habitually did during their long retreat, registered likely targets before their departure. In this case, streams and bridges were well marked on their gunners' and mortar officers' charts and the Battalion suffered casualties.

The next day the tanks continued to press forward but were eventually held up by a blown bridge. *'Battalion resting north of Rome on* [left] *bank of Tiber. Minchell my servant. Jocelyn holds conference of officers. Battalion moves forward to harbour area. Peaceful night.'*

10 June: 'Prepare for night attack. Grenadier Guards right, ourselves left. Objective Fornace and bridgehead on River Galantra. No opposition but stonked in gully before we start. Nebelwerfer (sobbing sisters). 8 platoon suffers 8 casualties + Sergeant Heap killed [my platoon sergeant]. *Rained: very wet. Dig in.'*

As usual the retreating enemy had registered likely targets and one of them was a well in the middle of a small valley with steep sides. It was our approach route into battle. The time was around 2000. I was only a few yards from the well up the northernmost slope nearest the enemy, but also a difficult target in terms of his trajectory. We had dug in and we heard, quite clearly the six-barrelled thump as the bombs were simultaneously fired from the mortar, each followed by the characteristic piercing shriek, hence the name 'sobbing sisters'.

Some of the guardsmen in my platoon had been near the well. Sergeant Heap, my platoon sergeant, just out from England, the replacement for Sergeant Wetheral, rushed to see what could be done for the wounded when a second salvo was fired. He remained near the well, despite the shrieking approach of the salvo, and was killed instantly. The stretcher bearers then, with their usual courage and competence, carried off the wounded as well as the dead. There were no more salvos, possibly because nebelwerfers could be spotted quite easily by our OPs.

My letter home commented: *'The fighting here has been terrific. No rest for weeks now. Since Cassino in fact. Except when I was LOB for four days. Unfortunately David Howard-Lowe was killed and Bryan Pugh wounded, both 3 Company officers and so I was called on immediately. The Commanding Officer, Colonel David Davies-Scourfield, was wounded and so were other officers. All in the same battle. Yesterday the Battalion did a night attack. We marched nearly 7 miles over rough country being heavily 'stonked' to begin with. We took our objectives and all was OK. I lost my platoon sergeant and also 8 of my platoon. We are now resting for a day in a most luxurious Italian house with all sorts of fruit and vegetables. ... My poor old beret has been through so many battles now, it has changed from its original khaki to a murky green! Everybody wears them out here. My service dress cap is at 'B' echelon and I haven't seen it since I went into Cassino.'*

I did not mention that in fact Number 8 platoon had lost three platoon sergeants in as many weeks and that the strength of the platoon had been reduced by half, although there were replacements, some recruited, *force majeure*, in the Middle East theatre who had not been through the Guards Depot.

For the next nine days we moved north. The countryside was exhilarating. Ochre-yellow corn was ripening in the sun, while vines were growing on the wire stretched between the fruit and olive trees. We moved each day. On 14 June reveille was at 2430 (0030). We left at 0130 for Terni where we took up positions beyond the town to trap the retreating Tenth Army but, fortunately for us, it failed to keep the rendezvous as it had passed through the day before. We then moved on to near Narni, sixty-five miles north of Rome, built on a rock nearly 800 feet high and taken by the Romans after a long siege from the Umbrians in 299 BC. We had no such problems.

I wrote: *'Our Company is situated in a most beautiful gully with birds singing and white oxen grazing in the fields. These oxen draw the farm carts and ploughs in the place of the more familiar horse seen in England. They are larger than the*

La Spezia

Bologna

Lake
Comacchio

*Adriatic
Sea*

GOTHIC LINE

Pisa

R. Arno

Leghorn

Florence

Rimini

Arezzo

'Cardiff Arms'
(Villa Pischiello)

Ancona

Lake
Trasimene

San Marco • Perugia

R. Tiber

Macerata

Porto San Giorgio
Fermo

Orvieto

Todi

Spoleto

Terni

Narni

*Tyrrhenian
Sea*

N

ROME

Avezzano

Frosinone

Miles

0   10   20   30   40   50

77

British bull and have immense horns which are rather terrifying on first sight. The people north of Cassino are ... more prosperous and, for cigarettes and bully beef, one can always get eggs, chickens and inferior 'vino' or red wine. The last-mentioned, although always (described as) 'buono', good, is not necessarily so when drunk! It is my ambition to visit Rome as soon as possible.'

On 14 June Jocelyn Gurney became a Lieutenant-Colonel and I bathed in a pond with David Pugh who preferred to do so in his birthday suit which attracted the attention of several Narni nymphs of impressionable age who were shepherded away by their chaperone.

On 15 June I met Robin Rose-Price who had become second-in-command. We also did firing practice just to keep our hands in. We were to need it within the week. More bathing in the pond. More spectators.

16 June: 'Shooting in the morning. Take leave party to Narni. Visit castle (and basilica). Buy 53 litre cask of vino for 500 lire [64 bottles for £1.25]. Very lucky to get it.' On this news, perhaps, "CQMS Cooper and 63 Sgt Thomas join company. Company sing-song [helped by my vino].'

A few days earlier the former Rhodes scholar, General Frido von Senger, had passed through Narni, 'completely of the Middle Ages. At Narni I was impressed by a basilica that was unusual in not being overlayed with seventeenth-century ornamentation. It still conveyed the potent charm of the turn of the millennium.' Narni stands in the Via Flaminia but its great bridge, originally built by Augustus with enormous arches, had been blown after the departure of the General.

In the bigger world, meanwhile, although German armies were retreating – and from 8 until June 20 the Battalion covered seventy-five miles – they had managed to extricate themselves from exceptional difficulties. At the last moment any breakthrough, which might have been, was blocked. Soon the withdrawal would slow down.

17 June: 'Leave 0330 harbour party. Position south of Todi. Very cold dirty journey. Win 2nd prize sweepstake with Tehran in Derby – 1500 lire (nearly £4).'

18 June: "Leave early in day with Bruce [Goff] in jeep. Spend most of day on side of road ... spend night in farm house. Farmer gives officers and CSM John beds. I share one with Dai Pugh to give CSM one [all double]. Sleep 8 hours."

18 June: The 26th Armoured Brigade was ordered to advance towards the north-east of Lake Trasimeno, bypassing Perugia, while 1st Guards Brigade was ordered to take the town and the strong points beyond. On the left were the Coldstream, 61st Brigade and tanks of the 17th/21st Lancers. On their right, due south of Perugia, were the Grenadiers among whose officers was George Lascelles who was wounded on patrol and taken prisoner. Waterloo Day had also seen his ancestor wounded at that battle on this day; and his father was wounded on the same date in 1915.

19 June: 'Move off 0700 hours. ... Leave farm in TCVs. Spend night in

vehicles. Raining hard.' This was at San Martino Delfino, two and half miles south of Perugia.

19 June: Both the Coldstream and Grenadiers suffered casualties from mines and enemy shelling.

20 June: At 0430 the railway station fell to the Coldstream and at dawn the Grenadiers reached the crossroads south of the town. Italians moved the trees which were blocking the road and stated that the Germans had evacuated the town. At 0800 the Grenadiers under Joshua Rowley entered Perugia to a rapturous welcome by the south gate and almost simultaneously, by a map-reading error (easily done), No 4 Company, Welsh Guards, under Francis Egerton, entered by the western route from the station. Both companies then withdrew to continue the battle while the inhabitants rejoiced.

Meanwhile, after sleeping in the TCVs, we breakfasted very early, washed and shaved and were driven by the indefatigable RASC drivers into battle. Our ten-day joy ride ended at 'Tulip', which was the codename for San Marco, just beyond Perugia.

Perugia is an old Etruscan town – an Etruscan entrance gate is in daily use – and is placed like so many Etruscan sites on a high point overlooking the valley whence 6th Armoured Division was advancing. The Grenadiers and Coldstream had attacked and removed the German defences south of the town and 61 Brigade had taken the high ground to the west. The Germans then withdrew two miles along the ridge near San Marco which the Welsh Guards were ordered to take and hold.

20 June: The initial part of the operation was handled in the very early hours of the morning by 'Fogg' (W.T.C. Fogg-Elliot), commanding No 1 Company on the left, and Alexis Cassavetti's No 2 Company took the road junction near Ponte d'Oddi on the right. There was no sign of the enemy. Bruce Goff and No 3 Company were ordered to pass through No 1 Company's position near Point 425.

Bruce, in the leading vehicle, overshot the narrow turning to our right and we had to turn round on the road heading west after the railway station, at a time when the enemy were shelling and mortaring the area and were registering on the road. We survived this manoeuvre and debussed at an angora wool factory which became Battalion headquarters. It was now a very clear day and the enemy had an unimpeded view. So for that matter did we. The tanks of 16th/5th Lancers were supporting us and as we went forward both the tanks and ourselves came under heavy shelling and mortaring. We were ordered to deploy on either side of the road but the tanks were forced to remain on the road because most of the land on either side was banked.

The leading platoon ahead of me cleared the defile between steep banks. After this there lay open ground which led, a quarter of a mile further on, to the ridge of high ground where San Marco was situated. Bruce Goff advanced to this defile with the leading tank, after ordering one platoon to clear the ground on the left which was done without too much opposition, while my own was to clear the right. Just before these operations began, however, we came under heavy machine-gun fire as well as intensified mortaring and shelling.

My objective was a modern red-brick villa graced with a tower which at that moment, despite its forty-foot prominence was undoubtedly being used as a German OP. The ground floor of the house, built alongside the second upper road leading to San Marco from Ponte d'Oddi, was about a hundred feet higher than our position on the lower road to San Marco. The villa had a drive approach from our lower road and a clear view down a re-entrant which had spurs on both sides. The drive followed the banks of the left-hand spur which began at the defile ahead of us, where Bruce Goff was now placed.

We were hidden from view just behind the right-hand spur as it touched the road. Thus, at the vertex of the inverted A formed by the re-entrant was the villa and the base was the road which wound its way from our position to that of the company commander's at the gap on the road between the high banks, one hundred yards ahead. There was a perfect German field of fire covering the re-entrant from the villa and the Spandau did not hesitate to let us know it.

As our somewhat more senior but opposite number put it: 'The thrust that develops from great depth ... finally ramifies into the fighting of handfuls of soldiers for a few blocks of houses or for the jagged part of some hill' (General von Senger).

It was my job to organize my handful of soldiers and take the place, but while I was working out the best approach, I distinctly heard the cranking and whining of a tank. It came from the direction of the villa. I presumed that, in addition to the Spandau, some of the shelling and machine-gun fire had come from this Panther or Tiger which was in the road behind the house and slightly to the right of it. It seemed to me that a right-flanking movement would get us on to higher ground and, in terms of the tank, into dead ground.

At that moment two tanks of the 16th/5th Lancers appeared. One proceeded to join Bruce Goff at the gap while the other, at my behest, moved off the road into the verges at the start of the re-entrant and most obligingly knocked a very large hole in the tower with its gun. It also machine-gunned the rest of the villa and fired one or two rounds to the right where the enemy tank was likely to be lurking. In the short moment of silence which followed we heard this tank moving off in the direction of San Marco.

However, while the tank officer and I had conversed, the enemy had registered the spot. Just as I decided that a better approach would be up the drive in a left-flanking movement, the enemy began shelling us with particular accuracy. I flung myself flat out onto the road against the bank while 62 Jones, my signaller, who was humping his large wireless set on his back, sank on his haunches next to me.

The shells were AP and not HE: that is to say they were constructed to pierce armour and explode. In this case they pierced the tarmac on the road, with the force of the explosion going downwards, but the ricochet of metal and road surface was hurled outwards in an arc. It passed over my prostrate self into the bank behind me, but cut straight into the chest of Guardsman Jones. He was killed instantly.

Now was the time to attack, immediately after the tank had done its bit and while it continued to give us covering fire, until we were too close to the enemy for the target to be fired on with safety. I ordered one section forward under Lance-Sergeant Brown and was about to follow him and, in turn, be followed by the other two sections – the rear one commanded by the new platoon sergeant, Abrams – when an equally new corporal, recruited from some other branch of the Army after Piccolo – that is to say, not a trained guardsman in any way – leading the section immediately behind me, asked in the middle of the field of fire of the Spandau, thus putting all our lives at mortal risk:

'Who is going to look after Jones?'

The timing of this question was tantamount to a refusal to go forward in the face of the enemy, an offence punishable by death. The tone reflected the thoughts of a stupid man who thought he was being clever. Seconds were vital. The whole attack could be aborted if we were caught in the open by enemy fire. It was this factor which saved his life. Not all of us felt brave all the time, but cowardice in the face of the enemy was best suppressed and disguising it by simulated sympathy for someone obviously dead was sickening and contemptible. It was also gross insubordination.

It was, therefore, not the Germans who nearly killed the corporal, but his platoon commander. My Tommy gun was slung over my right shoulder, naturally cocked and fully loaded. I brought it up slightly to shoot him on the spot. He saw the movement and froze. I then thought better of it. The others would be demoralized.

'Jones is dead,' I said, 'but you go and look after him.'

Later I thought that, in any case, I should have used my revolver. It was cleaner and made less noise. The windy corporal joined us later when it was over. I did not place him in close arrest afterwards. I was not feeling too well – the start of malaria.

This minor incipient mutiny settled, we advanced under cover of the trees behind Lance-Sergeant Brown's section which had moved to the left with a field of fire covering the left of the house. The tactic of the platoon commander in such a situation being in the middle of his platoon to keep control had been drilled into us at Sandhurst and in this case was correct. There was no doubt that Sergeant Brown was a Christian soldier. Within fifteen yards of where he and his platoon were lying low, a German stretcher party was carrying away a badly wounded man who had been shot by the leading man of the platoon. Sergeant Brown made no attempt to capture them and certainly did not open fire. In the former case he may have been right; we were not to know the number of Germans in the immediate vicinity and we could have taken on more than our exposed position warranted.

Meanwhile, I was leading the two other sections. As we approached the house I sent Sergeant Abrams round to the right to work his way from that direction, while the section remaining with me took as much cover as it could among the trees flanking the drive, ready to fire at the villa windows to keep the enemy's head down and prevent him observing the movement to our right. This movement, however, could come under fire in open ground if the windows facing in that direction, which we could not cover, were being used by the enemy, and particularly if his Spandau was still in working order, which I was tempted to doubt after the admirable support of the 16th/5th.

Sending my platoon runner, Guardsman Sparrow, to inform Lance-Sergeant Brown of my intentions and telling him, at the same time, that the remaining section and myself were going to move further to the right to try and cover the flanking movement, I moved towards a ten-foot-high surrounding wall which encircled the yard of the villa and stretched in a semi-circular manner from one end to the other.

Some of the enemy had, meanwhile, moved from the house to the sides and into the yard. We became aware of this when stick grenades were lobbed over the wall and from the road, around the right-hand side of the house. Stick grenades were not as powerful as our 36 grenades. They were not, of course, to be treated lightly, but a tactical withdrawal in open ground of a few yards was enough. In a room they would kill. Immediately following the explosions, a German took the risk of there being no one observing the top of the wall, having faith in the destructive and distracting power of his grenades, and put his head above the bricks. He saw me, but before he could duck he was dead. The .45mm soft-nosed Tommy gun bullet did not bounce off German parachute helmets at close range. In any case, he was hit below the rim. His face disappeared before he fell.

I felt we were winning. I threw one of my own grenades over the wall. Apart from killing or disabling anyone in the area, this made a considerable noise which was as good for our own morale as it was bad for the enemy's. In the meantime Sergeant Abrams had been working his way around the flank and I moved further to the right myself to support him. Then, a few inches from the corner of the house, at which point an ornamental rail separated us from the road, an arm stretched round to lob another stick grenade in my direction. As the man flexed his wrist to flick the stick at me, I fired. The grenade went off in his hand. However, we were in an exposed position as there were still Germans left in the house, the windows of which were above me because of the gradient. I moved cautiously into the open, covering the windows with my section.

At that moment a strange thing happened. A figure appeared on the crest of the hill to our right, approaching the section of Sergeant Abrams. He was shouting at the Germans in the house and obviously warning them, a little late in the day, that the enemy was at their gates. I was not even sure that he was German, but dared not take a chance. I gave him a quick short burst. He collapsed into the long grass and lay still.

Meanwhile, Sergeant Abrams was now in better cover and was closing on the right and claimed three kills. I moved swiftly to the left, ordering, just before this move, more grenades to be thrown at the right-hand corner of the house and pitched at the centre, on the road, where I guessed that there must be a front door, but we could not see it. This gave the impression of surrounding the place. Lobbing another of my own grenades over the high surrounding wall, thus increasing the impression of encirclement by these loud and demoralizing explosions, I then joined Lance-Sergeant Brown on the left and we stormed the side door, shooting out the lock. A terrified Italian inside shrieked,

'Don't kill me. Don't kill me. The Germans have all gone.'

He was telling the truth. We found only two bodies and a rather dazed prisoner. He had been hiding in, or had retired to, an outhouse, performing a natural function. Battle did, sometimes, have that effect on the human system.

I moved immediately on to a defensive position against counterattack, just across the road on a mound. It had a lovely view across the valley beyond and we began to dig in. Not for long, however, as the enemy had a lovely view too and began an accurate stonk. We may have dislodged his infantry, but the enemy artillery spotters were not in any way taking a siesta. We then became the defenders of the house we had attacked. However, we were shortly recalled by runner, there being no wireless operator, to join Bruce Goff and take up positions in San Marco where the second act and another battle was about to start, but it did not involve No 3 Company. We were welcomed by the inhabitants of San Marco, inevitably kissed by unshaven men but not so much by the women. We were then stonked for three days.

In the meantime Francis Egerton had arrived in the Corso of Perugia. Fruit, wine, flowers and kisses were showered upon him and his company, as well as one or two bullets from a few remaining Germans firing from an upper window. There were no casualties, but when the enemy were rounded up by Jim Jerman and his platoon the Germans were nearly lynched. *Mobile vulgus.* Nevertheless, the company extricated itself, with the prisoners, and was able to support Bruce Goff during his attack on the Villa Bossetti. Shortly afterwards the leading tank of the 16th/5th Lancers, who were always in support, was knocked out by a parting armour-piercing shell which resulted, luckily, in no casualties, including Bruce Goff who was nonchalantly leaning on it. San Marco – 'Tulip' – was cleared shortly afterwards. My diary entry was laconic: *'20 June: ... stonked. 62 Jones killed. Take house with aid of tank.'*

North-west of San Marco lay Montione (Point 532) beyond which stretched a four-mile broken ridge offering in its scrub, depth and rock considerable cover for the enemy in strength. Francis Egerton's company assaulted Montione with success but anticipated a counterattack. This materialized and, despite a tactical withdrawal, they were cut off.

21 June: Fogg-Elliot, his Company Sergeant-Major, Tremblet, and Sergeant John Essex were shelled and mortared as they tried to deliver rations to Francis Egerton's company. The non-commissioned officers were badly wounded. 'Fogg' was able to return over open ground and he and John Nichol-Carne, plus his platoon, then went back to capture the post which had caused the casualties and, at the same time, retrieve the wounded. Not surprisingly the enemy had other ideas.

Once more 'Fogg' and John Nichol-Carne passed through our lines, marching in single file along the road. John raised his head and eyes as a gesture of brave resignation when he saw me. Indeed, this little group on its rescue mission were met with accurate machine-gun and mortar fire and John's premonition was remorselessly fulfilled. CSM Tremblet and Sergeant Essex had been made prisoners of war.

John Nichol-Carne's platoon withdrew and the following day, 22 June, both officers were returned under blankets in ambulance jeeps, the Germans having respected the Red Cross. The whole Montione feature was finally cleared by a Grenadier battalion attack two days later.

Meanwhile, shelling and mortaring of San Marco continued for two more days and Geoffrey 'Glob' Evans, the Intelligence Officer, was badly hit and died of his wounds. Richard Sharples, one of Montgomery's ADCs, came to command No 1 Company. He later became an MP and was appointed Governor and Commander-in-Chief of Bermuda where he and his Welsh Guards ADC were murdered. Disgracefully, the Government of the day insisted that he be considered a civilian and not a soldier, despite his being Commander-in-Chief, thereby disallowing him the honour of being killed in the line of his military duty – as was his ADC – but allowing his heirs to pay death duties which would otherwise have been inapplicable.

On the 23rd, a strange and motley assembly of khaki-clad soldiers passed through our lines with PPA on their shoulder-flashes, heavily armed and

1. "At sixteen I joined the Home Guard" (p.5). The author wearing the cap badge of the Durham Light Infantry.

2. "I was ordered to get my kit and install myself with the Brigade Squad" (p.7). The author, 4th from left, back row, at the Guards Depot, Caterham.

3. 2nd Lieutenant Philip Brutton, Welsh Guards.

4. "We practised for two weeks before we mounted Guard on 3 February (1944)" (p.14). The author is marching behind Major Cecil Wigan.

5. "We then... began our approach to the foot of Castle Hill" (p.32). Seen from the ruins of Cassino; the Monastery is in the background. (*Picture Post*)

6.   "The Sherman tanks of the 2nd Lothian and Border House which were to take us out of the battle" (p.69). 8 Platoon, 3 Company, 3rd Bn. Welsh Guards, the author second from left.

7.   Men of No.1 Company, 3rd Bn. Welsh Guards resting near Arezzo (p.87). They are clad in canvas trousers, cap comforters, American khaki shirts and camouflage smocks.

trudging towards the enemy lines. They were Popski's Private Army, a parallel force to the original Long Range Desert Group, under the command of Major Popski, a Belgian national, which was to do, and had done, considerable damage to the enemy behind the lines. Only they, and presumably someone at Army Headquarters, knew where they were bound. When Tim Bolton advanced several miles north after the enemy withdrawal from the San Marco feature he found neither the PPA nor Germans, who were, as I had reported, members of the Parachute Regiment (under the command of Lieutenant-Colonel Egger, later to be captured by us).

24 June: 'Move to back area in large house [the Spagnoli wool factory]. *Central mess for dinner party. Brigadier was guest. Recommended Sgt. Abrams and Guardsman Sparrow for bravery. Learn Jim* [Jerman] *has gone to hospital.'* I was to go there myself on the following day.

An extraordinary number of gift parcels were sent home from this factory, whence the owners and staff were evacuated, being allergic to shelling by both sides. I still possess an angora wool pullover which I *bought* from the place months later. Also, years afterwards, I returned as a dinner guest of the owners but, bearing in mind the precipitous clearance of stock, thought it prudent not to disclose that I, or, more particularly, the Battalion, had been there before.

The recommendation of my platoon sergeant and my runner for bravery, within the platoon ration for other ranks of two, inevitably reflected unfairly on others equally deserving. However, their Military Medals were to speak for all participants but, of course, only they could carry the decoration.

25 June: 'Feel very ill [malaria]. *Temperature 102. Evacuated to 14th CCS, Todi. In same ward as Jim* [and John Retallack] *and Bernard Greer who has broken wrist and ankle through fall. Learn from Jim that Geoffrey* [Glob] *Evans has died.'*

Bernard's room in the Spagnoli house (which adjoined the factory) was on the first floor and had a balcony. Its distance from the ground was negligible — the sort of distance in assault courses we were taught to jump, landing on our toes and falling forward — but Bernard, exhausted from his duties at Piccolo (where John Jenkins, the Battalion Motor Transport Officer, had had to persuade him to leave his post in the Tac headquarters communications vehicle, as he had had no sleep for three days) and subsequent battles, was walking in his sleep and fell to the ground and broke his wrist. The ambulance taking him to Todi, twenty-eight miles away, then overturned and he was admitted concussed and with a fractured tibia in addition. The following day he was evacuated to a rear hospital, while Jim Jerman returned to the Battalion and I spent most of the day sleeping.

'Glob' Evans was the Intelligence Officer and had been wounded by shrapnel at San Marco. Three days later Tony Bailes, a friend from childhood days, serving in the D.C.L.I., was killed near Lake Trasimeno, but I only learnt of this when I wrote to him a few days later and his mother replied.

25 June: Christopher Carlisle, Coldstream, captured on patrol. A former fellow cadet, he was only with his Battalion a few days before capture at the head of his patrol. Some of his men behind him were killed. A typical tactic when a patrol is ambushed.

On 30 June I got out of bed and was well enough to visit Todi after six days in the CCS. This recovery from malaria was probably due to the bitter mepacrine pills we were ordered to take from the start of our going overseas. I wrote to my mother: *'John Nichol-Carne, a particular friend of mine, was killed the other day. Most distressing. I killed my first Germans on that day too* [in fact, the day before]. *Shot them with my Tommy gun when my platoon was clearing a house on the top of a hill ... it was being used as an observation post and we had to clear it. We did this and rejoined the Coy. The Coy. Cmdr., Bruce Goff, was congratulated by the General Commanding 6th Armoured Division. I must say, I didn't realize until later what a very difficult job it was because we were being shelled and mortared all the way and my mind was too busy controlling the platoon.'*

On 2 July I left hospital and visited Rome, after being granted five days convalescence. I was based at 'C' echelon which was also at Todi but used the mess of a battery of the 51st/152nd Light Anti Aircraft Regiment. At a later stage in the war they were to be converted into infantry as there appeared to be little of the Luftwaffe to shoot at.

On 4 July I wrote: *'Discharged from hospital ... truck going to Rome ... stayed Hotel Eden ... after lunch walked to Vatican ... man from Cooks showed me round ... Murals in mosaic from Rafael's drawings, gorgeous decorations and, of course, the magnificent tomb of St. Peter ... taxied to Colosseum ... Rome has also some remarkably fine modern architecture ... the Victor Emmanuel monument* [the wedding cake] *is an example ... it literally glistens in the sun.'*

On 6 July I was back in 'this delightful old Italian cathedral town' of Todi where my convalescence was proving thoroughly enjoyable. *'Plenty of time to write letters in the morning until coffee at 10.30 when I read and go out for a walk ... afternoon a snooze and more reading until tea at 4.30. The time between tea and dinner* [is spent] *chatting ... listening to the piano. After dinner a stroll in the twilight ... Feeling very fit and well again.'*

It was a strange, dream-like existence, a sort of Alice in Todiland experience. While I followed my leisurely routine, however, the war went on.

It was Field-Marshal Kesselring's intention to hold a line across Italy where Lake Trasimeno was in the centre. Equally, it was General Alexander's intention that he should be prevented from doing so and the enemy were pushed back to a line running from Ancona to Livorno (Leghorn), with Arezzo as its central point, nearly one thousand feet above sea level and defended by the 1st Parachute Regiment, our opponents at San Marco.

On 14 July 6th Armoured Division moved forward through the New Zealand Corps who had captured the south-eastern end of the six-mile mountain range which guarded Arezzo, and on 15 July 1st Guards Brigade entered the battle. The Grenadiers attacked at night, followed by the Coldstream who were in turn followed by the Welsh Guards who took the final objective, two peaks which flanked the road to Arezzo, suffering casualties from shell fire, but the enemy, still the Parachute Regiment, withdrew. On 17 July both Ancona and Leghorn fell and this new German line was broken.

Further west, Fifth Army had advanced 87 miles in the twelve days which followed the fall of Rome, 'a rate of advance that amounted to the pursuit of a defeated opponent. When XIV Panzer Corps took charge, the rate of advance was slowed down to thirty kilometres in the week from 16 to 23 June and to another thirty kilometres during the subsequent three weeks [up to 14 July]' (von Senger und Etterlin). This was an overall rate of withdrawal of 125 miles in just short of six weeks. The winter, Gothic Line defence was to run from south of La Spezia (near Massa) eastwards to the heights beyond the Futa Pass, Monte Verro and a line forward from the Battaglia feature to Rimini on the Adriatic.

In terms of other fronts, a few days earlier my diary entry read: '*8 July: Russians fighting on outskirts of Vilna. British at Caen* [where both the 1st and 2nd Battalions of the Welsh Guards were fighting]'.

11 July: '*Dai Pugh turns up with small amount of kit: all the stuff I don't want* [he arrived a day late having been to a party in Rome given by Vladimir Romanov]. *Report to Battalion. Colonel Jocelyn congratulated me on performance after Perugia* [San Marco]. *Arrive LOB camp* [the Cardiff Arms] *called Villa Pischiello on Lake Trasimene.*'

On the following day I heard that I had been recommended for the Military Cross. I also learnt that my mother had been bombed out, and that the Guards Chapel had been hit.

My letter home read: '*Sam Hall and Owen Lloyd-George are now out here. Sam received his second star on his arrival. I've only seen Sam so far but I am looking forward to meeting Owen again ... terribly sad about Guards Chapel ... Colonel Eddie Hay killed. Also another bomb landed on Esher Common during the sports ... many casualties* [including the wife of CSM Mineur killed, Cecil Wigan and Sandy Paget wounded].

'*Colonel Jocelyn* [told] *me* [that] *the General heard about* [San Marco] *and that Bruce and myself have been recommended for the MC. A newspaperman came down to interview me but I was in hospital; and got the story, however, from Bruce. Nothing will be heard for a month or so. These things often fizzle out.*' It did. I was Mentioned in Despatches. Bruce, most deservedly and for many other acts of bravery, received his MC, as did Francis Egerton.

'*Lake Trasimeno*,' I wrote to a cousin who was looking after my widowed mother (resilient, although bombed out; suffering from cancer of the thyroid but, after an operation, living for another thirty years, dying at nearly ninety) '[is] *of Hannibalian fame ... they used elephants not tanks ... how peaceful it all is ... lake large and tranquil with fascinating islands studding the glistening surface ... living in very large house in beautiful grounds ... property of the Marchese and Marchesa Bourbon del Monte Ranieri di Sorbello. They are a charming family and speak English perfectly ... villa luxuriously furnished and we dine in style. The Marchesa, like most Italian women, is rather beautiful but also very selective ... neither she nor her husband could have tolerated any others than ourselves.* [we, in fact, succeeded a German laundry unit but they kept to the back area!] ... *one of our officers* [Richard Llewellyn Lloyd — Richard Llewellyn who wrote *How Green was My Valley*] *remarked that the house was under military control and that she must consider herself very lucky not to have had it demolished like most others.*'

Later Richard Lloyd had the Marchesa's cook put in prison in Passignano for a month. The circumstances were as suspicious as Richard Lloyd was capricious. He was in charge of the mess. He also supplied the cook with Army rations. She taught him kitchen Italian wherever was most comfortable. They fell out. She called him names. He called in the police. The 'evidence' was there. The house, as he had inelegantly expressed it, was under military occupation. The cook returned to the Marchesa who has never forgotten the talented but complexed little man. It was David Gibson-Watt who recommended him for further extra-Regimental employment — anywhere.

15 July: Andrew Neilson, the Scots Guards company commander who fought at Piccolo, died of wounds. He had lost both his legs after stepping on a mine. His mother and his future wife had just been killed in the Guards Chapel disaster.

15 July: In contrast to the gallantry of Andrew Neilson, some deserters from another brigade were being held in Perugia and it was my duty and their misfortune that I was ordered to defend them.

16 July: '*Visit prisoners — three shits. Call at Palazzo Ansidei. Meet Barbara* [aged eighteen] *known as Babina* [di Torelli]. *In afternoon become very ill.*' My temperature must have been very high. It was neither love at first sight, alas, nor gaol fever, but malarial jaundice. The deserters were to be defended by Willy Bell, who, possessing more of the milk of human kindness than I did, no doubt did a better job but, hopefully, not too good.

On 17 July I was evacuated to a CCS in Perugia (having been found immobile in bed at the requisitioned Brufani Hotel by Willy Bell), then 58th General Hospital in Siena (about which I remember very little), then 59th General in Rome where I wrote to Kinka di Sorbello but the letter was returned as letters to civilians were forbidden (a later letter to her brother-in-law, Uguccione, who was serving with the Allies in 'A' force – he was half American – was to cause problems).

28 July: 'Evacuated by ambulance train to Naples [350 miles from the front]. *Very uncomfortable. This moving has made me much worse.'*

From 31 July onwards I began to improve and within three more days I was well enough to complain about the food.

On 2 August Sam Hall was killed north-west of Arezzo at Pian di Sco. I wrote: *'He hadn't been in the line very long but had been doing extraordinarily well ... One of his men* [Guardsman H. Thomas 31] *was sniped and he ran out into the open to tend his wounds (which were fatal – snipers seldom miss) and naturally was picked off himself.'*

Meanwhile, at the front, 1st Guards Brigade were advancing slowly up the Arno Valley towards Florence, while the enemy made an orderly withdrawal to the prepared defensive position along the Gothic Line, fifty miles north of Arezzo. There were no battles as such but there were casualties. On the left, across the river, were the Chianti Mountains and on the right the Pratomagno range in the spurs and re-entrants of which it was the job of 1st Guards Brigade to protect the flank of 6th Armoured Division as it probed and pushed its way up the Arno Valley towards Florence which was one of the main objectives of the Eighth Army, while Pisa and points north were principally those of the Fifth. When off duty, bathing in the Arno was encouraged and, as battlefields go, the Arno Valley with its ripening vines and its cornfields, golden-yellow pears and purple-orange peaches must have been among the best – while it lasted: but for some it was the end.

On 28 July Dai Pugh had patrolled five miles into enemy territory, and while the Battalion was based at Quarata, the Colonel-in-Chief, George VI, paid a visit to the area and, at the same time, Charles Haydon handed over the Brigade to a fellow Irish Guardsman, Andrew Montagu-Douglas-Scott. It was shortly after this that Sam Hall and his Guardsman were killed.

4 August: The Battalion moved forward and No 2 Company – an attached Grenadier company under David Willis, reinforced for five weeks the much depleted 3rd Battalion Welsh Guards – supported by two troops of tanks, captured Torre-a-Monte.

5 August: Major-General Gerald Templer, who had taken over command of 6th Armoured Division from Major-General Evelegh on 24 July, was injured while he or his jeep driver was trying to overtake a 3rd Battalion Welsh Guards 3-ton vehicle known as a portee (originally a 'porte-canon' which was once used to carry a 2-pounder anti-tank gun before being changed into an equipment-carrying vehicle). The Divisional Commander was injured when the sergeants' mess piano fell on top of him. It did not prevent him, however, from becoming a Field-Marshal.

6 *August:* Humphrey Leake, No 2 (Grenadier Guards) Company, was mortally wounded. Four days before, the Germans had abandoned Florence, or most of it, during the night and evacuated their general line of defence in the area on 24 August. They were also in the process of evacuating Paris on the same day. In the case of Florence, not all the city north of the Arno was evacuated and three Grenadier officers who crossed the Bailey bridge, constructed by the Royal Engineers, and armed with a pass signed by the Provost Marshal, apparently with some reluctance, went swanning in the direction of Via Magenta, which the Germans were loath to leave, and much to their surprise were captured: Derek Bond, my old instructor at the RMC, Joshua Rowley and John Pearson-Gregory, who escaped.

On 25 August the head of the Arno Valley was reached when Julian Martin-Smith's No 4 Company seized high ground near Altomena, while Tim Bolton with No 3 Company took the Grille feature further east. Ahead, rising at points to 5,000 feet, lay the Gothic Line.

Before taking on – with others – this formidable barrier, the Battalion was based at Podernuovo from 30 August in a villa known as Atrocity House where the soldierly reputation of the German Army was sullied by the massacre of nine women and children out of eighteen who had gone there for safety. This deliberate killing of civilians, often in retaliation for guerrilla attacks on German forces, was counterproductive. The Germans, never particularly popular, became hated and the lines of communication through the bleak valleys of the Apennines in August during the German withdrawal became hazardous.

Far removed from these activities in the northern Apennines, I was slowly recovering from malarial jaundice in the south of Italy in early August and began to take more interest in my surroundings. The sisters, naturally, were a centre of attraction, but surgical cases, the wounded, undoubtedly claimed their attention more than the merely sick who were segregated. In terms, therefore, of their emotions, as distinct from their undoubted professional competence, if wounds aroused their sympathy, jaundice certainly had the reverse effect. In any case, they were all older women, the youngest being twenty-one or two or whatever. There was, however, in terms of emotional preference towards the wounded, an exception, and she came to be known, ungratefully and ungallantly, as Thermopylae (Hot Gates) or more obscurely Point 480 (the date, BC, of the battle). She more or less had the field to herself and, not unnaturally, the lady was selective: rank, rather than physical predilection, took precedence. Rank could procure transport to Naples, even Rome, an officially approved hotel, restaurants, the odd night club and – shopping. In other words, Thermopylae sought not martyrdom at the front or indeed rear echelons with anyone under the rank of major, but rather recognition of her favours, even talents, by experienced men of the world, preferably nothing lower than a lieutenant-colonel. It was, therefore, obvious that sororal favours were neither coming my way nor was I attracted towards those portals. I even found it too hot to sunbathe, let alone be spurred to contemplating the amorous heights of Point 480.

On 16 August I had a haircut and the Lieutenant-Colonel in the RAMC 'mentions Sorrento'. I was now reading and writing copiously, so must have been getting better. The next day the Colonel 'promises Sorrento!' This was the British Red Cross Society Convalescent Home run by Eve Bowes-Lyon.

Not all were bound there: One of my companions was a subaltern facing a court martial. He had been driving an Army vehicle in which there were three nurses and two other officers. He drove along a road which approached a river crossing. The bridge had been blown. There was a diversion. He missed the diversion and he missed the bridge. All were killed except the man in the next bed. All were stripped of their belongings and their clothes and what could be salvaged from the wreck of the vehicle was removed by peasants. He was removed by ambulance.

18 August: 'News [reels] showed flying bombs.'

22 August, Tuesday: "Leave for [BRCS] Sorrento. Cross Bay [of Naples] in small steam boat. Meet Jack Baxter on board [Scots Guards contemporary]. He was wounded by mortar fire [and was later killed].'

I was to spend two weeks in the requisitioned hotel at Sorrento. The days were spent bathing and canoeing, eating – no doubt the wrong food – listening to the Devons' band, more drinking of wine than was wise with a jaundiced liver, listening to a small dance group which had, a novelty for me, an electric guitar. Given the state of Italian electrical wiring at that time and the fact that an electric guitar was not earthed, I was not surprised to hear that the guitarist's predecessor had been electrocuted.

My letter home read: 'My bedroom window has a balcony overlooking the Bay of Naples. In the distance is the port. The Bay itself is calm, warm, turquoise tinted and transparent. White sails and small craft are scattered near the shore while suntanned swimmers circle round them. Bathing is an absolute joy. One can borrow sailing boats or one-man canoes or anything in that line, very cheaply. The beach is made most attractive by Italian signorinas. At 21 or under, they're very easy on the eye but only a few maintain a respectable figure after the late twenties! One is absolutely free to do as you like. I report to the doctor in a week's time.'

On 25 August I sent some nuts and two dozen lemons to my mother. The next day I went to Capri with seven others, one of whom was with the Army Film and Photographic Unit; it takes all sorts to make an Army. 'Rowed *there and back by fisherman. Visit Blue Grotto; four eggs and chips at Hotel for lunch* [eggs were rationed in Great Britain, hence this regarding of eating eggs as a luxury, as well as being bad for the liver]. *See small and large beaches. San Michele* [Anacapri, Gracie Fields' villa] *etc.'* All by taxi: eight of us plus driver and guide in the same vehicle.

The boat trip cost us under £4 return. We were told that the Americans did not like strangers and we were required to lie down in the boat as we approached the island. I am sure that this was all part of the drama and the reason for our not taking the rival motor boat but choosing to be rowed there instead. However, we saw no Americans.

A cousin, Derek Wyburd, told me many years later that he had drawn up his destroyer alongside the Capri quay, having finished his duties off Salerno in late September, 1943, and spent the night in Ciano's bed (Mussolini's foreign minister and son-in-law who was shot on his orders). He was the first Allied officer to land on this five-and-a-half square mile island, and the first naval officer to land there during hostilities since Admiral Sir William Sidney Smith in 1808.

On 28 August I had a letter from Jocelyn Gurney which mentioned that Bruce and Francis had received their MCs and Sergeant Abrams and Guardsman Sparrow their MMs.

5 September: I left the BRCS by boat, reported to the transit camp and then the IRTD where, on the following day, I reported to James Cull (Welsh Guards).

7 September: 'Arrive Caserta for entraining. Visit the palace [Army Group rear headquarters where Harold Macmillan also had an office. His diary entries for this day cover problems with the Yugoslavs, both royalist and communist, and matters concerning Greece, the reoccupation of which was going to be far from easy with a civil war in the making]. *Leave Caserta in cattle trucks. Sleep on my camp bed. Pass through Cassino and battle zones.* [A young, newly arrived] *Scots Guards Officer informs me he was wounded in Wales!'*

9 September: 'Arrive Castiglione Formiento [probably Fiorentino on the rebuilt railway line between Cortona and Arezzo]. *Wait half a day for transport. Arrive CRU.'*

10 September: 'Breakfast 0745. Very cold now during night ... suddenly, as usual, informed about draft; leave for Battalion with Keith Jones and Paul Carr. Confusion in dark.'

11 September: 'Arrive 'A' echelon 0400 hours. Meet Gerald Farrar [Grenadiers, former fellow cadet] *and others playing cards.* [Also saw Billy Steele, Coldstream, now a major before taking command. He had been commandant at the RMC. Everyone seemed to be wandering around at this unearthly hour in what seemed to be a vast castello. There was no electric light, hence *"confusion in dark"]. Up 0900 hours. Meet Bruce. Colonel Jocelyn puts me in 2 (Dai's) Coy. Sgt Bolton my Platoon Sergeant. Country very beautiful [near Podernuovo] and very mountainous.'* Dai was David Gibson-Watt.

The day before, Sunday, 10 September, in these very beautiful and mountainous surroundings, General Mark Clark had launched his Fifth Army offensive. His objective was to break the German defences and cut Kesselring's principal line of communication in the Po Valley, Route 9 or the Via Emilia. Seven months later he succeeded.

VIII

The Gothic Line

THE APENNINES RUN THE LENGTH and, in some parts, the breadth of Italy. They have, therefore, been a natural line both of defence and division since the days of pre-history. Centuries before Christ, the northern part of the range formed the boundary between land occupied by the Celts (the Gauls) and other races further south, including the Etruscans and the Romans. The word *pen*, among other meanings, is the Welsh for top or summit; and Apennine, like Pennine, is derived from the Gallic word meaning summit or mountain top.

The Apennines were, therefore, an automatic choice by the German High Command for the site of a defence line running 140 miles from La Spezia, through the Vernico Pass, eastwards to the River Foglia and the cliffs between Cattolica and Pesaro, covering, in enfiladed construction, some 200 miles of actual fortifications. In terms of breadth, in the central sector, the range covered more than fifty miles of harsh and rugged ground through which Route 65 passed from Florence to Bologna over the Futa Pass at 3,000 feet with surrounding heights at 3,700 feet. This pass had been constructed under the direction of the Roman Consul, Gaius Flaminius, in 187 BC when he built the road, known later as the Via Cassia, from Arezzo to Bologna through the site of Florence, thus founding this city. More than two thousand years after its construction and like many of his predecessors, Field-Marshal Kesselring considered that this was the key to his defences in this sector against the inexorable Allied advance.

North of Florence the lower slopes of the Apennines merge into the dominating dark silhouette of the higher mountains. Cypresses, poplars, small villages clustered around their mediaeval churches and Renaissance castles on the green foothills, unchanged since portrayed in fifteenth-century paintings, all give way to rock, scrub and hog's back ridges as the going gets harder. Oaks, beech and chestnuts, vines, olives and maize are replaced by marginal holdings, small stone-walled pastures, some goats, a few peasants and the occasional wolf. As autumn set in, mist

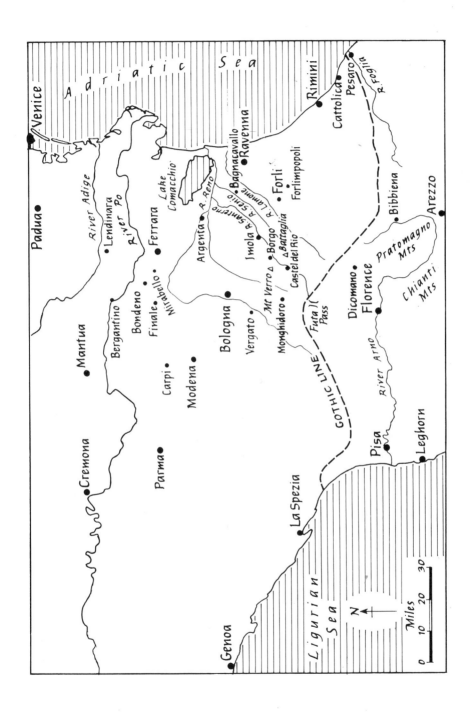

and fog clung to the peaks. Then came torrential rain, quagmires of mud and, later, deep snow and howling winds which drove the snow into dangerous drifts.

Meanwhile, eight new German divisions had arrived in Italy more or less at the same time as seven Allied divisions had left for Anvil, renamed Dragoon (Underlady might have been more appropriate), the controversial plan to invade the south of France. In terms of the Combined Chiefs of Staff's* Mediterranean strategy of attracting German forces away from Overlord and the Eastern front, twenty-five divisions were in Italy, nineteen in the Balkans and eleven in the south of France, a total of fifty-five in the Mediterranean area. That said, however, 15th Army Group was likely to be too weak to carry out Alexander's plan of reaching the Po Valley before the autumn and then advancing north-eastward into Austria via Ljubljana and Fiume (Rijeka), after landings in Yugoslavia. Nevertheless, there were some reinforcements: a Brazilian division, a not fully effective 92nd US Division, a divisional-size formation of anti-tank and anti-aircraft artillery units converted into infantry and five Italian Combat Groups of small divisional size who proved to be good soldiers. Alexander did not entirely rule out reaching the Po Valley. Indeed he might have done so had it not been for the weather.

In fact the rains came early, but even if they had not, and speaking only of my own experience in the Apennines, the Po Valley and the Alps, I think the intention was admirable, but the execution would have been difficult. On the other hand, General John Harding, then Alexander's Chief of Staff, held the opposite view, as did General Mark Clark, certainly an experienced realist by now in mountain warfare. These views were held in spite of losses to the Anvil/Dragoon expedition. Furthermore, both were enthusiastic in supporting Alexander's initial plan to launch an attack through the Futa to take Bologna and cut Route 9, the Via Emilia, although this plan would mean, at first, an inactive role for Allied armour. In the event, the bulk of Eighth Army was transferred to the Adriatic, less XIII British Corps The offensive on this front was launched on 26 August with three corps – the Polish, Canadian and British V Corps, together with the New Zealanders – on a thirty mile front, comprising ten divisions, 1,200 tanks and 1,000 guns.

On the Fifth Army front, the great assault, as mentioned earlier, was launched on 10 September. An advance was made after heavy fighting. On the right 8th Indian Division and 6th Armoured were pushing forward and my diary entry for the 12th is self-explanatory: *'Delay in departure owing to traffic congestion. Christopher Thursby-Pelham 2i/c. Frank Hughes in company.*

---

* The Combined Chiefs of Staff headquarters was based in Washington. It comprised the United States Joint Chiefs of Staff and the British Chiefs of Staff.

99 Williams [formerly with Pip Bankier] *my servant. Sgt. Bolton my Platoon Sergeant.'* Two days later I wrote: *'At the moment I'm camping on the side of a mountain – a mere molehill compared with the Gothic Line, but don't worry, things are going surprisingly well. Alexander is truly an admirable commander-in-chief; I do wish they'd promote him to Field-Marshal.'* In fact he was soon to be promoted and his promotion was ante-dated to the fall of Rome in order to preserve his seniority over Montgomery who had been made a Field-Marshal before the Normandy invasion. My concern for the promotion of the commander-in-chief was also extended to my own level of command: *'I wanted my old platoon back and tried very hard with Bruce, but Colonel Jocelyn put me in Dai's company... needed experienced officers* [other subalterns were newly joined]. *Fortunately I was in Cassino with two sergeants in the platoon.'*

The move on 14 September gave us our first sight of the Gothic Line. Pushing forward, however, from Dicomano to Bavello and Villore in the Alpe di San Benedetto, the formidable defences had been deserted (wired and concreted, I would not have liked to assault them), following German withdrawals. They had, however, retired to higher positions.

15 September: 'Arrive in new area. Billeted in farm ... move into better billet ... my platoon convoy mule team, under Raymond Buckeridge, to No 1 Coy on top of mountain. A long, long trail. Return to base by 0030.'

16 September: 'Billeted in vestry. Church wrecked by Kraut vandals. Commandeer honey, pigs and sheep – all stray. [Provided change from Army rations.]'

Also on this day a patrol discovered the enemy in strength on Monte Peschiena (4,000 feet).

Sunday, 17 September: 'Coy moves to house near Figline. Road from previous billets to Dicomano under shell fire. Wright, Francis Egerton's servant, killed. Francis wounded. Chris Thursby-Pelham adjutant. Keith Jones [1 Coy] missing. [Wounded on patrol. POW only six days after joining the Battalion].'

The Brigade had been suddenly withdrawn from the Peschiena feature and we were now on our way into the line north-east of Bibbiena on the side of Monte Penna, another sector in the Gothic Line in the Alpe di Serra.

19 September: 'Leave in advance in carrier which breaks down. Recce hill feature ... stonk on neighbouring knoll. Relieve 1st D.L.I. My platoon on summit of hill. Very cold and somewhat damp in my slit trench.'

20 September: 'On hill all day. Men are tired. Lockyear (coy. cook) does platoon cooking. No shelling.'

21 September: 'Very cloudy. Mountain enveloped in mist. Owen Lloyd-George and self* [in] *very close shave with S mines.'*

S mines were nasty little things with three prongs protruding above ground which, when stepped on, were propelled upwards and either blew off the foot or exploded at stomach level. Owen and I were strolling on the reverse slope of high ground when we left the path and entered a re-entrant which led to the crest of the hill, the idea being to have a cautious look at enemy-held features in front. I was leading and Owen was following me when instinct prompted me to look closely at the ground.

'Don't move,' I said. 'Look at the ground.'

We saw a field of these mines. We were surrounded by them. Miraculously, we had not stepped on any. We tiptoed back to the path with exceptional care and the incident, like so many close calls in war, was dismissed. Sadly, such minefields undoubtedly killed many Italian peasants whose unstinting help, largely unrewarded and at great risk to themselves, to escaped Allied prisoners of war was among the greatest acts of self-sacrifice and human charity in Italy during the War.

A week later David Gibson-Watt and Owen were sitting on a wall and David was about to jump down.

'Don't move!' said Owen. There, again, was a field of S mines which they had escaped treading on when they approached the wall.

'What made you look down?' asked David.

'Instinct,' said Owen.

The 3rd Battalion Welsh Guards then moved five miles north-east of Bibbiena on to the forward slopes of Monte Penna, facing another sector of the Gothic Line defences and one which up till then had been held by the enemy. But here again our penetrations elsewhere were compelling the enemy to retire.

'On September 22nd, three days after their arrival, a Welsh Guards patrol climbed 4,000 feet to the top of Monte Vescovi'. (*Welsh Guards at War*).

On reading the above, I thought: 'Poor fellows: what a hike!' Patrols were not an attack, even fighting patrols, in the sense of being supported by artillery, mortars, machine-gun fire and/or smoke, at any rate as a preliminary action. Their point was to seek information and sometimes fight. Often, too, like Tim Hayley on Mount Orio, or more recently Sam Hall, Gerald Seager and Keith Jones, to mention only four subalterns, they could end in death or capture. Their fate, nevertheless, conveyed information, preferably by their remaining alive. That is why there was always a form of patrol rear echelon which could, with luck, report back in the event of the total eclipse of the forward elements. In the case of Monte Vescovi it was a strong patrol of platoon strength. It was only on reading my diary that I realized that it was I who had led this patrol with my platoon as ordered by David Gibson-Watt under instructions from the commanding officer. It *was* a hike too!

22 September: 'Sudden notice to move. Very pushed. Coy advance over mountains. Attack feature with platoon. The place was 5,000 feet up.'

I see that I used the word *attack*. These were obviously my orders and there was no supporting fire or smoke. We approached the summit over open ground, mostly scrub which offered limited cover but nothing to rejoice about if we were subjected to enemy fire of any kind. The ground was green and the going soft after rain. The sun was shining; a lovely day if we could stay alive.

The approach, in fact, was a form of plateau and the summit, as it appeared to us, was a thickly wooded hill with quite a few rocks and boulders, behind which we prayed that there were no Spandaus or Schmeissers. The platoon was spread out, each section covering the others. Of the alternatives — a direct frontal attack up a form of path leading into the unknown or a right-flanking attack leading, eventually, equally into the unknown — I chose the second. I left Sergeant Bolton with one section to cover us. He had a good field of fire, effectively straight up the approach track to the feature and to his right above us. I led the other two sections round to the right but suddenly, as we turned a corner, we saw a steep escarpment. It was solid rock and, to all intents and purposes, perpendicular. There was no question of climbing it, even if we had had grappling irons and climbing ropes. I was about to order our doubling back to our starting point when a voice at the top of the rock face said:

'They've all gone, sir. You can come in the front way!'

It was Sergeant Bolton, technically at fault for having disobeyed orders but 100% right for using his initiative.

The enemy had *'just left, which was most considerate'*. We knew that he had just left because we could smell the dugouts: the diet of the intermittently washed German soldiery included garlic sausage which, when exuded through the skin and the field-grey uniform, produced an unmistakeable smell of 'Kraut'. Also, in this case, their fires were still burning and the ersatz coffee in one hastily abandoned tin was still warm. We were careful in case it was booby-trapped. None of us drank coffee in any case. The position was a strongpoint held by about half a dozen men, but with a Spandau and Schmeissers they could have proved difficult to dislodge and there could well have been casualties.

23 September: '*Commanding Officer and Dai very pleased about attack. Relieved by LAA changed into infantry. What confusion!*' They arrived in a straggling column of bewildered men, no doubt missing their heavy weapons which, thanks to many factors, they had hardly ever fired in Italy. A further entry for *23 September:* '*In large sumptuous house near Arezzo. Feet very bad.*' Before and after this climb and attack my feet caused me no trouble whatsoever, which was a tribute to my feet and to the Army boot. However, at a point lower down this Vescovi feature, I was walking with difficulty and being helped by Sergeant Bolton. Our two-wheel-drive transport was still some way away but not the company commander's four-wheel-drive jeep. The driver and the company commander had met further up and they then drove past Sergeant Bolton and myself without stopping. David Gibson-Watt looked at me with vague curiosity and I have often wondered what, if anything, was passing through the mind of this kind and considerate commander. The pain, probably a tendon, which forced me to hobble painfully back to base had luckily not brought me to partial immobility either before or during the attack and was, in itself, of minimal importance compared to what might have happened had the enemy stood and fought.

30 September: 'Owen attends O group in middle of dinner.'

1 October: 'Recce group [for Battaglia]. *Bring on company* [as 2 i/c]. *Americans very kind. 2 Coy in reserve. Civilians, Americans and British all in one house, also ducks, pigs, cows and horses. Indians outside with mules.'*

The prelude to our going on to Monte Battaglia (over 2,500 feet) was a long journey by road, across Bailey bridges and along ravines where surging, ice-cold torrents had begun to cascade on to the road, washing away the surface. Often the precipitous drops on the side of the road forced the drivers to choose a pothole rather than take the risk of approaching too near the edge which could well have given away. The journey, via Borgo San Lorenzo, took several hours and I was not a little relieved when we debussed near Castel del Rio to prepare ourselves for a long, long climb.

Battaglia had fallen to the American 350th Infantry, in the US 88th 'Blue Devils' Division, during the afternoon of 27 September, in the sense that they were led through mist and heavy rain by members of the partisan 30th Garibaldi Brigade to the peak of this mountain, proving for one vital moment that their partisan claim to be in possession of the area was valid. Their chances of holding the feature against German re-occupation − it was obviously through a muddle and misunderstanding between enemy commands that the position had been evacuated − were likely to be nil.

During one week of fighting, beginning on 20 September, the reserve 88th Division, under Brigadier-General Paul 'Bull' Kendall, had made remarkable progress down the rocky Santerno Valley, fighting its way towards Imola. Mark Clark had decided that the seizure of Imola would do more to trap the German Armies there, in accordance with Alexander's master plan, than a successful debouchment near Bologna, even if this were to be possible, bearing in mind Eighth Army's slow progress in the deteriorating weather conditions and their being met by stiff enemy resistance.

The 88th Division advanced rapidly and captured Castel del Rio on the morning of 27 September and became engaged in heavy fighting on two mountains, Pratolungo and Carnevale, with Battaglia − meaning battle in Italian − about to become the third. On the right, where the British XIII

Corps were fighting in increasingly difficult and mountainous country, the British 1st Infantry Division was moving down the upper reaches of the parallel Senio Valley with the intention of clearing Palazzuolo which lay along Arrow Route on a road where the Germans had carried out extensive demolitions. Palazzuolo fell to the British 66th Infantry Brigade (Brigadier Martin Redmayne) on 25 September.

The reason why the Germans created a vacuum on Monte Battaglia which the enterprising partisans filled remains unresolved. What is certain is that no sooner had the Americans – Company C of the 2nd Battalion, 350th US Infantry – installed themselves in the ruins of the old robber baron castle on the peak of the mountain and dug themselves in, when the first German counterattack was launched in heavy mist before dark. A second counterattack the following morning after an all-night bombardment nearly succeeded but was beaten back. The third counterattack made by some units of the 44th and 715th Infantry Divisions, following small probes into the American positions during the day, came in the afternoon, but was beaten off. In the evening another American company arrived with ammunition and much-need rations carried by mules.

A fourth counterattack was made on the morning of 29 September when the enemy penetrated the castle but were driven off with grenades. This was followed by an intense amount of shelling and mortaring and a fifth counterattack on the 30th and a sixth on 1 October, by which time the defenders were being heavily supported by reinforcements from other units in 350th Infantry. Also, on the flanks to right and left, British and American forces had closed the earlier gaps which the enemy had tried to exploit. Nevertheless, bad weather had grounded the air forces for three days.

This was the current situation when the reconnaissance group arrived on Battaglia on 1 October, the day of the sixth counterattack. The Welsh Guards were to sustain, together with the Grenadiers, the seventh and then the eighth of these remorseless and determined enemy assaults on this vital feature in the German line of defence where enemy troops had been drawn from the Bologna section.

On 2 October, the day the Battalion arrived on Battaglia, the US II Corps' thrust had reached Monghidoro, under twenty miles from Bologna and from where the Alps, now covered in snow, were visible. Mark Clark was optimistic, but Alexander wrote to Field-Marshal Maitland Wilson on the same day: 'It [the advance] is a slow and costly process and my fears are now that we may not be just quite strong enough to carry it through. I am reinforcing Fifth Army by giving them 78th Division for XIII Corps. It is my last remaining fully fresh division.'

Six days earlier he had written to Maitland Wilson: 'The trouble is that my forces are too weak to force a breakthrough and so close the two pincers.

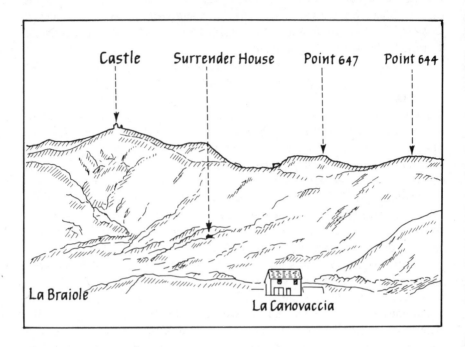

The Grenadiers were in the castle and the Coldstream were on the south-east slopes. The Welsh Guards were spread out along the windswept and rain-soaked ridge with standing patrols between their positions. After an intense bombardment, the enemy launched a pre-dawn attack on 11 October. The German intention was to occupy and hold "the maintenance route" to Monte Battaglia. The detailed objectives — confirmed by captured documents — were La Braiole, which was a farm in the gully, Point 647, Point 644 and La Canovaccia. The assault was made in two waves. Mountain mist, consequent confusion, determined defence and heavy counter-bombardment drove the enemy back with heavy casualties. The end of the attack came when seventy-five of them surrendered. Casualties in 1st Guards Brigade were comparatively light but had been heavy during the days preceding the battle.

The advance of both Armies is too slow to achieve decisive results unless the Germans break and there is no sign of that.' Nevertheless, Alexander never lost faith in total victory in Italy. He prevented the withdrawal of two further divisions from his command in the winter and achieved his objective in the spring. His realism was instinctively shared by his troops in the front line as we carried out our orders day by day.

2 October: 'Full moon. Dai [Gibson-Watt] mending road with platoons. Raining all day. I'm left behind to cope with mules. Muddle through. 88 mules to cope with. Up all night with Owen L − G coping with mules.'

The Battalion convoy reached the debussing point at 1500 and started a seven-hour trek, arriving at their positions facing the enemy at 2200. The 'road' was in fact a track, steep, rough, narrow and in parts extremely slippery because of the rain. It was also being shelled and mortared. Carrying spades as well as weapons, wirelesses and other vital paraphernalia made it no easier; and Battaglia was the highest point on this particular ridge, its castle on the peak being reached by crawling on hands and knees and scrambling up the approach slopes in some sections with the aid of ropes.

The approach from the rear position was a knife-edged ridge with vertiginous drops on either side. The Germans were occupying positions further along the same ridge as well as other narrow strips which splayed out at right-angles to it. The six German counterattacks had left both American and German unburied dead littered around the position. On 2 October the Welsh Guards took over the defence of this causeway approach route, well registered by German mortars and buffeted by piercing wind and rain.

The slit trenches were full of freezing water, which was not conducive to the same feeling of well-being as the warm embrace of the Arno in August. The causeway was, in places, only a yard wide and not, therefore, an easy target to hit; but slit trenches could not be dug along such narrow stretches and where they were, on each side, was often where the bombs and shells were inclined to fall and where the rain was certain to trickle in rivulets, creating a hip bath where and when it was least needed.

On 3 October, the Coldstream relieved the Americans on the south-east slopes and on the 4th the gallant Americans in the castle were relieved by the Grenadiers. Casualties in the 88th Division had been high: between 21 September and 3 October it had lost 2,105 men killed and wounded.

3 October: 'Leave 0400 hours with two mules, picking up mortar kit. Mud is terrible. Sun appears for rest of day. Get off track at dawn as it is under observation. Mules now organized. Indian muleteers pinch all my platoon kit.'

The rain not only made the man-mule tracks extremely arduous − and worse after sun had dried the surface making it more difficult to extricate the foot (hopefully together with the boot) and more difficult for the mules − but it filled the slit trenches which afforded the only shelter against enemy shelling and mortaring. There was only one track and this was used each night by 150 mules and 100 men.

The wounded had a bad time being evacuated. Even with stretcher-bearer relays every quarter of a mile, the carry took three and a half hours from the most advanced point on the causeway and the journey was both arduous and dangerous.

3 October: John Pearson-Gregory, leading the Grenadier reconnaissance party, badly wounded.

4 October: Two companies of Grenadiers under Tom Hohler and Victor Budge relieved the Americans in the positions furthest forward around the castle hill and were in turn relieved by two other companies under David Bonsor and David Rollo. Their Commanding Officer, Colonel John Nelson, ordered reliefs to be undertaken every seventy-two hours which he considered to be the maximum time that any man could maintain his full faculties under such conditions. As it was, losses were running at an average of ten men a day as a result of enemy shelling.

4 October: 'Escort mules to Tac HQ (4½ miles of mud, mules and mortaring). I do not like the way the Yanks bring their dead back slung over mules like sacks of silage.' [Practical, nevertheless. Also stretcher-bearers were fully occupied with the wounded.] *Frantic search for Brigadier's present to the Commanding Officer — 2 bottles of whisky.'* None of us, in the sense of the term, drank in the line. Our exclusive beverage was hot tea or cold water, of which there was no shortage.

On one of these trips I had some difficulty in finding the way and opened the door of a peasant house where I found an American obviously exhausted and sitting behind a medium machine gun with a field of fire comprising myself and the stone wall behind me.

'I'm looking for the forward company — the front line,' I said.

'Don't ask me, sor. We're only the medium machine guns.'

He was very near the front and he was lucky that I was not one of the enemy. Another recollection of our time with Fifth Army is of a jeep that had fallen off a track. This was no problem. Our allies simply brought up a machine to haul it out, restored it to us and gave us another one as well. The Battalion, in fact, had several jeeps with the same serial number which John Jenkins, in charge of transport, was careful not to have in the same convoy, at any rate nose to tail. It was said that so many jeeps were being unloaded at Naples that a bottle of whisky procured one vehicle.

5 October: 'Return in early hours, having found Commander's whisky; [but] as cork is sealed, cannot reward self for trouble and loss of sleep [he had to wait until the following night for it to be delivered]. 88 S P [Self Propelled] gun has eye on farmhouse which is a bore. (I knew 88 mules were unlucky!)'

In fact, we could hear this gun creaking slowly forward. There was a heavy mist and very bad visibility. After a considerable amount of snail's-pace manoeuvring, it fired one shot. The shell landed in the Indian camp. There were casualties. It then withdrew. I never knew why we did not take out a fighting patrol to locate it and kill the crew before they killed us. The real danger would have come from its local defence − infantry posted ahead of the gun. The thought crossed my mind to volunteer but I had had no sleep and I was not feeling at all in fighting form.

This same feeling of approaching sickness weakened my resolve when I was asked to identify some of our fallen who were under blankets, lying alongside a score of American dead. It was an American medical orderly of about my age who had the kindness, seeing my hesitation, and expertise to do the job for me. Apart from our shoulder flashes, we always wore the usual identity discs.

6 October: '*David Gibson-Watt thinks I've got jaundice. Evacuated to 4th CCS, Borgo San Lorenzo ... under canvas, sleeping on stretcher. Nurses are wonderful under such conditions* [mud, duckboards, cold, rain and multi-seater latrines]. *Very badly wounded officer admitted (Teller mine).*'

7 October: '*Diagnosed by doctor. Same trouble as last summer.*'

8 October: '*Have caught bad cold and feel far worse than before admittance. Food and orderlies good.*'

Letter home: '*I am now in the 4th CCS with a recurrence of my former illness. It is* **not** *serious ... convalescent fortnight* [insufficient] *... doctors themselves said three months ... [difficult to] recuperate in wet mud and cold on the summit of the Apennines.*'

9 October: '*Evacuated to 108 South African Hospital, Florence.*'

9 October: The peasant house where the Grenadier battalion headquarters was situated was shelled, killing Douglas Berry, the Intelligence Officer, and others. Tom Streatfield-Moore was wounded. An enemy patrol then killed the sentries and attacked the position, throwing grenades through the window and wounding Mike Jenkins and ten other ranks. As John Nelson, commanding the Grenadiers, remarked later: 'It was difficult commanding a battalion in the line with a telephone in one hand and a pistol in the other.' A grenade landed under his table, but did not explode.

11 October: Dawn attack after intense bombardment by three German battalions of which two did not leave the start line. The third, which came in a little after 0400 hours, comprises two companies of the 1st Battalion 577 Gr. The German objectives were the approach route along the narrow causeway to the castle, La Braiole farm in the gully, Point 647, Point 644 and La Canovaccia.

The initial attack came round the west side of the Battaglia feature, but in the thick, early morning mountain mist both German companies lost their way and intermingled. Nevertheless, they attacked No 1 Company

Grenadiers, under Tom Hohler, which was placed on the western slope of the castle hill, but were beaten back after intense close combat.

At the time of the attack the Welsh Guards were due to relieve the Grenadiers in the castle that evening and Alexis Cassavetti, Paul Carr and Corporal J. McGhan were returning from their reconnaissance when they were challenged by the standing patrol below Point 647 and simultaneously were confronted by a party of Germans of whom four were killed by the standing patrol while the Welsh Guards party returned safely.

Shortly afterwards, at 0500 hours, the enemy attacked La Canovaccia after a heavy preliminary bombardment of mortar and machine-gun fire. La Canovaccia contained a platoon of No 3 Company, Welsh Guards, as well as company headquarters, the Regimental Aid Post and the Grenadier Advance Headquarters. The enemy were beaten off by a section under Corporal D. F. Burgess while our 3-inch mortars put down punishing fire in front of No 3 Company's lines. At the same time No 1 Company's machine guns were shooting across No 3 Company's front. These Welsh Guards company positions had been well sited by Colonel Jocelyn Gurney.

Meanwhile, further west, in the gully below the causeway, a Welsh Guards standing patrol under Lance-Sergeant C. Wilcox was overrun by a second enemy assault and, in anticipation of its return, Jim Jerman's platoon in La Braiole did not fire until the enemy were almost on top of both them and the nearby Grenadier 3-inch mortar platoon, which lost three men. When the fire order was given, the enemy were beaten off and suffered heavy casualties.

Then a second phase developed when an attack was put in against No 1 Company Welsh Guards positions. The enemy penetrated dangerously close to the very top of the ridge near Point 647 where a platoon under Willy Bell was placed. The enemy were driven back with withering fire from both Grenadier and Welsh Guards machine guns, mortars and small arms as well as a heavy barrage of shells from the Ayrshire Yeomanry. The Germans asked for an armistice under a Red Cross flag to evacuate their wounded. Half an hour was granted; but, as it turned out, after an extra quarter of an hour's grace, a white flag appeared and one officer and seventy-four men surrendered to No 1 Company Welsh Guards.

The battle had been witnessed by Major-General Sir H. C. 'Budget' Loyd, Commanding the Brigade of Guards; the casualties were relatively light in the whole Brigade during the battle − as distinct from those derived from the constant shelling, mortaring and direct attacks which preceded it after 1st Guards Brigade's arrival on Battaglia − and numbered thirteen in all. The Welsh Guards lost the standing patrol plus three men.

11 October: The Welsh Guards relieved the Grenadiers in and around the castle. Sixteen men were placed within the keep. Like Cassino, they were surrounded not only by the immensely thick walls but also by the detritus of destruction and death which had resulted from two weeks of bombardment and assault. On a clear day − and there were not many when we were there − the Bologna-Rimini road, along which no vehicles passed in daytime, could be seen, also the great plains of the Po valley and, beyond, the Alps.

These two attacks were the last which the Germans attempted against Battaglia, but they clung on to the ravines and cliffs which formed the militarily formidable rock fault, known as the Chalk Vein or Vena del Gesso, which separated this gaunt mountain from the Po Valley.

12 October: 'John de Rutzen killed.' John was commanding Support Company. He was caught while driving his jeep by the shrapnel of a stray shell which had missed its mountain-top target and descended to hit the backbone of a mule and exploded. Dai Pugh and Tony Wrigley were wounded. So, too, was Dicky Sharples and his soldier servant while visiting Andrew Gibson-Watt's platoon, when they were inadvertently shot by the Bren gun of a suddenly awakened sentry.

14/15 October: The Battalion came out of the line. Four days later, we relieved our successors and found that the Germans had withdrawn. The castle became a rear position and the Welsh Guards left this sector on 24 and 25 October, crossing the Santerno Valley near Fontanelice, going into the mountains further north, where they stayed until relieved on 31 October. Eleven days later the Battalion returned to Battaglia for a week − no casualties − and returned to billets in Palazzuola, then to new billets at Greve, some fifteen miles due south of Florence where I was to rejoin them.

The weather conditions, which were appalling at the front, also endangered the lives of the wounded evacuated in the rear.

17 October: 'Leave 108 [South African Hospital] *for airport. Driver loses way. Arrive at midnight. Tent full of badly wounded.'*

18 October: 'Thick fog. Spend whole day at airport. Eventually taken by ambulance to 31st General, Arezzo. Americans would not fly after fog had lifted in the afternoon. Considering there were very bad surgical cases waiting, this seems a little inconsiderate.'

I have no idea why the Americans would not fly. I remember quite vividly the roar of their engines as they tried to land in the fog, coming in as low as they dared and then pulling away, circling and trying again many times, but in vain. Next to me were one or two badly wounded men whose lives could well depend upon their being evacuated to base hospitals with the equipment and facilities to handle their cases. We had been supposed to fly to Naples.

24 October: 'Evacuated to 58 General, Perugia. Polish women driving trucks.'
There was no such equivalent in other Allied forces.

28 October: After heroic advances, Fifth Army were ordered to dig in and wait for the spring before renewing their attacks, already within sight of their objective, Eighth Army continued to advance, step by step, and reached the shores of Lake Comacchio.

8 November: '*Tim Mitchell (CG) dead* [with whom I had served as a cadet]'.

9 November: '*Jack Baxter* [Scots Guards] *killed.*' Also a former fellow cadet.

13 November: Alexander broadcast to the partisans that the coming of winter enforced a pause. In fact, a bitterly cold winter lay ahead.

Field-Marshal Kesselring had suffered head injuries in an accident and was out of action for three months: ironically, it was a German gun being towed out of a side turning which collided with the Commander-in-Chief's motorcar and scored a direct hit at point-blank range. Colonel-General von Vietinghoff-Scheel took over command of Army Group C and was careful to avoid his own artillery.

On the Adriatic front, Eighth Army captured Ravenna on 5 December, despite ammunition shortage. Earlier, on the same day as he broadcast to the partisans, Alexander signalled Maitland Wilson that Eighth Army had only enough shells for a fifteen-day attack in December, while Fifth Army had a reserve for ten. Nevertheless, Eighth Army made the slog to Lake Comacchio while the Germans entrenched themselves on the banks of the Senio. No one knew it at the time, but the scene was set for the great attacks of the spring and the fall of Bologna on 21 April.

18 November: I wrote home: '*Have visited the Sorbellos in the country. Gian di Sorbello is vice-prefect of Perugia and is mending all the bridges of the Province* [Umbria: with Colonel Owen, 52nd CRE, billeted in his house. Sorbello was a qualified engineer] *The Regiment first met the family months ago.*'

19 November: '*Up early shooting* [at Pischiello]. *See Gianni's hideout from the Gestapo* [in a reed hut in the woods]. *Climb to top of mountain. See Sorbello Castle (built about 900 AD originally).*'

20 November: '*Return to convalescent depot (my whisky ration given to Major Murray, the officer commanding).*

28 November: '*Field-Marshal Alexander in Perugia. Gian is interviewed about bridges in the Province.*' This was the only time I saw him, or rather his back. I saluted.

I was, at this time, officially based at a convalescent depot in Perugia where there was nothing to do except give my cigarette and alcohol ration to the commanding officer. The hospitality of the Sorbello family was particularly kind. They and their family were to become lifelong friends. In the subterranean regions of Palazzo Sorbello in Perugia there is an Etruscan well: in other words the site has been occupied for at least two and a half millennia, and in the town itself, the Arco di Augusto is one of at least five known Etruscan gates, despite being named after the Roman emperor. The French occupied the town in 1797, it suffered three earthquakes in the nineteenth century, was seized by the Austrians in 1849, joined United Italy under duress in 1860 and was co-liberated by the Grenadiers and the Welsh Guards in 1944; but sadly no plaque records this event, no Piazza Capitano Francisco Egerton or Joshua Rowley or Via Tenente Giacomo Jerman has been so named – to date.

2 December: 'Hitch-hike to Pischiello. [Meet] *Gian's mad father now in his 80s who betrayed his sons to the Gestapo* [they were half-American] *and ended up in prison himself* [released by the Allies].' This was a clear case of senile decay and very dangerous indeed for his family and their possessions.

4 December: 'Go to Rome in Henrico Salivetti's car. Breaks down (10 hour trip).'

I wrote that Rome at night was dangerous. Italo-American deserters indulged in profitable nocturnal hold-ups and robberies. I always carried a revolver, either my service revolver or a small pocket-size Biretta which I had acquired.

5 December: 'Arrive at Uguccione's flat [brother of Gian]. *I am not allowed into civilian restaurant – Alfredo's. Kinka di Sorbello and self go to Orso's. Kinka posing as English and in ENSA* [the well-known Welsh soprano from Swansea]. *Very pleasant.'*

The receptionist was suspicious: 'We had to turn away a Baronessa.'

'Well, do you want me to sing?' asks the Marchesa.

'No, no! You're English all right.' Welsh would have been more accurate.

The headwaiter then recognized her but was addressed, with heavy winking, in English (he had been at the Savoy) and with a broad smile we were given a good table.

7 December: 'Go to transit camp with Ferrante. Collect rations [Ferrante di Cavriani, Kinka di Sorbello's brother].'

The transit camp was just outside Rome and we went in Ferrante's small car. I had decided to indent for rations covering myself and a certain number of hypothetical soldiery in order, primarily, that I should repay a considerable amount of civilian hospitality with the gift of British bacon. I approached the matter with caution. Not so Ferrante. Carried away by the sight of so much bacon, as if he was in the food department at Fortnum and Mason he began asking the Lance Corporal behind the counter whether or not he had back bacon, not too fat as he preferred lean and could the rashers be sliced thin?

'I think I'll indent for whatever you have available and I'll take a few tins of baked beans,' I interrupted, anxious to scale this foraging foray down to size, sign quickly and depart even more quickly. Ferrante finally understood the situation. I declined the corporal's offer to help me carry the carton to the car – there should have been a truck – and we drove out through the gates. The corporal is now certainly chairman of a grocery chain.

8 December: 'Dine at Alfredo's in a suit of Ferrante's [who had had bacon for breakfast].'

9 December: *'Prices rocket high. Bread riots; black market quite blatant. Poor are suffering* [Those crops we saw near Rome in June must have been cornered].'
10 December: *'Visit Palazzo Venezia and see unique art collection, stored in Vatican for safety during campaign.'*
11 December: *'Leave Rome in Henrico's car. Hitch from petrol point in two South African vehicles which separate. Kinka's baggage therefore temporarily lost on other vehicle. Great distress.'* Through Military Police channels I located the luggage in Florence. The unit was entirely Basuto who were totally honest. As we sat in the back of their 15-cwt truck, an American jeep followed us for a short while. Painted underneath the windscreen were the words 'Never a Dull Moment'.

Meanwhile the Battalion had settled down to a routine, five days in the line and five days at Greve. Life, therefore, was evenly divided between the cold and wet conditions of the mountains and the warmth of Florentine hospitality and its adjuncts. The Welsh Guards even arranged a dance and no doubt it was only one among others. The facilities for all ranks in Florence were well organized, cinemas and restaurants included, with the basic cost of a pasta meal being within everyone's means.

Nothing very much of consequence occurred at the front with the exception of a Coldstream attack on 4 December on Monte Penzola which they captured after a considerable amount of enemy resistance. In the Welsh Guards, Jim Jerman and Bryan Pugh were ordered to create a small diversion on the flank while this more serious operation took place. This involved two platoons of No 3 Company.

Inevitably all supplies beyond a certain point were brought up by mules and the organization of this was put into the swiftly expert hands of Joe Gurney from his base at Sant Apollinare at the south end of the ridge which culminated in the mountains of Acqua Salata and Verro, where I was due to arrive before very long. The jeep-head was at Sassoleone but sometimes the route was flooded.

Joe Gurney established contact with the Indian Mule Company and from his base the kit which had been transferred to jeeps was then put onto mules, the number of which he would require being conveyed to the Mule Company. Company representatives were told how many animals they would be allotted. The Guardsmen adapted quickly and the whole operation made the early efforts — indeed pioneering efforts of Owen Lloyd-George and myself — seem very amateurish.

I had been invited by the Sorbellos to spend Christmas at the 'Cardiff Arms' (Pischiello) which I gladly accepted as the alternatives were not so attractive.
23 December: *'Dress Christmas tree* [at Pischiello].'
24 December: *'Attend Midnight Mass.'*

25 December: 'Excellent lunch with pre-war champagne, light tree. Give Gian socks and gloves, Kinka stockings, also [presents] *to maids: calendar and money etc. Canadian cake* [from my uncle] *very popular. Receive pencil.'*
Letter dated 28th: *'On Christmas day we had ... lunch: game, porcetta, champagne. In the afternoon we lit the Christmas tree which Kinka and I had dressed. The children's presents were laid out underneath. Carlo (5½) and Roberto (3½) received aeroplanes and children's books. Silvia (1¾) a tea set.'*
27 December: 'Leave Pischiello. Hitchhike back to Perugia. Find major has been sacked for drunkenness over Christmas. Evidently he had drunk all the whisky.'
29 December: 'Interviewed by doctor. Apply to leave soon. Received pass to visit Civitella Ranieri [another Sorbello castle near Umbertide].*'*
Saturday, 30 December: 'Leave for Civitella Ranieri.' Despite the best efforts of Colonel Owen, Gian di Sorbello and their team of engineers, the bridges on the main road were not fully restored. Instead we went by the mountain route via San Marco and Parano, a distance of twenty-two miles in bad weather conditions for civilian cars — and one motorcycle (Georgio Rappini).
31 December: 'Castle very old (12th century) and quaint. Rather cold, snowing. Other guests included Sorbello family [Ludovico di Sorbello, now the Conte Ranieri, was the owner], *Gipsy Lawrence (a nurse), Colonel Owen, Valaria* [dell'Adorazione] *etc.'*

The castle was, and is, square in shape, with an inner courtyard, private chapel and egress holes in the upper battlements, not for Juliet to drop notes to Romeo but for the dispatch of boiling oil. Outside was a weather-worn statue of Roger the Dog, a Condottiere ancestor of the 13th century who returned one day to find his castle occupied by erstwhile allies. He reoccupied the place by the usual tactics of guile mixed with bravado. Recently the castle was struck by an earthquake, but the present owner, Roberto, then aged three-and-a-half, had the place restored almost as quickly in comparative terms as Roger the Dog had regained it.
1 January, 1945: 'Snowbound in castle until 3 January. Return to Perugia.'
4 January: 'Dance in evening at Palazzo Sorbello.'
5 January: 'Arrive convalescent depot at 0400 ... put luggage in RE mess ... truck will meet me at Pischiello.'
6 January: 'Twelfth night or Befana [Epiphany: the manifestation of Christ to the Magi].*'*
7 January: 'Kinka distributes Befana presents to peasant children (the idea being the parents give chickens etc. back throughout the year [mezzo-mezzo system].*'*

The mezzo-mezzo system, now no longer practised, was prevalent in most parts of central and southern Italy. Basically, the seed, threshing facilities, central organization of the estate, the land and the cottages were provided by the landlord and he received in return half the produce. Of course, by the time an estimate had been made by the peasant and another by the agent

111

— it was important to have a fairly honest agent — the owner may or may not have received his share which was in lieu of rent. Chickens were also part of the arrangement — raised on corn and land provided by the owner — and were presented occasionally to the larder of the big house, where the kitchen was carefully supervised by the housekeeper or the owner's wife, for this was Italy.

On an estate of, say, one thousand acres under one form of cultivation or another — olives, vines, fruit trees, cereals, tobacco, animal husbandry and so on — with another thousand acres of woodland, there might be as many as thirty to forty peasant families who were self-supporting after paying their dues in kind. It was not until the late 1950s that customs began to change: now the cottages are empty or sold to foreigners.

Undoubtedly the saddest factor to have disappeared is the sight and the noise of the white oxen with their harness bells tinkling and their slow plodding across the fields and vineyards, a country scene witnessed by Etruscans and Romans, Lombards and Italians until thirty years ago. Now tractors have replaced the oxen and six or maybe ten men represent the independent labour on the estate. The ceremony I witnessed on 7 January, 1945, was a custom going back into time immemorial, but one of the last of its kind. On the following day my world changed too — from the peace of an ancient custom to the troubled world of modern warfare from which I had been absent for two months.

IX

The Apennines to the Adriatic

THE JOURNEY FROM the northern shores of Lake Trasimene to Florence in the 15-cwt Royal Engineers truck then took four and a half hours. It can now be done in under an hour.

8 January: 'Lunch with Joe Gurney, Owen and Malcolm Richards. Visit Cathedral with Owen ... go to cinema ... dine at Savoy with Owen, Hugh [Arbuthnot] *and Tom* [Dubuisson]. *Visit Hugh's cousin's flat. Meet Tim King and Gerald Farrar* [former fellow officer cadets].'

9 January: 'In No 1 Company (Tim Bolton).'

10 January: '46 Jones (Bernard Greer's servant) now looking after me.'

13 January: 'Transfer with 46 Jones to No 2 Company (James Cull, Charles Brodie-Knight, Frank Hughes and Kenneth Witter).' The company was billeted near Greve at Colligale in the wine-growing district and based upon a small house on the estate of the viticulturist, Count Rossi-Scotti.

14 January: 'Charles [Brodie-Knight] *leaves for the "hill"* [Monte Verro].'

15 January: 'Company leaves 0500 hours. Go to Florence after lunch.'

Florence was very largely untouched by the war as a result of a general desire expressed not only by the Florentines themselves but also by Field-Marshals Kesselring and Alexander. The bronze doors of the eleventh century Baptistry were walled up and many treasures dispersed for reasons of safety. The thirteenth century Cathedral (Duomo) of Santa Maria del Fiore I had already seen with Owen Lloyd-George and I took the opportunity when in the city of also visiting the Palazzo Vecchio and other places of renown, including museums, in what could be seen at the time.

On a less recondite level, there were also such sights and places as Harry's Bar, the Music Box, a place called *'Numero Sette'* which, for better or worse, I never entered and the Excelsior Hotel which I did. There, on 18 January, I bumped into my cousin Michael Bankier, now ADC to Lieutenant-General Sir Sidney Kirkman, XIII Corps Commander, who was to write, following Mick's death after the war, that he worked with exemplary efficiency.

23 January: 'To bed at 0400 hours. Up 0800 hours. Drill parade. Only officer present — others asleep. Commander [Jocelyn Gurney] *and Lorna Twining to dinner … also Charles and James* [Cull]'.

Lorna Twining had been widowed twice in the war. Her second husband, Dick Twining, had been killed serving with the Battalion at Fondouk in North Africa. 'Lorna Twining,' wrote Squiff Ellis in *Welsh Guards at War* 'went out to minister to the comfort of her husband's Battalion and of others in the 1st Guards Brigade. They all know this and bless her.' Lorna married Desmond Chichester in the Coldstream after the war. A son was born to them. She died in childbirth.

February 4, Sunday: 'Leave early for front. Long ride in TCV. Gruelling climb in mud for miles and miles. Under command of Bruce [Goff]. *Spandaus fire as we approach position* [the Pimple]. *Recce forward of position to study minefields. German recce patrols.'*   The approach to Verro — other than being the longest, as it was the furthest — was the same in principle as the approach to any of the mountain features whither the Battalion had been sent since October: Battaglia, the Penzola ridge, Acqua Salata which was further north and finally, on 26 December, the furthest north of all, Monte del Verro with its most prominent and exposed position, the Pimple, said to be the most forward point in the Allied line. Opposite us were our old antagonists, the Parachute Regiment, and they welcomed us with bursts of Spandau fire, but, on the first night, no shelling. Although waning, the moon was fairly clear and slightly to my discomfort I could see the stars, which meant that the Germans might be able to see us as we had not put down smoke for the good reason that it was quickly blown away by the ice-cold mountain winds.

After the experiences of the first winter in Italy where cases of trench feet and frostbite were quite common, winter clothing had been issued which included thick white socks, string vests, wind suits, heavy pullovers and, just as the ground began to thaw and the snow disappear, white camouflage snow suits. I remember ordering the men not to wear them. The intention was good, had they arrived earlier, but the effect at that moment could have been fatal.

The reconnaissance of the forward position to study minefields was both pointless and dangerous: the Pimple was surrounded by minefields which we had laid. It was a small exposed position on the crest of the foremost hill of our lines, about twenty yards in diameter and approached with caution through a taped path — the tapes not always being there — with mines on either side. It was on the left flank of the company position and the German lines were across a steep, snow-covered valley about a mile away as a bullet could travel. On our left was a re-entrant dividing us from the unit on the adjoining feature, half a mile distant. The position, in other words, was entirely exposed. In order to inspect the minefield I left the inside perimeter where there were about ten slit trenches — two men to a trench — crawled underneath the barbed wire, making the target as difficult as possible for any enemy sniper and, without any precise idea of where the minefield actually lay, checked that it had not, at least, been lifted from under our noses and that it still existed, presumably under the snow. I then asked myself, 'What next?'

The question was answered almost immediately by two thumps in the distance — mortars firing — and the shrill whistle and whine of the falling bombs as they landed unpleasantly close, showering me with snow and mud and, in the process, also exploding one of our mines. I imagine that Bruce Goff had said, 'There's the Pimple. You'd better check the local defence.' Well, I had done so and I wondered who was going to clear all these mines, 3,000 feet up in this wilderness, when the opposing armies had departed.

Shortly after my minor foray the Germans sent out recce patrols. Now, if the Pimple commander had nothing more than his loyal band of fellows, his compo rations and his weapons to hold him firm in his isolation, he also had immediate command and immediate attention in so far as DF (Defensive Fire) was concerned and my signal on the 'blower' that enemy patrols were sighted 500 yards twelve o'clock in front of our position brought down just about everything to disturb the sleep of the guilty and the innocent, even in the agricultural centre of Imola only five and a half miles away in the Lombardy plain. The recce patrols duly retired. The German artillery then returned the compliment the next day and the following day and I began to feel sorry that I had started it.

5 February: 'Sniper active. Heavy [enemy] *stonk on forward slope.'* This was just in front of us: I was waiting for it to creep forward, which would have meant an attack. My platoon went on even fuller alert, for there was little sleep and even less movement on the Pimple by day. At night we slept by rota with stand-to at dusk and dawn. The company latrines were to our right on the reverse slope of the neighbouring position and were liable to be shelled. In fact, the anticipated attack came in nine days later.

Also on *5 February: 'German paratroop deserter comes into company lines.'* We watched this lone, grey-green-clad figure as he wound and plodded his way across the valley where there was deep snow. He was unarmed and gave as his reason for deserting that he was the only man in the section who was not a non-commissioned officer and thus received all the chores and fatigues as his daily lot in military life.

The last brief entry for *5 February: 'Commander visits "Pimple" with Tom Dubuisson, Intelligence Officer. He asks why he wasn't challenged and it was explained that visitors usually didn't cross the minefield* [which, despite a slight surface thaw, was frozen].' He was a little too surprised to pursue the point. In fact, as he approached, we were all looking the other way, towards the enemy. He had made a short cut from the company lines on our right and, indeed, through the minefield.

6 February: 'German attack on outpost of neighbouring division repulsed, mostly by our DF.' I remember this attack not so much because we had a front-seat view from a higher and more forward position but because of the wasted effort. It had begun at dusk after a heavy barrage, a considerable amount of smoke and then flares to light the way through the smoke. I have my doubts whether the infantry on the ground could see as well as we could, 500 feet higher up and half a mile away. The objective was no great feature but a lone, sturdy, stone-built cottage used in more peaceful times by shepherds, built on the crest of a lower ridge which quickly sloped into the same great valley which divided us from the German lines. It was a sort of half-way house which nobody wanted because it had no purpose and, more to the point, was not so easy to defend. Then came the day, or the dusk, when someone wished to make his name and, at the cost, I believe, of quite a few casualties, the place was taken from a German patrol who happened to be in the house at the time. They put up, as paratroops were inclined to do, a sturdy defence until they withdrew from a battle which was incurring unjustified casualties. The next night, however, they returned but were beaten off by our mortars and artillery. The Germans then shelled us.

7 February: 'Quite a heavy stonk on various company positions ... not so cold as usual. Sleeping as usual in slit trench. Guardsman S... deserts to enemy. Probably temporarily insane.'

Guardsman S... was not insane at all. The story which emerged later, after he had been picked up by the Military Police in Rome, was that he was being accused by his comrades of having stolen some of their kit and had been assured, in consequence, that there could be an accident in the front line. Whether there is the remotest truth in any part of this story is wholly unknown to me. What is known is that this Guardsman suddenly leapt out of his slit trench and ran towards the enemy, unarmed. This fact was immediately reported through the chain of command and on reaching 'Sunray' (Colonel Jocelyn Gurney) he ordered not only the Battalion DF to bear down on the spot where it might be assumed the deserting Guardsman would be crossing, but the whole DF of the Division and any other back-up that could be demanded. I was able to listen in to all this on my own wireless set which suddenly became monopolized by the Commanding Officer shouting, 'Kill him! Kill him! Kill him.' The young fox had doubled back. Meanwhile, the most incredible din deafened us all, not only of the guns themselves, quite some way back, but the crash of shells and mortars only a few yards in front of us. In addition, our medium and heavy machine guns were being brought to bear on the target area. The Germans must have thought we had gone mad.

8.   "Battaglia had fallen to the American 350th Infantry during the afternoon of 27 September" (p.100). The ruins of the castle.

9.   "The rain made the mule tracks extremely arduous" (p.103). The sergeant is dressed for muling.

DAMN FINE FISHING OLD MAN!

10. "The episode became the subject of a cartoon, drawn by Lieutenant-Colonel Val ffrench-Blake, commanding the 17th/21st Lancers" (p. 123).

11. The author (right) with Captain Christopher Thursby-Pelham, of fishing fame (p.123).

12. South African bridge over the River Po near Ferrara, April, 1945 (p.130).

13. The author (right) with John Davies on the return from Austria to Bologna (p.149).

14. Captain Philip Brutton, Welsh Guards, after the war.

8 February: 'Quite heavy stonk on reserve platoon positions.' Also on this day Corporal P... formerly of the Household Cavalry and noted in the history books as being a central figure in the case known as that of the 'Horse with the Green Tail' ('come round to the stables after I've dismounted and I'll show you a horse with a green tail.' The young lady later alleged she was shown more than she considered appropriate, and Corporal P... received eighteen months in the Glasshouse), asked leave to speak to me. This approach was considerably formal, given the circumstances, even for the Brigade of Guards, and Sergeant Pugh, who was sharing my slit trench, and I looked up to find Corporal P... standing stiffly to attention, on the skyline and impervious to enemy attention. I thought the very least that I could do was to match his bravery, so I too got out of the trench, stood facing him and said, 'Yes please.' He saluted. 'My nerves have gone, sir. I ask leave to report to the Medical Officer.' It was granted. He had ceased, like the Corporal at San Marco, to be of any use. He saluted, turned smartly to his right and marched off, while the whole platoon, who had inevitably heard this discussion, whinnied and neighed at him softly.

9 February: 'Very cold day indeed ... mud up to knees and much further in places (both mules and men have been suffocated). Relieved by Coldstream (Ian Skimming, and two former fellow cadets, David Shenton and Tim Makeig-Jones.) Return to mule base takes hours [in practice, it was usually five to six hours].'

It was during our long plod from the Pimple to the start line − the mule base − after we had passed the command post where the Battalion commander slept in a stone trough or manger, that I sank into the mud up to my small pack.

Two facts were clear: first, there was no leverage to extricate myself and, secondly, further effort would have only meant my sinking lower into the mud. I was, in consequence, pulled out by members of my platoon who formed a human chain which began on firm ground somewhere on the side of the track. Given the fact that the length of a man's legs − say up to his knees − and an equivalent measurement for a mule are a fraction of the overall height of either man or mule, I am unable to say why the mud was so deep unless certain sectors had been repeatedly shelled.

10 February: 'Leave start point 0300. Arrive Colligale 0800. Find Paul Makins in Battalion [Company Commander at R.M.C. (Mons) and younger brother of Colonel Willy].'

17 February: 'Frank [Hughes] *returns from hill. Colonel Jocelyn accepts me for regular commission.'*

The trek up the 'hill' on St. Valentine's Day, 14 February, was to be the last for the Battalion, which had arrived there for the first time on 26 December and where it witnessed on New Year's Day the German celebration of firing tracer bullets into the sky in the form of a gargantuan V which was followed by the laconic response of one round fired from every gun, around 2,000, on the Allied side.

On 15 February German artillery and mortars were firing considerably more than one round each; and under this heavy shelling, CSM 98 Evans was killed and eight Guardsmen wounded in the outposts held by No 4 Company under David Gibson-Watt. Two of his forward platoons, commanded by Henry Cottom, were then attacked by fifteen to twenty enemy paratroopers who had been observed creeping across the snow up the valley towards their lines. Automatically DF fire was called down and, as they approached closer, they were met with Bren and rifle fire as well as grenades. After twenty minutes the attack was called off and the enemy withdrew. There were several German dead to be seen the following day but, except under the protection of the Red Cross, to venture forth and bury them was impossible as the position was closely observed by the enemy.

22 February: 'David Gibson-Watt, David Wroth and Peter Leuchars visit. Company party. David G-W ends by dancing on the table.'

23 February: 'Reveille 0300. Leave Colligale 0500. Very cold in 5-tonner. Tea break very near Pischiello [Cardiff Arms]. Arrive Spoleto 1500. In billet with Jim Jerman, Andrew Gibson-Watt and Tony Walker.'

1st and 24th Fourth Guards Brigades assembled in Spoleto in order to reorganize and prepare for the spring offensives. North of the Apennines the German Tenth and Fourteenth Armies were doing the same thing. Bologna was not the headquarters of either Army but it was the equivalent to Florence in terms of recreation and local leave facilities. The German XIV Panzer Corps was responsible for its defences against both the Allies and two groups of Italians who were also at each others' throats – the fascist Blackshirts and the largely communist partisans.

Our journey to Spoleto from Greve on 23 February was to take us, after a two-week stay there, to the Adriatic and our participation in the final defeat of the German Armies in Italy. As Alexander had reported to the Combined Chiefs of Staff: 'In December, 1944, sufficient forces were still available in the Italian theatre of war to undertake an offensive, although several divisions had departed for France.' Several German divisions had also departed, but the Armies which remained on both sides represented two formidable opposing forces. The two Allied Armies totalled around 560,000 men; the Germans mustered 491,000. Eighth Army alone had 1,220 pieces of artillery against the Germans' 665; and 1,320 armoured vehicles were facing the enemy's 400. In the air the advantage was absolute and on the ground the Italian partisans, often led by Allied ('A' Force) officers such as Uguccione di Sorbello or British SOE and equipped by air drops, were beginning to bite.

The plan of the Chiefs of Staff to withdraw a further two divisions was cancelled after reading a summary of the situation from Alexander which had been brought by hand to London by General Gruenther who was now Chief of Staff, 15th Army Group, the gist of which was that the German lines were extended and the Allies held the initiative because of their air and armoured superiority and their mobility. 'For lack of fuel, the Germans have become extremely immobile. In consequence, I firmly believe we have a great opportunity of winning a first-class victory on the Italian front' (from *Alex* by Nigel Nicolson).

The plan which evolved was discussed with Mark Clark whose duty it now was to work out the details with Alexander's new Chief of Staff, General Sir William Morgan, successor to John Harding, who was now commanding XIII Corps, in which 6th Armoured was serving, in Eighth Army.

24 February: 'Battalion in barracks except Support [Company]. Officers in billets. Central officers' mess Commanding Officer's birthday. Chris Thursby-Pelham joins company as 2 i/c.'

26 February: 'Officers' photograph. Subalterns' drill parade with Drill Sergeant John [formerly CSM No 3 company]. *(Not awfully good: probably out of practice). Andrew Gibson-Watt breaks arm in Eton* [Field] *game.*

27 February: 'Platoon training. 20th birthday.' There appears to have been no particular celebration.

28 February: 'Drill parade.' The two Guards Brigades in Spoleto participated. The 24th were soon to serve under 56th Division command, while 1st Guards Brigade remained in 6th Armoured (3rd Grenadiers, 3rd Welsh Guards and the 1st Welch Regiment).

1 March: 'March past Major-General Murray, commanding 6th Armoured Division. My platoon judged as having a high standard of drill.'

As we settled into Spoleto there may have been fewer draftees in my platoon than others: that is to say men who had been drafted into the Battalion to make up our strength after the heavy losses at Piccolo and who would not have had the same standard of drill as those who had passed through the Guards Depot and the Training Battalion. In fact, there were no more drafts of Guardsmen coming out from England owing to the overall shortage as a result of casualties in Italy and North-West Europe.

Initially there had been three Guards Brigades in Italy: 201 (6th Battalion Grenadiers, 3rd Coldstream and 2nd Battalion Scots Guards) landed at Salerno on 9 September, 1943, under the command of Brigadier Julian Gascoigne, and was later ordered on 5 November to capture Monte Camino – which eventually fell to a corps attack – and then to fight along the Garigliano during the winter. Secondly, 24th (5th Battalion Grenadiers, 1st Scots Guards and 1st Battalion Irish Guards) landed on 27 September at Salerno under the command of Brigadier Malcolm Erskine, and then on 22 January, 1944, at Anzio, where it lost eighty per cent of its strength. The

1st Battalion Irish Guards ceased to exist as a fighting force. Thirdly, 1st Guards Brigade (3rd Battalion Grenadiers, 2nd Coldstream and 3rd Battalion Welsh Guards) landed at Naples on 5 February, 1944, and held parts of the Garigliano line.

In March, 1944, 24th Guards Brigade was withdrawn from Anzio and in April was amalgamated with 201. Three battalions went home to prepare for Normandy: 6th Grenadiers, 2nd Scots Guards and 1st Irish Guards. The new 24th Guards Brigade comprised 5th Grenadiers, 3rd Coldstream and 1st Scots Guards.

On 12 April, 1944, the 1st Household Cavalry [armoured car] Regiment landed and was placed under command of General Anders' Polish II Corps.

After the fall of Cassino 1st Guards Brigade rejoined 6th Armoured Division and 24th Guards Brigade joined the 6th South African Armoured Division, advancing northwards on an axis parallel to that of 1st Guards Brigade some thirty miles to the west. It spent the winter of 1944/45 in the Sette Valley after being ordered to abandon its attempt to push forward along Route 6620 under the prevailing weather conditions.

During the reorganization at Spoleto the 5th Battalion Grenadiers and 3rd Coldstream (24th Guards Brigade) went home and were replaced by 2nd Coldstream from 1st Guards Brigade and 1st Battalion The Buffs. The Grenadiers and Coldstream both left some men behind to make up the strength of those which remained. In 1st Guards Brigade, the 1st Battalion The Welch Regiment replaced 2nd Coldstream, while 3rd Grenadiers and 3rd Welsh Guards retained their place. 1st Guards Brigade stayed in 6th Armoured Division. 24th Guards Brigade joined 56th Division and was to face hard fighting as an infantry brigade in the Argenta Gap. It was finally transferred to 91st US Infantry Division stationed in Venetia Giulia.

Meanwhile, S Company, 1st Battalion Scots Guards, under its company commander, Richard Coke, which had long been serving with the 2nd Battalion Coldstream Guards and had fought with great distinction, went home and rejoined its regiment. To return, however, to 1 March, 1945, Spoleto:

'St. David's Day dinner for Guardsmen. Party in the mess and sergeants' mess. General and Brigadier Gerald Verney present [having replaced, respectively General Evelegh and Andrew Scott].'

Saturday, 3 March: 'Leave 1100 for Pischiello. Make Perugia in 1¼ hours. Perugia to Pischiello 25 minutes. Motorcycle pretty good (Pischiello now 9th Armoured Brigade Headquarters).'

Sunday, 4 March: 'Gian helps people off island in Lake [Trasimene] *during shooting practice. 300 in all embark in DUKWs. James Cull and Julian Martin-Smith turn up* [return with] *self and bike in 15 cwt.'*

6 March: 'Letter to Uguccione [serving in 'A' Force in the mountains with the partisans].' This letter was to cause problems.
7 March: 'O.C. company. James goes on leave.'
10 March: ' "[As] Improperly Dressed".'

'As Improperly Dressed' was a revue held, not in the old Roman theatre but in the Teatro Nuovo 'at seven o'clock'. It may be noted that it was not at 1900 hours and it could well be described as the forerunner of the Spoleto Festival – so far shamefully unacknowledged – and was written and produced by Captain C. R. S. Buckle, Scots Guards, who also played the part of Sally, the White Sultana, an act which sent a current of embarrassment through the lower limbs of the Higher Command ('Damn fellow must be pretty odd') who squirmed in their seats as much as the Captain writhed and gyrated, snake-like, on the stage.

These critiques, were, however, foretold in the programme's 'Press Comments':

'This sort of thing would not have been tolerated in peacetime.' *The Household Brigade Magazine.*

'A revolting mixture of smut and sentiment.' James Agate in the *Sunday Times.*

'... the bottom ...' *Pravda.*

After which followed the request: 'Please adjust your dress before leaving.'

The Musical Director was Major H. J. L. Green (Coldstream Guards) who was later promoted to Brigadier, despite it all. The Business Manager was Lieutenant D. E. C. Price, Scots Guards, later to be knighted and an M.P. Wardrobe, including the Sultana's jock strap and bra: Lieutenant Lord Herschell, Coldstream Guards, last seen lunching in the Upper House after clocking in. Assistant producer Lieutenant M. E. Howard, Coldstream Guards. Theatre Manager, Sergeant Pollock, Scots Guards. The Compère was CQMS Davidson, Scots Guards.

A platoon sergeant in our company, Sergeant Thomas, 63, a man of great wit and charm, played in many of the acts. He was to lose a foot five weeks later, after stepping on a mine.

Meanwhile, in Bologna, General von Senger und Etterlin arranged for the Opera to re-open and ordered – arranged is his word – the soldiery to attend, as had the British and Americans in Naples. He also arranged that Italian variety troupes were created and sent to the rest camps in compensation for his closing the brothels, which the General regarded as serving the needs more of those based in the rear than at the front and that, in any case, VD was no less rampant either way.

In Spoleto the British Army command did not have to deal with the additional problems which faced von Senger, namely the SD, the SS,

Italian Blackshirts and Red Bandannas, although they were a little put out by the White Sultana, the snake they had let out of the box office.

Sunday, 11 March: I left Spoleto at 0930 for Porto San Georgio on the Adriatic in charge of the recce party for No 2 Company. The officer in charge of the whole party, Raymond Buckeridge, was confronted with such confusion that in the end I found my own billets for the company. Meanwhile, we slept in the transit hotel in Macerata after a subalterns' party in the officers' club which got out of control. As a result, the Town Major in this military backwater, up to this moment more concerned with curing his own hangovers than exuding sympathy for those incurring their own, wrote to his superiors the following day stating that the only adjective he could ascribe to the affair was 'outrageous'. We agreed. He was obviously not going to be of any help in resolving the question of billets for the Battalion, if indeed he had anything to do with it, but he knew the area.

12 March: I found a billet for the company between Fermo and Porto San Giorgio, some forty kilometres from Macerata (map p.77).

13 March: '*Move to villa* [which had been requisitioned] *and prepare for* [the arrival of] *the company. Evacuate school. James* [Cull] *very pleased with billets.*' Indeed, his advance party had secured a delightful villa, situated on a small estate where the owners played their part with good grace.

14 March: '*Lay on canteen and sergeants' mess. School and theatre no longer requisitioned.*' I also went to see Contessa Giulia Vinci in Fermo, with a letter of introduction from the Sorbellos. Her small palazzo in the town had been requisitioned by 1st Guards Brigade headquarters, but she continued to hold bridge parties in the afternoon in her gilded and very grand *salone* on the *piano nobile*. Her husband was a prisoner of war in India and I had been warned that she was not necessarily pro-British. In the event, she was most hospitable.

16 March: This was a day during which two problems arose. The first was the outcome of the subalterns' party five days earlier and took the form of the matter being raised by the adjutant, Francis Egerton. He also had to inform me that a letter I had written to the gallant Uguccione di Sorbello in 'A' Force had been opened en route. I had given it to the owner of the billet in Spoleto and addressed it to Palazzo Sorbello to await his return. I had mentioned my visit to Pischiello with his brother, Gian, and the evacuation of the islands in Lake Trasimene − some of the islanders leaving their homes for the first time − and their evacuation by DUKWs. This was, apparently, a military secret.

The letter had been passed to a certain Major-General Heydeman, who to everyone's amazement was British and not German, a red-faced officer, I heard, who wore jodhpurs which he whacked with a riding whip; a *tertium quid* in charge of the Umbrian area who was due to hand over his responsibilities to civilian control. The matter had been passed down to Brigade headquarters and I was duly marched in to see the Brigadier, *chez Guilia Vinci*, who delighted Jocelyn Gurney and myself with a Freudian slip when he referred to the ungallant general as 'von Heydeman'. I saluted, marched out and mused on the confusion of Allied Military Government in Italy: in Rome mixed restaurants were forbidden; in Perugia they were encouraged. The military and telephone exchanges were connected, yet the post was not and, apparently, written communication between the two groups was forbidden, even at that date with Italian troops fighting alongside us. DUKWs were obviously a dangerous topic in the eyes of General (von) Heydeman. I wonder if he knew what they were? We were to ride on them crossing the Po. Perhaps that was the secret, and their use during the Comacchio operations.

18 March: 'Christopher Thursby-Pelham and Joe Gurney go fishing.' This trip nearly added to the long list of war widows. The point was that it was Christopher's intention to kill — catch is hardly the word — the fish by exploding a bundle of gelignite sticks and, furthermore, to set off the charge electrically, by means of a battery. Water is known to be a reasonably certain conductor and to the surprise of no one except the two men in the boat, the Adriatic proved to be no exception. Christopher created his electrical circuit. The wires touched the rudder. The gelignite did not sink. The boat blew up. There were casualties among the fish and Christopher and Joe joined them in the drink, suffering nothing more than badly bruised backs, a small hole in their pockets to pay for the boat and a major rocket from the Commanding Officer. The episode became the subject of a cartoon, drawn by Colonel Val ffrench-Blake, commanding the 17th/21st Lancers. The cartoon found its way to Brigade Headquarters which prompted a Demi Official note from the Brigade Major, John Buchanan, Grenadiers, to Francis Egerton, the adjutant, whose notes reveal that he was largely but not wholly informed about the matter. The matter itself, indeed, was getting blown up. But then officers were supposed to die gallantly in battle and not inadvertently in fishing boats.

22 March: 'Colonel Jocelyn in hospital.'

23 March: 'Garden party with 17th/21st [Lancers].'

24 March: 'Place guardsman in close arrest: absent from post while on guard.' Eve tempted Adam with an apple, but the raddled nymph in the woods below the drive to the house was offering her services to more than one man, indeed to all the company. James Cull caught wind of this and immediately called an 'O' group of those officers present — and luckily all were accounted for. After a short discussion, it was decided that the best action was inaction and, other than the poor man who happened to be on duty when the temptress arrived, everyone and everything returned to the *status quo ante.*

The 'O' group was dismissed.

Sunday, 25 March: 'Morning service conducted by Malcolm Richards.'

26 March: 'Company attack. GOC visits company as smoke grenade bursts outside [his] car; he asks James Cull if scheme has started yet! Do we usually behave like that?! Letter to Bertie Bankier after his farewell letter to Regiment.'

Bertie's successor was Colonel Sammy Stanier whose wife was engaged throughout the war in organizing the distribution of comforts and necessities for prisoners of war and Guardsmen at the front. Her husband had recently commanded 231st Infantry Brigade in north-west Europe and he was due to arrive at the Battalion on 7 April.

28 March: 'Owen [Lloyd George] goes home for grandfather's funeral.'

29 March: 'Brigadier Gerald Verney addresses officers.'

Good Friday, 30 March: 'Malcolm [Richards] holds service in the morning which is, as usual, short, good and to the point.'

Jack Hosegood invited me to dinner but was delayed. Meanwhile, Hugh (Pullthrough) Nisbett entertained me and offered me a drink in the form of Gordon's gin which was rationed. The second glass, perforce, had to be Benevento gin which would have been better named Hoochinoo (the American Indian tribe that distilled the original Red Man's Revenge) for indeed hooch it was. After jaundice I would imagine that a thimbleful was already too much. The soup course passed without a hitch, but soon the choice lay between blackout or exit. I rose, thanked Peter Clifton, the Commanding Officer and, accompanied by Jack Hosegood, I left. There was a long passage to negotiate at the end of which I could see Guardsmen Pritchard and Norrice and the 15-cwt truck I had ordered to meet me. In the passage, however, there were suits of armour, stationed in rows on either side, like some ghostly mediaeval guard of honour formed by the Condottiere and Gentlemen of Fermo. It was essential, with the remaining seconds of consciousness which I felt were left to me, neither to collapse nor to lurch into any one of these suits of armour as the domino effect would have made an awful noise. In a final concentration of effort I managed it. My stretcher-bearers saluted and bore me into the truck, then carried me to bed.

Easter Sunday, 1 April: 'Attend Communion held by Malcolm [Richards]. Lunch with James plus padrone [of the villa] and wife ... dine at Grenadiers' mess in the evening [and stick to wine].' I apologized to Peter Clifton.

2 April: 'Up very early for exercises with tanks. Cross river.'

Another river, the Senio, was also crossed when 8th Army established a bridgehead as a preliminary to the great attack on 8 April.

7 April: 'Field firing. Colonel Sammy Stanier here. Rugger match in the afternoon. Officers' photograph. Interview with all officers [and senior NCOs] by Regt. Lieut. Col. Dine at Giulia Vinci's. Most enjoyable.'

A week later, Saturday, 14 April, Colonel Sammy was batting for the

Regiment at Supreme Command Headquarters: 'Lunched with the Field-Marshal [Alexander]. General [Sir Edmond] Schreiber [Governor of Malta] was there. Also the Lieutenant Colonel of the Welsh Guards, who spoke very well of Julian Faber — which gave me great pleasure. [Faber was Macmillan's son-in-law].' Extract from *War Diaries* by Harold Macmillan.

8 April: 'Pick James up at Battalion HQ. Talk with Colonel Jocelyn.' He was a gallant and inspiring commander, sadly about to leave us.

On this day, 8 April, the Eighth Army launched its massive attack against the German Tenth Army which was soon, in conjunction with the Fifth Army, to result in nearly half a million men laying down their arms and, also, not a few laying down their lives.

9 April: 'Say goodbye to Giulia Vinci.'

Fermo, the villa at Porto San Giorgio, the beach, bathing and even the military exercises, so very necessary to keep us all in fighting trim, had been a delightful interval before the final drama, for everyone on both sides knew that the war must end soon. The question in everyone's mind, although not expressed, was are we — am I — going to fall at the last jump or will we — will I — pass the post?

Before dawn the next day, Tuesday, 10 April, reveille sounded at 0330 hours. We breakfasted. We embussed. We were off to battle.

125

X

The Po, the Alps and Austria

THE FINAL ATTACK which Eighth Army launched against the German
Tenth Army on 8 April was shortly to be followed by the double punch
delivered by Fifth Army which came down from the Apennines and attacked
the German Fourteenth Army south of Bologna.

The Senio, Reno and Santerno Rivers were rapidly crossed. The enemy
was being remorselessly rolled back just as Fifth Army launched its attack.
On its right flank was X Corps, flanking the Polish Corps in Eighth Army.
Further west was XIII Corps, then US II Corps and US IV Corps. Opposing,
on the Bologna front, was the German XIV Panzer Corps with four divisions
and LI Mountain Corps to its right further west. The attack on this front
developed on 14 April and came as a surprise against the left wing of LI
Mountain Corps and the right wing of XIV Panzer Corps, held by 94 Infantry
Division which was thrown back together with the untried 8th Mountain
Division. There were hardly any reserves – mostly transferred to the Eighth
Army front – and the result was that this point had become the weakest,
despite its artillery concentration, in the German defences. This was
immediately exploited by General Truscott.

The US 1st Armoured Division passed through the village of Tole which
lies beyond Vergato, overcame the mobile German anti-tank defences, left
the north slopes of the Apennines behind them and debouched into the
plain. Fifth Army had now fought its way through more than fifty miles of
mountain defences during the winter campaign, often at heights around
3,000 feet in appalling weather conditions, as 1st Guards Brigade were only
too well aware. It was now into tank country and making the most of it: the
US 10th Alpine Division and 88th Division fought their way towards the
Via Emilia between Bologna and Modena. The whole line on this part of the
front was pierced while the Germans withdrew as best they could.

In both Fifth and Eighth Armies, the armoured divisions were now
blasting their way through to the Po, pulverizing German defences south of
the great river. Most if not all the bridges had been destroyed by Allied air
attacks, the approach roads bombed and largely blocked with burning

vehicles. These shock waves obviously presaged the end of the struggle. It was, nevertheless, still a very dangerous game for the fighting man on either side, as we were all well aware.

10 April: 'Reveille 0330 hours. Leave the Fermo area ... arrive [Forlimpopoli] *south of Forli at 1300 hours. Hear news of big attack. It's all started again like last summer. Let's hope we finish it this time.'*

11 April: 'Sharing tent with Frank Hughes. Col. Jocelyn leaves the Battalion. Teal [Ashton] *also leaves.'*

I wrote home: *'Col. Jocelyn has now left us* [to take up a staff job on 12 April]. *I'm really very sorry indeed, almost too sorry for words. He was a brilliant and brave leader. A most charming and understanding man and a great help to myself. He was a strict disciplinarian and ruthless with failure, especially officers. His successor is Col. Robin Rose-Price who used to be our 2nd in Command last year. He is at the moment in France on the Staff. A very brilliant man. I like him a lot. At the moment Julian Martin-Smith is commanding as Acting Temporary Lt/Col until Col. Robin arrives.'*

16 April: 'Leave Forlimpopoli at 0630 ... in forward concentration area [Bagnacavallo]. *Roads very dusty. Farm buildings mostly totally demolished. Visit Lugo* [three miles west of Bagnacavallo] *and Senio river* [which ran between the two] *in jeep with James* [Cull].'

17 April: 'Learn routes by heart. 63 Thomas [a platoon sergeant] *loses his right foot on mine. Corporals Morgan and Fleming slightly hurt ... all this whilst swanning on Senio.'*

Sergeant Thomas' wit did not desert him while lying on his stretcher: 'My best foot, too!' he told us. We were very sorry indeed to lose Sergeant Thomas. He was not my platoon sergeant, who was an equally memorable and reliable man, Sergeant Neagle, among whose predecessors, one had been wounded at Cassino and three had been killed. One after San Marco, I had recommended for a decoration which he received.

18 April: 'Move to new area.'

19 April: 'In assembly area ... move to forward area. [Our] harbour area now Argenta Gap [five miles or so across flat dry land which lay between Lake Comacchio and the Reno − effectively the penultimate river to cross before the Po]. *Kraut plane drops 2 bombs rather close.'* Slit trenches had, as usual, been dug and we dived for them as the whoosh of the bombs signalled an unpleasantly close explosion which indeed shook the ground around us with seismic shudders. It was to be the last of my several air-to-ground encounters with the Luftwaffe during this war.

20 April: 'Breakfast 0500. Move to company positions 1000 hrs. Snipers cause a few casualties in forward companies, 160 prisoners pass through our hands [of which 40 or so were taken by the Battalion and 100 more the following day].'

To date 6th Armoured Division had been in reserve. Now, however, with the Argenta Gap firmly in our hands, the 26th Armoured Brigade was ordered into the vanguard supported by the Welsh Guards. (1st Guards Brigade, as mentioned earlier, now comprised 3 Grenadier Guards, 3 Welsh Guards and 1 Welch Regiment. Also in 6th Armoured were 61st Infantry Brigade as well as 26th Armoured.) The objective was now to strike for the Po between Ferrara and Bondeno at the small town of Mirabello. At the same time Fifth Army was fighting its way north towards Modena, Carpi and San Benedetto on the Po, further west; both Armies branching out to meet each other – not inappropriately – at Finale Emilia on the Pinaro, twelve miles south of the Po and ten and a half miles west of Mirabello where I was to lead the attack to take the town.

By the evening of the 20th the Battalion held positions along the far bank of the Reno at Traghetto, Malvezzi and Borgo Cortili, the first two places being flattened after air bombardment on the 19th. On our right flank the Welch Regiment had a tougher fight for the Combalina Canal which they crossed but were counterattacked by German armour which, while they engaged it, was in turn outflanked by the 17th/21st who, luckily, had found an unblown bridge and rushed it. Their tanks then broke through the German defences and did not stop until reaching Renalico five miles further on. The Welch Regiment then succeeded in their second attempt to cross the canal, established a secure bridgehead which the Grenadiers passed through and the Germans withdrew north-west towards Mirabello, ten miles further north.

21 April: 'Move 0630. Find all animals on farm burnt by Krauts. Also one girl killed, another wounded, a third raped. Move forward to village where one man [was] deliberately killed by German throwing grenade.'

We had advanced rapidly in conjunction with the armour amidst the sombre scenes and all-pervading dust of motorized warfare on dry ground: ruined towns behind us, now more open country with burning farmsteads and dead animals in the fields, mainly horses and cattle, their bellies bloated, lying on their backs, their legs stretched stiffly skywards and occasionally exploding from the pressure of built-up internal gases; knocked out half-tracks and guns and mainly German corpses lying unburied on this headlong advance.

We also met despondent straggling columns of German prisoners, trudging southwards; and, incongruously, excited civilians showering us with flowers and vivas as we passed through their lives in a few seconds.

22 April: '[There had been considerable enemy resistance before, during and after the breakout from the Argenta Gap.] *Learn Robin Rose-Price arrived. Move to forward area. Prepare for night assault on Mirabello. No 1* [Paul Makins] *and No 2* [James Cull] *companies assaulting.* [I am] *in carrier. Am leading vehicles in Battalion. Relieve Rifle Brigade. Stonked on way in. No casualties, thank God* [heavy shelling and mortaring. Always unpleasant, but particularly when exposed in vehicles, the engines and tracks of which blocked the noise of approaching missiles]. *Exchange of fire with Kraut ambulance. Corporal Robinson wounded.'*

My memories of Mirabello are confined to its lack of architectural distinction, one wide street, and the fact that we arrived at night. Then, after relieving the Rifle Brigade, we fought our way, luckily without casualties, except for Corporal Robinson, down the street. I was 2 i/c company in the battle and as such had a particular job of being close to the wireless while James Cull, as company commander, led his troops forward in the classic street fighting, house-clearance tactic of covering fire and movement, grenade lobbing, smoke cover and a keen eye, whenever possible, for avoiding booby traps and mines. Two-inch mortars and PIATs were also very useful and the Bren was invaluable. We also brought up a flame-thrower against which no sensible soldier would stand and sizzle if he could possibly avoid it.

What we were doing exchanging fire with an ambulance, I have totally forgotten. I can only assume that it had abandoned its basic role, had not removed the Red Cross and then its occupants opened fire on us. We had been seen off by Christopher Thursby-Pelham [LOB] who waved frantically as we departed which I thought was singularly unmilitary but it did not prevent him from becoming a distinguished Brigadier in the post-war Army.

Corporal Robinson was wounded close to where we were. The mortaring and shelling was quite intense and I remember seeking shelter under a staircase, feeling like a civilian. The reason was first the mental association (I was first bombed when I was fifteen years old) and, secondly, in all the war in Italy I had never been in a house worthy of the name during a battle; and my memory of Battaglia reminded me that they were very unsafe, a point which was rammed home when we shelled and shot up the villa at San Marco. I had always been in a slit trench or unpleasantly exposed, but never in a house. I was also feeling frustrated at having to hang around, although in general I enjoyed being 2 i/c in battle.

In the event, the *coup de feu* — *coup de grâce* would be inappropriate — was given by Paul Makins (No 1 Company) at the break of dawn with a little help from the flame-thrower. In so far as the enemy was concerned, he withdrew from the frying pan towards more fire nearer the Po, pursued by the armoured brigade which battled on to capture Bondeno, after cutting the railway line between Ferrara and Bologna.

The armoured brigade then wheeled left towards Finale, where they saw two jeeps approaching them with cerise-coloured sheets on the bonnets and driven by Americans. The Fifth and Eighth Armies had met. Some 7,000 prisoners of war were forced into the armoured embrace of the Americans, and 6th Armoured Division reached the Po on 23 April, St George's Day, fifteen days after the initial assault.

23 April: 'Town [Mirabello] *cleared, except for odd sniper. Use flame-thrower to get them out. CSM Williams and self acquire goose and side of a pig for* [the] *company. Derby Yeo* [manry] *reach Po. 16th/5th link with South Africans. Swan in Mirabello looking for Krauts.'*

24 April: 'Still in Mirabello and likely to stay until tomorrow. New Zealanders passing through. Terrific chaps and quite wild. One sells German car for 40,000 lire [£100] *receives 20,000* [while the balance is being collected] *and drives away.'*

On the 24th, after a reconnaissance, the Grenadiers crossed the Po against light opposition. They were followed on the 25th by the Welsh Guards. The day before, while waiting for orders to advance in Mirabello, I wrote home:

'I'm thoroughly enjoying life as second in command [in battle]. *I always travel in the carrier, arrange all the maps, decipher codes and do all sorts of interesting things. The only trouble is you can't hear a shell or a mortar bomb with the noise of the tracks. Thereby preventing one from baling out into the nearest ditch!'*

25 April: 'Cross River Po ('Rupee') 0930. Brigadier describes it as a great victory … very little opposition. Swan forward about five miles. Very little destruction.'

The Welsh Guards crossed in twelve DUKWs and I remember the approach north of Porporana as we rumbled our way down the approach road, then slid into the water and were across this wide and exposed stretch of river without any covering fire or smoke but, equally, without mishap. We clambered up the other side and de-DUKW-ed.

It was also on this day that the commanding officer, now Robin Rose-Price, David Gibson-Watt and an officer from the Ayrshire Yeomanry, together with Sergeant Emrys Davies and his platoon mounted on amphibious tanks, made a five-mile dash to the Bianco Canal where the advance route of the Battalion crossed over a bridge at Castel Guglielmo. The next transriparian exercise was to cross the Adige. The idea was to capture the bridge intact to save the Royal Engineers the trouble of building one and to accelerate the Battalion's advance. Alas, the enemy had other ideas. The bridge blew up just as the first tank was about to cross.

Five days before we crossed the Po, General von Senger und Etterlin was vainly trying to organize his disintegrating corps. Such was the Intelligence reaching Allied headquarters from SOE and partisan sources that the location of his new headquarters was known and promptly bombed. He emerged unscathed, though the cattle bolted, the neighbouring house ignited and his washing ended up in the trees. He pulled out.

By this date, 20 April, XIV Panzer Corps and its right-hand neighbour, LI Mountain Corps, were no longer contiguous. The Fifth Army advance had reached San Benedetto on the Po, the 94th Division had 'completely vanished', the commander of 65th Infantry Division, Lieutenant-General Pfeiffer, was killed at the Finale bridge and Colonel General Graf von Schwerin, Corps Commander opposing us near Ferrara, surrendered with all his staff, saying that the military situation was hopeless. On the night of 22 April, when we were engaging the enemy in Mirabello, General von Senger had to decide whether to surrender south of the Po with his staff or cross the river. On the 23rd, the day the Derby Yeomanry reached the Po and we were clearing Mirabello, von Senger found a ferry at Bergantino further upstream and crossed at dawn.

At the same time I wrote home: *'There are thousands of prisoners coming in. I'm really very sick of seeing them. I don't think they're all crack troops. The Germans now often leave their poorer troops behind to delay us, while their crack troops retire "to fight another day".* [My personal experience in the past was that it was more often the other way round].' Indeed at this moment a disciplined company of parachutists under a young officer surrendered to Andrew Gibson-Watt's platoon. The officer said that they would only do so to Guardsmen. He added that he had taken part in the capture of Derek Bond and his brother officers in Florence. His men produced some wine, the Welsh Guardsmen some cigarettes; family photographs were exchanged, and as Andrew wrote, they generally behaved 'like long-lost brothers'.

In the crumbling Greater Reich Himmler tried to surrender on 24 April to the United States and Britain only. This was refused. On 26 April United States and Russian forces met in central Germany at Torgau.

27 April: 'Reveille 0330 hours. Move forward to area of Adige. Assault crossing of Adige by 1 and 2 Companies cancelled.' I wrote: *'1st Guards Brigade were the British assault troops over the Po. Together with the New Zealanders we were the first Eighth Army troops to cross.... It was a strange feeling embussing into DUKWs (Ducks) on land, driving a quarter of a mile straight into the river and across 200 yards of water, then streaming ashore on the other side.'*

On 27 April the Battalion was ordered to clear Lendinara on a tributary of the Adige and two miles from the main river; whereupon, Jack Hoffmann with his carrier platoon engaged several of the enemy in and around the cemetery where a number had taken up positions irreverently behind the mausolea and monuments to the local dear departed, to whom several of these last-ditch derring-dos were soon to be dispatched, before the remainder decided to surrender in unwitting emulation of their superiors at Caserta.

We were then ordered to the Adige where a German sniper nearly parted the hair of the commanding officer at the site of a would-be crossing. Then, after a short interval, a party of fourteen Germans appeared and attempted to cross this partly destroyed bridge. We opened fire, killing one and wounding three. The rest surrendered. These were the last shots fired by the Battalion in Italy. At this time, however, the last Guardsman to be killed was in the mortar platoon. The 3-inch mortars were set up at the edge of a wood which was acting as camouflage. The order to fire was given, but the angle of the barrel, fixed in accordance with the range, was too steep to clear an overhanging branch of a tree. The Guardsman was mortally wounded by the mortar bomb he had himself placed in the barrel. I saw him being taken to the care of Dai Morris, the Medical Officer, in a carrier and in the arms of Malcolm Richards, the Padre, but he closed his eyes for ever on this earth before getting there and was taken into the arms of God.

28 April: 'German resistance in Italy is practically over.' Mussolini was captured and executed by partisans on this day.

On 28 April the German military plenipotentiaries arrived at Allied Forces Headquarters, Caserta, to sign the military surrender documents. The first moves had been made earlier by German representatives in Switzerland of SS Oberstgruppenführer Karl Wolff, the senior SS General in Italy, and Colonel-General von Vietinghoff-Scheel, Commander-in- Chief, through the intermediary of Lieutenant-Colonel von Schweinitz.

The delegation was received by Alexander's Chief of Staff, General Sir William Morgan. The surrender terms were unconditional. The Germans returned to Bolzano on 30 April saying that they might have exceeded their powers and that their signatures required confirmation. General Morgan accepted. The plenipotentiaries returned to a certain state of confusion within the German Higher Command. Kesselring maintained that von Vietinghoff-Scheel had begun by exceeding his powers in the first place and retired him. A certain General Schultz, whom nobody seemed to know, replaced von Vietinghoff. Then Wolff was placed under arrest by Kesselring. Then everyone became friends again and Wolff was released and was once more in direct touch by radio with Caserta who were sticking to the agreed date.

Despite an excellent signals platoon under Dick Kingzett and first-class signallers within the company, the Welsh Guards were not informed of the wavelength of these transmissions and there was no time to search the ether for the chance to eavesdrop on such conversations sent *en clair*. Instead the Battalion took to prayer:

29 April: 'Church service with Malcolm. Clearing exercise: 2 prisoners and five horses. Col. Robin hoped it would be our last operation in War. I wonder! Sharing billet with Chris [Thursby-Pelham] *in Lendinara.'*

30 April: 'Arrive at Noale [between Padua and Treviso] *... tremendous welcome by populace.'*

1 May: 'Reveille 0400... guard POW camp.'

This was the day that Hitler shot himself and Admiral Karl Doenitz became head of state. Also on 1 May Tito's communist partisans entered Trieste just before the New Zealanders and were advancing into Venezia

Giulia and the Austrian region of Carinthia. On the same day, too, General von Senger gave orders to General Haug of LI Corps and to General Heidrich of 1 Para Corps as well as to XIV Panzer Corps to lay down their arms. None questioned his orders.

On 2 May radio messages were sent out from German Headquarters at Bolzano *en clair* ordering all units to surrender. There was a public announcement worldwide at 1830 and one hour later Winston Churchill spoke in the House of Commons saying: 'It brings to a conclusion the work of as gallant an Army as ever marched and brings to a pitch of fame the military reputation of a commander who has always enjoyed the fullest confidence of the House of Commons.' Allied forces were approaching the Brenner Pass and the German Tenth Army had quite literally been annihilated.

2 May: 'POW includes General in SS (4th on black list) [I had a close look at him: he flinched as I approached. He was standing, together with other prisoners, but ignored by them, in an outhouse] *also Divisional Commander of 65th* [and the combined 305th Infantry Division: Major-General von Schellowitz particularly asked me that he be not handed over to the Americans and could his ADC accompany him. I assured him to the best of my knowledge that the answer to the first question was that he was likely to remain as a British POW and the answer to the second was that he would be held with other Generals but without ADCs] *10,000 prisoners in cage.'*

3 May: 'Uguccione di Sorbello turns up again.' He was awarded the Italian equivalent to the Victoria Cross by the Italian government for his work with 'A' Force.

Also on 3 May there was more trouble with Tito and cables were winging to and fro from Caserta and London with Churchill insisting on a firm military stand and that Tito be brought to heel. Meanwhile he took Fiume. Alexander was at first not too sure how to handle the matter, even doubting whether the British soldiery would relish shooting up these communist partisans. For once Alexander was out of touch with the rank and file and was rebuked by Downing Street. The situation was taken in hand and other than those territories which were ceded to Yugoslavia by Italy in accordance with the postwar settlement, Tito and his partisans were eventually thrown out.

My entry for 3 May ends with the laconic statement: *'46 Jones tight.'* Guardsman Jones, who never drank, had been persuaded to celebrate. At lunchtime he arrived with my mess tins, duly filled with what the company cook had provided. It took him, however, a full two minutes to cross two yards. With a superb balancing act he managed to keep the food in the tins while his knees bent and then straightened out as if he were trying to cross the deck of a storm-tossed ship. I was quite hypnotised. He then bowed low

— with great dignity — I was sitting on my camp bed — presented me with my humble fare as if it were caviar on gold plate, hiccupped, apologised in a very slurred voice, straightened up, about-turned and managed to make the opening through the door and disappeared. He was wholly forgiven. Who was I to cast a stone?

4 May: General von Senger und Etterlin arrived at the Florence headquarters of General Mark Clark to discuss the details of handling the prisoners of war from two German Armies. A British liaison officer, John Profumo, provided him with an English breakfast while Mark Clark provided a three-room house with bathroom and kitchen, where the 'full American rations' could be put through the culinary process. Twenty-two officers accompanied him. He returned to Bolzano after nine days' work and went on to his headquarters at Matterolo. On 22nd May 'I and my adjutant Count von Cramm were fetched from Matterolo and so I went into captivity as leader of the huge POW camp at Ghedi.'

4 May: SHAEF announced the surrender of all German forces to Field-Marshal Montgomery.

4 May: '*Move to Udine … columns of Chetniks* [Royalists] *escaping from Tito whom we are preventing* [from] *progressing further.*'

4 May: 91st Guards Brigade sitrep, concerning last-ditch resistance from the German SS Mountain Division, first at Ospedaletto and then at Venzone: '*Two Italian partisans who approached a cave in which some dozen German officers were sheltering were killed at point-blank range; whereupon all German officers were liquidated by one of our WASP flame-throwers.*'

5 May: '*Tito is causing a great deal of trouble.*'

This was our first encounter with the Yugoslav communist forces. Tito had refused to place his partisans under Allied command. In the end he withdrew from the more sensitive areas; but the Welsh Guards became intimately involved in handing over non-communists to both Tito and Stalin after we had entered Austria.

I wrote home: '*I managed to recondition an abandoned German car, which I've been running about in! Everybody has something or other, but unfortunately we are not allowed to take them over the border, so I've got rid of it. I exchanged it with the partisans for a very streamlined radio. We've been guarding prisoners of war — 10,000 of them, including an SS General on the black list* [also] *a Divisional commander and his entire staff. The interpreter was Lieutenant in the artillery. Do you remember my telling you after the battle of Monte Piccolo where Pip was killed, we pushed forward to Arce? During the* [day we] *experienced the* [most intensive] *artillery and mortar stonk. It was so heavy and concentrated. The interpreter was the man responsible! A small world, isn't it? He was a most charming man and in the hotel business before the war. The last days have been spent keeping the peace between Tito's partisans and Mihailovich's Chetniks. All*

Yugoslavs but holding different views! All hated by the Italians, I think because Tito is a little [too] keen to occupy Italian soil. We are, therefore, preventing any further trespassing.'

7 May: 'Germans capitulate [German generals sign surrender terms at Reims].'

7 May: General Mark Clark, 15th Army Group, signalled General McCreery that Eighth Army would only accept the surrender of German forces facing them. Germans opposing communist formations – Soviet or Titoist – must surrender to them.

8 May: '[VE Day] *Reveille 0100. 3 W.G. enter the Greater Reich. First town Villach. "No fraternization order." Germans freed POWs: Yugoslavs, Russians and British, all intermingling.'* VE Day was a civilian celebration. We heard about it later!

8 May: General Mark Clark ordered General McCreery to occupy the British zone with maximum speed and extend before the arrival of the Russians and Yugoslavs. He also ordered the use of artillery or air arm, as distinct from employing British infantry and thus incurring casualties, against Germans who refused to surrender.

It goes without saying that I was wholly unaware of any higher echelon orders or activities in Austria at the time – a fact which I shared with many considerably more senior to me – other than those orders which were given to me through the chain of command or which I gave at my own humble level or those orders which affected me or the effect of which I could see with my own eyes. I will, however, occasionally refer to Higher Command signals in the text so that the reader may more easily follow the sequence of events.

On 9 May I wrote to my mother: *'Yesterday we entered Austria – the Greater Reich! The Alps were incredibly beautiful. The sun shining on the glistening peaks, the snow sparkling like crystal flakes. The rich colours of the lower slopes, greens of every shade inter-mixed with copper beech. We are not allowed to fraternize. In the town we are occupying there are German troops still walking about prior to their imprisonment by their own troops (there are so many it takes time). There are also many freed POWs: French, British, American, Russian, Poles etc. Also Tito (who's a bloody nuisance). Many of the Germans are armed still, mostly because they fear attacks from Tito. Last night I was sent to investigate a report of a shooting match between German troops and civilians. I entered a German company* [area] *and found it exactly as it would have been had we not been there* [i.e. at this stage the situation in many sectors remained at the status quo ante]. *I've been driving all sorts of cars for the last week: Mercedes-Benz and Lancia being my favourites.'*

In addition to Germans, Yugoslavs of different political colours, creeds and tongues, the Cossacks, the Austrians themselves, the British Army (in this sector) and freed prisoners of war, there were also refugees. A friend of mine, now living in Zurich, arrived aged twelve with members of her family from Hungary, fleeing from the Russians. They had abandoned all their possessions except those which could be loaded on to wagons and drawn by four strong horses. Many arrived with nothing except a worn pair of shoes; but for all it was a terrible and desperate moment.

Nevertheless, thanks to V Corps staff work and the presence of the Red Cross as well as Allied Military Government, conditions were never, in terms of organization, to become Brechtian, except during some of the expulsions. Nor was there any animosity on the part of the ordinary British soldier towards either the refugees or those who had fought for the Germans or towards the Germans themselves. In other words, to use a First World War expression, there was never any 'anti-coal-scuttle-helmet' sentiment of any kind. There was simply sympathy for the unfortunate and the defeated.

10 May: 'Relieve Jim Jerman guarding road blocks [against Tito incursions]. *Spend most of day* [after my tour of duty] *driving Austrian girl in Mercedes.'*

Fraternization was still officially forbidden, but the Underground Fraternization Movement was formed (the UFM) and many local liaisons fructified at this time. Battalion headquarters were well within the law: they were installed in a schloss at Rosegg owned by a branch of the Liechtenstein family which provided the excuse that they and their friends were not Austrian but Liechtensteiners. On the other hand, some took the regulations seriously: Tim Bolton, I remember, fresh from morning exercises and a swim in the Wörther See, objected to my playing a more leisurely game of ping-pong with a delectable young Austrian who was devoted to the game and potentially to the Welsh Guards.

10 May: V Corps Commander, Lieutenant-General Sir Charles Keightley, accepted the invitation of Marshal Tolbukhin to come to Voitsberg where the Soviets demanded the handing over of named Czarist (Cossack) officers. Most were non-Soviet citizens who were not differentiated but lumped together in one 'Wanted' list. This date was the beginning of the tragedy which involved the transfer of 73,000 victims to the communists, both Russian and Yugoslav. I was to transfer the first 200 to Yugoslavia, men, women and children. Then, the next day, I handed over 2,000, three per cent of the total. Such were the priorities in Austria that playing ping-pong with an eighteen-year-old Austrian was *verboten* but jettisoning 2,200 Yugoslavs to their fate was strictly according to the rules.

12 May: 'Tito still making aggression. They are purely brigands and looters. Bathe in small lakes near house. Sudden order to move.'

12 May: President Truman cabled Churchill. Both leaders then warned off Stalin and Tito. The problem which now remained was clearing Tito out of Carinthia and Trieste. Within six days he ordered his troops out of Austria.

Meanwhile, General Keightley was in close touch with Soviet forces who were showing no signs of aggression other than their offering an excess of pre-luncheon vodka.

13 May: 'Whole company in school building. All Guardsmen sleeping in beds. Some with sheets [there were eiderdowns, but the gift parcels home became both numerous and bulky at this moment]. *Baths and showers downstairs; electric light, wireless; only Tito spoils the fun.'*

13 May: The 'fun' of Austria, as compared to war in Italy, certainly in no way applied to the 73,000 unfortunates who were soon to be expelled in the wake of the political advice given to General Keightley at Klagenfurt. On this day Harold Macmillan, as Resident Minister, flew north with Alexander's concurrence. He then advised the return of the Cossacks, and stated in his diary that handing them over would mean their being enslaved, tortured or murdered, but to refuse would offend the Soviets. He also thought – or wrote that he thought – that refusal would break the Yalta Agreement. In deciding to advise the handing over of Russians who were not Soviet citizens, he not only broke the Yalta Agreement (in a different sense to his meaning) but also ran contrary to the spirit of his own cable to the Foreign Office of 27 July, 1944.

I visited the Viktring camp at about this time, where 30,000 people were gathered as a group, and also another large camp in the Drau valley, the Peggetz camp. Like the one at Viktring, it was full not only of soldiers, but older men, women and small children romping around the fields. Yet again, all felt safe in British hands. Nearly 2,000 (about two-thirds) of the officers were non-Soviet citizens, as were many of the older men, together with their women and children.

Proud and exceedingly well-disciplined, the men in the Cossack camps I visited wore loose, long dark blue or dark green caftans with crimson, light blue or yellow shoulderstraps. The Cossack Guards wore short red or blue tunics with caps of the same colours. They were all superbly mounted, but, except for the Guards, without spurs, only carrying whips. Their headgear was a conical cap of curled black Astrakhan wool with a cloth top of red, light blue or yellow. My brother officer, Jim Jerman, in No 3 Company Welsh Guards, was ordered to hand over a large batch of these Cossacks, but saved only a doctor who was acting as an interpreter and whom the female Soviet representative or commissar insisted was a Russian and should board the train. Several lambskin caps were given to Jim Jerman. One was an officer's, the others had belonged to the men, one of which he gave to me. It had a red cloth top, blue quilting inside with a German label.

14 May: 'Duty officer. Scenery beautiful: greens of all colours with the mountains in the background.'

14 May: Stalin and Tito were informed that the spheres of influence agreed at Yalta must be respected and that the Yugoslavs must clear out of Austria. *If* Soviet military support for Tito had ever been contemplated, the idea was certainly dropped from now on.

14 May: Following Macmillan's recorded advice on his return to Caserta, Lieutenant-General Robertson, Chief Administrative Officer at AFHQ, sent off his crucial signal to Eighth Army ordering that all Russians were to be handed over to the Soviet forces and that all Yugoslavs who were in uniform and had been fighting with the Germans were to be handed over to Tito. Despite previous and subsequent contradictory signals from AFHQ, this order was to be the basis of V Corps' expulsion orders and, with few exceptions, the consequent dispatch of 73,000 people.

Government policy, it is pertinent to mention, which had been clearly signalled to AFHQ at Caserta and had been passed on, was that (a) no one other than Soviet citizens (who were to be screened: otherwise, quite obviously, the order had no practical meaning) was to be returned to the Soviet Union in accordance with the Commonwealth-Soviet Repatriation Agreement signed at Yalta on 11 February, about which Macmillan was briefed in detail by Eden in Athens four days later, and (b) *all* Yugoslavs of whatever creed, language group, political affiliation – pro or anti-German, pro or anti-communist – sex, uniform or past history were to be evacuated and thence to await a Government decision. This order was dispatched from London on 29 April, 1945.

In so far as the Russians were concerned, among the six Cossack groups, totalling nearly 70,000 men, women and children, there were thousands of *non*-Soviet citizens, particularly the old Czarist officers, whom Stalin was most anxious to receive and execute, as well as thousands of women and children in whom he had little interest but received all the same, because the Cossacks were returned by V Corps as military formations, plus families and dependants and not screened individually.

Concerning the Yugoslavs, the thinking behind V Corps signals and actions was to clear the area in case of a showdown with Tito whose incursions into Carinthia were becoming a serious menace – more political than military; but nevertheless the need was obvious to free troops from guard duty and road blocks, should such a need arise. The strange factor in this case was the handing over of Tito's enemies to Tito – in order to facilitate fighting the same man and expelling his troops from Austria!

15 May: Following Robertson's signal, an agreement was made between Tito's emissary and the BGS V Corps, Brigadier Toby Low, and preparations were made for its implementation: among other details, 11,000 Croats were to be returned to Yugoslavia immediately. I handed over the first two groups.

It has been posited that the evacuation, as ordered a few days earlier, to Italy would have blocked the lines of communication. It did not appear to me to be so at the time, but someone in a better position to judge, Nigel Nicolson, 1st Guards Brigade Intelligence Officer in Austria, wrote to me recently: 'The "clogging-up of the L of C" argument is quite wrong, as RASC lorries were returning daily from Austria empty, and the railway was working Klagenfurt-Trieste. In fact the whole Ukrainian Division was sent back this way.'

In the event 33,000 Yugoslavs were handed over. As my victims were Yugoslavs, my percentage of returnees was around seven per cent of the total and forty per cent of the number handed over to Tito by the Welsh Guards. In addition, the Battalion was ordered to hand over thousands of Cossacks.

15 May: 'Take ex-French POWs to Villach. All cars have now been handed in. Bathe in Lake [Wörther See]. *Spend afternoon on Dai Morris'* (the Medical Officer's) *speed boat.'*

It was also on this day that British forces refused the surrender of 200,000 Croats and 300,000 Germans at Bleiburg, and consequent refuge for the Croat women and children. From a military viewpoint and in terms of orders affecting V Corps, the refusal was technically and tactically logical. The result, however, was a massacre.

16 May: 'Visit Brigade Headquarters. Tea with Mick [Bankier, who had become ADC to Kirkman's successor at XIII Corps, Lieutenant-General Sir John Harding. At that moment he was about to become ADC to Charles Keightley at V Corps].'

16 May: Alexander's Chief of Staff, General Sir William Morgan, was in Klagenfurt at V Corps headquarters. He was briefed on the current situation and asked Eisenhower by signal to accept POWs and Russian refugees in preference to handing the latter over to Stalin.

17 May: Macleod, Robertson's deputy at AFHQ, ordered 15th Army Group and Eighth Army to evacuate all Chetniks and dissident Yugoslavs infiltrating areas occupied by Allied troops to Italy. This order confirmed Churchill's order of 29 April and the AFHQ signal of 2 May. It superseded Robertson's own signal of 14 May. No known evidence exists that it was forwarded to V Corps. McCreery initialled it undated.

17 May: Robertson cabled the Combined Chiefs of Staff in Alexander's name and asked for direction concerning the disposal of Cossacks and Yugoslavs.

17 May: Alexander signalled General Eisenhower asking him to accept 109,000 Germans and 46,000 Cossacks. Alexander would evacuate the Yugoslavs. Eisenhower agreed and confirmed this to Churchill who had also cabled him.

17 May: The Soviets, in their turn, courteously agreed to accept all Soviet citizens in British hands; yet six days earlier they had demanded – with a typed list of names, some in capitals – those whom they knew were not Soviet citizens.

17 May: V Corps, acting on Robertson's signal of 14 May and not that of Macleod's of 17 May, ordered that *all* Yugoslav nationals in the British zone were to be handed over to Tito's forces. Robertson's signal was restricted to Yugoslavs in uniform who had fought for the Germans. They were not to be told of their destination and the transfer was to be done soonest.

Thus at the highest military level on 17 May AFHQ's orders were to transfer all Yugoslavs to Italy and at the same time Alexander was trying to transfer the Cossacks to SHAEF where the Geneva Convention of 1929 prevailed over Yalta: i.e. *these* Russians were regarded as being German troops and therefore were not liable to repatriation even if they were Soviet citizens (and many were not), while at the lowest military level, my own, I was ordered to proceed with my platoon and the Derbyshire Yeomanry (one tank) to Rosenbach to execute the reverse, as far as the Yugoslavs were concerned. Meanwhile, V Corps were actively engaged in the details of handing over the Cossacks to Marshal Tolbukhin.

17 May: '*Move to forward road block with platoon. Gerry Hamlyn, Derbyshire Yeomanry in support. Liaise with Tito in Rosenbach on the frontier. Stop all trains.*'

Tito was, in fact, represented by a slim communist colonel, Lieutenant-Colonel Hocevar (later Yugoslav Ambassador to Poland) who had met Brigadier Toby Low two days earlier. He was dressed in a smart dark green uniform which he might have obtained from the Royalists. He wore polished boots, a fore-and-aft cap, Sam Browne belt and pistol. We spoke English.

'*Stop all trains*' – coming from Yugoslavia. No one left Austria for Yugoslavia at that moment with any degree of free will. Indeed the tunnel was used only days before by thousands of refugees groping their way into Austria from Yugoslavia. The Colonel was interested in taking into his far from politically tender hands the former Croat Government who were due to arrive the next day, although at that moment I was unaware of the fact. In the meantime, I was billeted with the local schoolmaster, a rather retiring and diminutive denizen of this frontier post on the edge of the forest, with a thinly grown moustache who, on seeing me, disappeared into his sanctuary like a fieldmouse sniffing the air and finding the scent inimical. It must have been difficult for him to adjust to the intruding presence of the British Army, when his life up to that moment had been spent teaching lederhosened lads and their pigtailed sisters about the authority of the State and other matters. Perhaps the authority of his spouse was less remote: she was explicitly welcoming and immediately adaptable. A well-upholstered, bosom-heaving, beaming Brünhilde, her hair in plaits, thirtyish and wearing near traditional dress, she showed me my room as if I were her personal guest. Soon the *Frau Schulmeister* indicated she was sadly frustrated and wished to tell me the details, despite the language barrier. She got, as it were, things off her chest; and I gathered she repeated her story with increasing ardour and appropriate mime to my successors who, dutifully in turn, expressed their acute understanding of her husband's unfortunate misunderstanding of the problem which apparently faced them both.

18 May: The precise reason for my being in Rosenbach under the shadow of the Karawanken Alps with a tank and my stalwart platoon under command became more evident when I received orders on the field telephone to hand over members of the former Croat Government, which had been installed by the Germans. They were to be accompanied by their families. The village was at the Austrian end of the Ljubljana (Loïbl) tunnel and a train had come into the station which nestled next to the mountain base like a toy in a model railway. Then, in the afternoon, a convoy of 3-ton trucks carrying at least 200 people arrived from, I was told, Vienna. They had fled there after the withdrawal of General von Loehr's Army Group E from Yugoslavia. They proffered me notes in English written by well-wishers in Vienna, or perhaps by themselves, pathetically explaining who they were – Professor this, Doctor that – and that they were not Nazis but simply patriots who were anti-communist. This was the crux of the matter and this was their last chance to escape. If they had piled out of the transport and taken to the hills behind us – the mountains leading to Yugoslavia were in front – I would not have given the order to kill them. Perhaps I would have gone through the motions of ordering shots to be fired over their heads. This is hypothetical. They made no effort to escape. They were herded into the waiting carriages, carrying suitcases and small children and helping the elderly. They began their long journey in an unlit train through the tunnel to Yugoslavia and their deaths.

Two weeks later, one man made his way over the mountains and, this time, returned as a refugee. He told the following tale: the anti-communist Croats had been lodged in an hotel. After lunch the next day, on orders received from Belgrade, they were put up against the garden wall and mowed down with machine guns. The refugee, who lost all his family – his wife, mother and three children – was in the lavatory at the time of the executions. In the pre-haste or post-haste of the killers searching the hotel, he had been overlooked. He had stayed where he was until dark and clambered back over the mountains, praying that the British would not send him back again. They did not. Nevertheless, 33,000 non-communist Yugoslavs were returned to their fate at Tito's hands; and some 3,000 Russian officers, plus their women and children, who were not Soviet citizens, as well as 940 Germans, were handed over to Stalin in the next three weeks. These figures do not include some 37,000 Cossacks who had fought with the Germans against Stalin, also with their women and children, nor 200,000 Croats, again with dependants, who were respectively transferred to Soviet Russia and refused surrender at Bleiburg on 15 May and subsequently massacred.

18 May: 'Tito becoming most aggressive. Extradition of Chetniks and Croats most nauseating: although war criminals deserve to be shot (as they certainly will be). Prime Minister of Croatia included in the bag.' It was the winner, of course, who judged who was a war criminal.

18 May: 1st Guards Brigade Sitrep for 18 May, written by Nigel Nicolson, stated that about 2,000 Croats were being evacuated the following day; among them would be many women and children. They were to be taken in TCVs to the Welsh Guards' area. They were said to be unaware of their destination. (Those dispatched yesterday were aware.)

19 May: 2,000 Croats were handed over by my platoon and myself to Tito. The strange British subaltern again appeared as he had done the previous day, this time accompanied by two British officers whom I sensed were on Corps or Divisional staff as they were not guardsmen. I was to learn many years later that the subaltern was Lieutenant Robert Finlay Lochhead of 6th Special Force, the SOE liaison officer between Tito and V Corps. He was accompanied by Major John Mennell of 6th Armoured Division and a Corps staff officer. 6th Special Force was under Major Charles Villiers, Grenadier Guards, the best man and closest friend of V Corps BGS, Toby Low, and a man, in the course of his allotted task, in very close touch with Tito.

19 May: Macmillan flew to England at Churchill's behest.

19 May: Colonel Robin Rose-Price wrote in the Battalion War Diary: 'Evacuation of Croats begins. Order of most sinister duplicity received i.e. to send Croats to their foes.' 1st Guards Brigade Sitrep read: 'The transfer was efficiently organized by both 3 WG and the Tito Major, the latter showing considerable tact in clearing away all Tito soldiers from the area with the exception of himself.' This was correct, if tact be the word. The Tito man I saw was a lieutenant-colonel, perhaps not the same man. Anyway, the Croats were handed over and my place was taken by another officer and another platoon, as a result of this V Corps order, after the transfer of the 12,000 Croats, the 17,000 Slovenes being held at Viktring and the 4,000 Serbian Chetniks who were to follow. This made a total of 33,000 men, women and children who were surrendered to Tito.

19 May: 'Receive and write letters. Have a drink with owner of house. F. M. Alexander appears to have taken Tito in hand.' This last phrase was an ill-informed entry, because what I did not know was that Tito had ordered his men out of Austria on 18 May and his representative had signed an agreement this day at Klagenfurt, the sequel to his earlier visit. It does, however, show that at my level we were reasonably aware of what was happening and, equally important, what was not happening or likely to happen on the ground. The agreement involved Tito's forces withdrawing south of the Yugoslav-Austrian border and Tito would receive 'all Yugoslav nationals now in the Corps area who had been fighting in uniform with the Germans, and their camp followers [specifically defined by Corps as "someone who is dependent upon the soldiery"].' Altogether the Welsh Guards handed over 5,000 of the 33,000 who were sent to their deaths via the sinister Rosenbach railway tunnel, and thousands more to the Russians.

20 May: 'Return to Coy. Bathe in Lake [Wörther See].' It was a fine day with little wind and I decided to go sailing. I had, however, been warned that the Wörther See had a dangerous reputation for sudden storms and this expedition ended by my pushing the boat to the shore while my companion held on to the rudder. We were luckily not very far out when the storm broke suddenly upon us.

Thus, despite the appalling events which were taking place, life in Austria for the Army was singularly pleasant. There were, for example, untold numbers of horses in the Corps area at that time. One day, James Gresham, the Second-in-Command, and I went to one of the Cossack camps and James selected a splendid looking animal which he considered would be a good steeplechaser without ever having seen it jump. (I was to learn later in Palestine that James knew a great deal about horses.) The horse was roving with scores of others in a large and verdant Austrian field, its coat beautifully groomed, its tail swishing away the spring flies, and its head alternately tossing up and down and then nibbling the grass. It was then carefully harnessed and placed with much care in a makeshift loosebox and taken to Battalion headquarters where there was no shortage of those who were capable of the highest standards of horsemanship.

In due course the animal won every race or steeplechase for which it was entered and when the time came for the Battalion to leave Austria on 30 June it was commandeered by the Army commander, Dick McCreery. This was, of course, a sad day for grooms and all who were directly concerned, not least the commanding officer who was no mean horseman himself and who supervised the handing over of the champion to the cavalry regiment detailed to transport the handsome bay to McCreery's headquarters near Udine.

On arrival, Sir Richard McCreery inspected the animal which had been brought before him and said something about appearances not being everything – indeed, appearances in a horse are pretty well everything – but his suspicions, at first only implied, were soon confirmed when the horse he had received not only failed to win any race or chase, but more or less stopped to nuzzle the spectators – for it was a very friendly horse which liked sugar – or nibble the grass when it was supposed to be taking the fences and galloping ahead of the field. In other words, the original had been nobbled and this animal switched in its place. There was a court of inquiry. Witnesses came from the Battalion with details of markings. The cavalry regiment responsible for its transportation was naturally questioned. No one ever discovered how and when the switch occurred, whither the horse was taken, or whether it ever ran a race again.

In our own company the horses were not champions — they would have been commandeered — but were adequate. We had a former German RSM at Potsdam as our head groom — until he had to leave for his term as a POW — and once when a bay mare I was riding bolted towards the stables he witnessed my being unseated. The animal was fifty yards from our lines and we were trotting down a slope which led to her stable when, with the bit between her teeth, she suddenly bolted. A holm oak loomed up with a low overhanging branch against which I hit my head. I promptly came off but kept hold of the reins, and remounted. Our Potsdam instructor remarked that my control over the animal could be questioned but not my courage. In fact, I had not the courage not to remount, given the standing of this witness and, of course, the honour of the British Army, let alone the Regiment. Nevertheless, I avoided the horse in future.

21 May: I was the duty officer in our peaceful company backwater, peaceful for us, that is, not for the deportees. Thousands of Yugoslavs had already been handed over and were to continue to be handed over until the operation was halted definitely by Alexander when he arrived on the scene on 4 June, twenty-seven days after V Corps headquarters were established at Klagenfurt. Meanwhile, the Cossack operation was about to begin with the specific intention of including non-Soviet citizens.

21 May: Brigadier Toby Low issued the V Corps 'Definition of Russian Nationals'. This was arbitrary selection by military formations and had nothing to do with screening. In fact, individual cases were not to be considered *ab initio*.

21 May: V Corps staff officer, Major-General de Fonblanque, discussed details of the transfer of the Cossacks with the Soviets.

21 May: McCreery received notice of Eisenhower's acceptance of the Cossacks. This would eliminate any problem he might have had in his mind about the matter, following V Corps communications. The Combined Chiefs of Staff were also informed. McCreery, however, had already proposed his own Allied policy. He asked AFHQ for 'proper principles' to be consolidated and what was the current 'approved policy' following orders and counterorders to which he himself contributed four days later on 25 May.

21 May: Eisenhower signalled to Alexander the details of the agreed Cossack and German POW evacuation.

22 May: General Keightley held a conference with his senior commanders about handing over the Cossacks in cattle trucks.

22 May: Macmillan returned to AFHQ after a brief visit to England.

The reader will note that every effort was being made to save the Cossacks by evacuating them to Eisenhower's command as part of the German Army, where the Geneva Convention prevailed, thus obviating any local agreement made by V Corps whom the Soviets would concede was subordinate to AFHQ, whether or not they were upset. Also, coincidental or not, after Macmillan's return the policy considered vital at the time, 'not upsetting the Russians', took precedence over any humanitarian intentions. Even so, Alexander tried to mitigate the blow by forbidding the use of force, a point which his Chief of Staff, General Morgan, reiterated and who even went into details about the evacuation, as if hinting that it was to be carried out. Who, among the Cossacks, would volunteer to be handed over to the communists? Alexander replied to McCreery's signal, with a copy to V Corps. McCreery disregarded it.

22 May: V Corps instructed divisional commanders to shoot Cossacks in order that the hand-over might be carried out.

22 May: 'Take five Poles to ex-PW's cage near Klagenfurt. Chetnik POW fails to turn up. Who blames him! Going home back to slavery.... still a few of Tito's boys left.'

23 May: Brigadier Low, V Corps BGS, left for England. He was soon elected to Parliament as a Conservative Member.

23 May: Alexander signalled McCreery that no Yugoslavs in the hands of Allied troops would be returned against their will and that all Yugoslavs would be evacuated and screened.

24 May: V Corps War Diary noted that the transfer of Croats to Tito was completed. The transfer of Serbs and Slovenes at Viktring camp had begun.

24 May: V Corps issued its order 'Return of Cossacks to Soviet Forces'.

24 May: 'Visit Jim Jerman in evening. See Colonel Jocelyn [Gurney] now wearing DSO at Tac HQ. He offers to post letter to Sorbellos.'

25 May: 'Exercise "Rattling". Rounding up of all suspects [including Tito stragglers]. Spend day in carrier.'

25 May: Colonel Gerrett, 15th Army Group Liaison Officer at V Corps, signalled that he had been assured that the 42,000 Cossacks to be handed over were all Soviet citizens. His orders were to oversee those who were not to SHAEF − or all of them.

25 May: Eighth Army, acting on the signal from General Morgan, AFHQ, ordered V Corps to return all Soviet citizens but deleted the provision of not using force.

While these human dramas were taking place around us, within the Welsh Guards' lines there were church parades, drill parades, cricket matches, sergeants' mess parties, Guardsmen's outings, officers' dinner parties, riding and the rounding up of Tito's stragglers prior to their expulsion from Austria, less their loot.

26 May: Tim Bolton, speaking for all Welsh Guardsmen, albeit without their knowledge, concerning the handing-over of non-communists, told the Commanding Officer, Robin Rose-Price: 'This is so totally distasteful that we are not going on doing it.' All ranks would have agreed with him.

27 May: By this date nearly 5,500 Serbs had been transferred to Tito.

27 May: The Welsh Guards held a thanksgiving service which I attended.

28 May: Under V Corps auspices, the Cossack officers were deceived by a fictitious invitation to attend a conference with Field-Marshal Alexander.

29 May: I was told that Cossack officers, many of whom were not Soviet citizens, were handed over to Stalin's representatives at Judenberg.

29 May: The transfer of Chetniks to Tito was completed. The Welsh Guards had a drill parade.

30 May: I heard that the Red Cross were protesting vigorously about the Yugoslav forced repatriations, threatening to withdraw unless these transfers were stopped. The Welsh Guards had a second drill parade — 'showing best battle dress'.

1 June: Brother officers told me that V Corps had abandoned all pretence of not using force and that there were scenes of panic, desperation and violence at Peggetz camp. Jim Jerman told me that after their officers had been handed over, the men were stoic and resigned to their fate. Indeed, I remember seeing them herded in large groups and being guarded with the minimum of force.

3 June: I heard from my cousin Mick Bankier, now ADC to Charles Keightley, V Corps Commander, that Alexander had given notice of his arrival in Austria.

4 June: I also heard that screening had been introduced, under orders from V Corps, for the first time.

4 June: Field-Marshal Alexander arrived in Austria and ordered that Yugoslav repatriation be halted forthwith.

4 June: '*Chat with Princess Liechtenstein aged 85* [born 1860].'

7 June: I heard a little later that on this day an enquiry had been instigated by Field-Marshal Alexander. It was conducted by a Liaison Officer from Eighth Army and was not very high-powered.

10 June: '*Bitten by dog while on motor-bicycle.*' This black brute, although possessing only one of the fifty heads of Cerberus, was twice the size and half as house-trained as Conan Doyle's Hound of the Baskervilles. Indeed, it had obviously been reared in a bear pit and schooled by the Gestapo. Its master was ruminating outside his farmhouse, set back some fifty yards from the road. The animal was crouching by the side of its keeper and was either not restrained or let loose; whereupon, it raced towards me, barking and snarling. I had either to shoot it or shoot past it. I chose to accelerate. It chose to bite my right leg, but its nasty yellow teeth luckily sank into my battle dress. I opened the throttle wide. It clung on, and neither teeth nor battle dress would give way — a tribute to the hardiness of both. Eventually it gave up, a very battered brute. It may, of course, have been simply and basically allergic to motor-bicycles, but I suspect it was its master who was allergic to the British Army.

12 June: 'Spend whole day forage hunting.' At Klagenfurt, where V Corps headquarters were situated, there was a German-administered centre for the storage and distribution of fodder. The old soldier at the centre behind the desk, a German Quartermaster, on hearing my request, demurred. In simple German I had deliberately doubled the number of horses and the number of days they needed to be fed. When he refused, I changed my line of approach, halved the amount and ordered him to authorize my Guardsmen to start loading immediately. I still have his chit. The horses were grateful. The Potsdam RSM was impressed.

13 June: V Corps Commander, General Keightley, received a courteous but cautionary message from General McCreery at Eighth Army, the gist of which was that what had been done was now in the past, but in future screening must be enforced and under the guidance of the Allied Military Government's Displaced Persons Branch. Given that he had received and passed on to AFHQ V Corps' 'Definition of Russian Nationals' on 21 May and also received their signal asking to use force on May 23 as well as visiting Austria the following day, it is inconceivable that he was unaware of Keightley's actions. It was as much a signal to himself as it was to Keightley.

13 June: 'Collect money from James Pugh.' This was a collection of notes varying from German occupation drachma to German occupation currency in every known Balkan and Italian denomination and, for all the bank teller or his management in the Banca di Venezia was to know — where I was to hand it in — it might have included a promissory note from Eskimo Nell or money from any Monopoly board. The facts were as follows: the Guardsmen had persuaded (or had been offered by) German prisoners of war that an exchange of these otherwise worthless notes for cigarettes (NAAFI and free) or other perquisites such as soap was an opportunity which would not come their way again. The end result was that those who obtained these pieces of paper received a registered share in no less than £3,000, as I later understood the figure to be.

The Allied Control Commission in Italy, mindful of the chaos caused by inflation in enemy-occupied territory after the First World War, had guaranteed good value against any currency handed in. Consequently, after a gap of three weeks or so, another officer, to whom my receipt had been given, collected the equivalent in Allied occupation lire. I was then to lose £20 on a bet with a Lance Sergeant who ran a book on the first post-war Derby with the backing of his newly acquired liquid assets.

14 June: 'Up 0545. Leave for Venice. Make Venice in quick time in big

[Mercedes] *car. Stay at Palazzo Mare.'* The car, I think, 'belonged' to Jim Jerman who had avoided it being commandeered by someone more senior and was later to hide it in the upper loft of a barn by driving it up a ramp, nearly emerging through the wooden side at the far end. I often wondered what the farmer did with that Mercedes, which could not, without a British registration number, be brought back home.

Besides Jim Jerman, there were also Jack Hoffman and my soldier servant 46 Jones in the car and I drove this vehicle down through the Alps to Venice without a hitch, having blind faith in its earlier German maintenance. It was a magnificent car with a canvas roof and I drove it along one of the earliest autostrada from Venice to Padua, with the canvas roof inadvertently undone and consequently streaming behind me to the total joy of the motor-car mad Italians.

I parked the car in something then practically unknown, a multi-storeyed car park, before taking the boat to our hotel on the Lido. I also handed in the pieces of paper which had been entrusted to me at the Banca di Venezia e America. As the bank no longer appears in the Bankers' Almanac I hope this was not the beginning of the doors being closed and its sinking into the lagoon.

The week at Venice was rather neglected in terms of touring the unique and inestimable sites of this city. Nevertheless, between pressing social engagements in which British nurses, a trip to Trieste, a Venetian called Graziella and a trip on a gondola are prominent in the record, such places as St Mark's, the Bell Tower and the Doge's Palace were both inspected and appreciated.

We had moved from the Lido to comfortable but small single rooms in the Luna Hotel, and Jim and I – we must have lost Jack Hoffmann and 46 Jones momentarily – had dinner with Graziella and her cousin, both girls expressing interest in the higher confines of the Luna, or concurring with our interest in their being interested, which we satisfied by ascending the staff staircase, there being a rule in British-run hotels about the place being restricted to military personnel; and by no stretch of the imagination could Graziella or her cousin be described as military. She could, therefore, not be introduced by the front door. The problem which faced me in the morning, after the curiosity of Graziella had been satisfied, was how to escort her downstairs when the staff staircase was being used by the staff bearing breakfast, some of whom might have recognized her.

A military hotel required a military decision. The best and only practical escape route was the front staircase. Just above the entrance hall, where the Hall Porter was prince of his domain, the stairs branched left and right in a grand sweep, the right being nearer the Hall Porter's desk. The next problem was that the Hall Porter was a distant cousin of Graziella and scandal at all costs must be avoided. A tip could not have closed his eyes or shut his mouth. How, therefore, to distract his attention as she slipped down the stairs and out of the front door? I returned to the room and collected the breakfast tray. Graziella followed me. We were in the shadow of the staircase. The Hall Porter was answering a telephone call but facing the hall. I said goodbye to her, then lobbed the breakfast tray to the right of the Porter's desk as she slipped down the stairs to the left and, like a young gazelle, reached the front door, while her startled cousin gazed with astonishment at the breakfast tray which had landed at his feet. Graziella paused for a second at the door, blew a kiss, waved and was gone. I was in the shadow, went upstairs and hoped no one would check where one breakfast tray was missing. No one did. I left the hotel at 1600 hours with my companions, dined in Udine and reached our base in Austria at 2300.

30 June: '1st Guards Brigade leave Austria.'

1 July: 'Off again via Conegliano, Padua.'

2 July: 'Arrive Fano.'

For all ranks the next twenty-seven days were spent bathing and sunbathing by the shore of the Adriatic. The Brigade's return was delayed because our ship, the *Georgic*, was given to the South Africans, who had done their best to burn down Naples — accidentally, of course. They were not the only ones to indulge their high spirits.

26 July: 'Party in evening at Pesaro. Meet some of the 52nd L.A.A. Owen and Hugh [Arbuthnot] *let down tents at funfair. OC funfair rings up Battalion afterwards: very rude and insulting remarks.'* (What could he have said, one wonders!)

27 July: 'Everybody very worried about the Labour Govt. Has the country gone mad? Does it not realize that the war is not over?' We were going home before being sent to Japan. As I was under twenty-one, I had no vote.

29 July: 'Leave Fano by train.'

30 July: 'Pass through Cassino. Arrive Naples in morning. Staying at transit camp. Visit Naples.'

2 August: 'Drive to Sorrento. Orange Grove [in Naples] *in the evening. Nearly have serious accident in jeep.'* In fact, I nearly turned it over while driving down the main corso of Naples after dinner. The traffic islands were unlit. Suddenly, one of them appeared a very short distance ahead — the headlights of jeeps were always limited in the distance they illuminated — and as I swerved, the jeep keeled over. It was touch and go whether it was going to overturn. Had it done so, the passengers, Paul Makins, Dick Kingzett and the Guardsman driver, might, with luck, have been thrown clear; but the driver was always stuck behind the wheel and usually killed. A courteous American Military Policeman arrived in his own jeep; 'I think, sir, that it would be better if the driver drove.' I did not dispute his wisdom.

August 4: '*Lunch with Paul* [Makins] *and Dick* [Kingzett]. *See "Tosca" at Opera House.* (But not, this time, in the Royal Box, like last year: offered me in absence of C.-in-C.)'

5 August: '*More officers arrive, mostly Camerons en route for the Far East.*'

6 August: '*Go to Naples and Sorrento. Three meals on the black market — about £6 in total per person — with Dick* [Kingzett], *Mark Gilbey and Willy Bell. Bathe. Meet a Wren called Lavinia Lascelles* [sister of someone with whom I was to serve at 1st Guards Brigade headquarters in Palestine: Johnnie Lascelles. We were close friends. He died in 1951 aged 28. Their father was the King's Secretary.]'

7 August: '*Duty officer. Receive letter from Kinka and 35 Lewis.*' These were to be the last letters I was to receive in Italy. Well over one hundred were sent to my mother and an equal number received. Equally, many others were written and many were the replies.

9 August: '*Leave Naples at 1800 hours. Ship crowded.*'

10 August: '*Japanese surrender offer announced. Ship full of Indian officials and wives. Sleeping on deck.*'

12 August: '*Japan surrenders. Thank God for that!*' Six days earlier the atomic bomb had been dropped on Hiroshima. On 8 August the Soviet Union had declared war on Japan and invaded Manchuria. On 9 August a second atomic bomb had been dropped by the Americans on Nagasaki.

18 August: '*Arrive Southampton.*'

19 August: '*Disembark. Arrive Caterham* [the Guards Depot].' Our disembarkation was welcomed by an excess of zeal by His Majesty's Customs officials which I thought then and think now was out of place.

20 August: '*Lunch at Guards Club* [in Upper Brook Street]. *Meet Mother. Col. Robin* [Rose-Price], *Elydir* [Williams], *James and June Cull at Club. Learn James, John Davies and self* [have been] *mentioned in despatches.*'

22 September: [after leave, I rejoined the 3rd Battalion] '*Arrive Selkirk*' in the Border Country.

25 September: The Colonel of the Grenadiers, HRH Princess Elizabeth, inspected her Regiment.

26 September: The Colonel of the Welsh Guards, Lord Gowrie VC, inspected the 3rd Battalion.

27 September: Appointed '*Intelligence Officer and Education Officer*' with '*separate office* [which had] *a fire and a wireless.*' The education duties were clear. I was less sure about my Intelligence duties. Who were the enemy — the Scots or the English?

1 October: The Major-General commanding the Brigade of Guards, 'Budget' Loyd, visited the Battalion. Owen Lloyd-George visited my room. He picked up my Luger pistol, correctly cleared the chamber, pointed the gun at the floor, squeezed the trigger, and the bullet which had lain dormant — entirely my fault — since more active days was propelled through the floorboards and embedded itself in the bedside table in Johnny Davies' room. Johnny, who had been lying on his bed at the time, reading no doubt some book with a peaceful and relaxing theme, enquired if there were any more to follow. This was the definitive last shot fired by the 3rd Battalion.

15 October: I left Selkirk for the Guards Depot where I stayed for three months before going to Palestine, via the gradually diminishing 3rd Battalion now stationed at Great Missenden, Buckinghamshire. There, in February, 1946, a farewell dinner was held with four friends, among whom was Owen who, while en route to the restaurant, lit the fuse of a thunderflash — more a grenade than a firework — in the back of the car. Party pranks can go awry. This was clearly an example: neither the rear door nor the window would open. The fuse time was about thirty seconds. My door opened. I snatched the nasty object, threw it outside and it exploded in mid-air. The door hit the bank of the narrow country lane. It was now hanging on its hinges which was better, however, than our being in a similar state. Like the thunderflash, the dinner went with a bang and we returned to base safely. The 3rd Battalion had always lived dangerously.

My stay in Great Britain had not lasted long, perhaps luckily. I had been away on active service, whither I was returning, for nearly a year and a half, which was not nearly as long as others. On the other hand, I had not only returned, but done so in one piece. Some, alas, had not. This was the sacrifice that they and the fallen had made for their country and their Regiment.

Epilogue

THE 3RD BATTALION WELSH GUARDS left for North Africa on 5 February, 1943, and returned to Great Britain on 18 August, 1945. It served just over two and a half years in Africa, Italy and Austria. One thousand men went out; there were one thousand casualties; and one thousand men came back. The list of fallen for the whole Regiment, three battalions, was 633 officers and men.

In terms of country over which the 3rd Battalion fought, the contrasts were extreme: the hills and wadis of North Africa; the extreme cold and rock-strewn exposure of Monte Ornito (Cerasola); the total desolation of Cassino; the hot, dusty battles of the Liri Valley, permeated with the stench of death; the long four days of battles before Arce — Monte Orio and Monte Piccolo; the pursuit beyond Rome: more casualties near the Tiber as the Germans turned to fight hard rearguard actions; the days spent just beyond Perugia in taking enemy-held positions at San Marco (Tulip); the patrolling and assaults before and after Arezzo; the approach to the Gothic Line and the bitter battle of Battaglia; winter lines held on mountain tops which, to reach, took eight hours in motor transport and then almost as many on foot to the front; the mule trains and the mud, the evacuation of casualties and the problems of supply; the final assaults and the advance across the Po Valley; the crossing of the Alps and, finally, the dreadful job of handing over the Cossacks and the Yugoslavs.

Yet, our thoughts as we left the valley of the Drau in Carinthia, with its lakes, forests, green fields and surrounding mountains, were that we were going home. Some of us also bore in mind, as we wound our way through the Alpine pass, which was not so easy for the carrier drivers, that this was the way the Gauls and Germans — Goths, Lombards, Franks, Ghibellines, Austrians and the Wehrmacht — had arrived, and that the last horde of these northern invaders had been driven out with great sacrifice by the Allied armies of which we had formed a part. No less than 200,000 men had died in the battle for Italy — 110,000 Germans and 90,000 Allies. In addition there were civilian casualties and the wounded of both sides.

Some of us knew, as well, that this was only a peaceful interval before being sent to the Far East to fight and defeat the Japanese who were already being rolled back in Burma and on the high seas. Some 500 enemy warships had been sunk; a million Japanese soldiers were isolated in their various combat zones and, for many months, B29 bombers had pounded the harbours and ports of the Japanese mainland. A B29 fire-bombing raid on Tokyo had, alone, killed 200,000 people. Allied battleships had moved in to shell the principal cities, but no one was under any illusion about the problems involved when the Japanese mainland was attacked.

Two major landings had been planned, unbeknown to us at the time, to take place in October, 1945, and February, 1946. There were nineteen fully armed Japanese divisions allotted for the fanatical defence of the fatherland, backed by 4,000 kamikaze pilots and an even greater number of aircraft. The headquarters for the defence of South Japan was situated in Hiroshima and, on the Allied side, planners had forecast a million casualties in the assault force of which half were likely to be fatal. Then came Little Boy, the atomic bomb that killed 200,000 at Hiroshima, followed by Fat Man which wiped out 140,000 at Nagasaki — the same figure as those killed in the 1923 Tokyo earthquake. The end came quickly, just over a month after we had left Austria. The combined Allied fleets alone had lost 400,000 men. Japan's war dead numbered 2.5 million, while their opponents suffered 10.5 million killed alone, including soldiers and civilians. The Great East Asia War which the Japanese had launched from Hiroshima had ended where it began. So, in the event, we did not go to Japan: the 1st Battalion Welsh Guards went to Palestine (where I joined them for a few months later on 1 March, 1946, and where Staff Captain, 1st Guards Brigade, escaped two assassination attempts by Jewish terrorists). The 2nd Battalion went to Germany and the 3rd Battalion was disbanded in Great Britain.

Meanwhile, in the Principality of Wales at Island Farm Camp, Bridgend, on the Glamorgan coast, a prisoner-of-war camp for high-ranking officers was established. Among the officers were Field-Marshals Brauchitsch, Manstein and Rundstedt and our distinguished opponent in Italy, Colonel-General Frido von Senger und Etterlin. In his book he wrote of the kindness of those for whom he was working as a gardener at Merthyrmaur House, Bridgend, until his release. General von Senger's old college, St. John's, Oxford, made arrangements for his son to visit him, but he was released before this could take place. However, both Captain B. H. Liddell Hart, the military historian, and Kurt Hahn, founder of Gordonstoun where the Prince of Wales was educated, visited General von Senger during his captivity.

The neighbouring estate to Merthyrmaur, Penllyn, was owned by the father of two Welsh Guards officers and remains in the family — John and

Frank Homfray, the first being killed serving with the 2nd Battalion in Normandy. Nevertheless, entirely without rancour, both Captain and Mrs Harber Homfray not only behaved with impeccable courtesy, but it was even thought that occasionally a mount was found for a general or two, in order that they might ride to hounds.

Those of us who had survived remembered those who had fallen throughout the world in this titanic struggle. We also remembered, in particular, those whom we had known and those with whom we had served, together with their families. More recently, we have thought of the losses and the gallantry in the Falklands. We are also mindful of a Welsh motto: *hwy clod na hoedl* – Fame lasts longer than life.

APPENDIX I

The Four Battles of Cassino

THE FIRST CASSINO BATTLE, with the intention of breaching the Gustav Line, began under the orders of General Alexander commanding 15th Army Group and General Mark Clark commanding Fifth Army with the French attack under General Alphonse Juin on 12 January, 1944, against the German positions in the mountains north-east of the town in the upper reaches of the Rapido. The objective was to take Atina and then move into the Liri Valley, thus outflanking Cassino, and turn the Line.

The immediate approach to the Gustav Line had been defended along the Reinhard Line, lying in front of Cassino, and at the cost of some 15,864 Allied casualties. German XIV Panzer Corps losses were equally heavy. On 15 January the US II Corps, under General Keyes, captured Monte Trocchio.

On 17 January General Richard McCreery's X Corps crossed the Garigliano at its mouth and established a bridgehead. Upstream, adjoining the flank of the American 36th Division, only one company got across. The high ground remained in German hands.

The banks of the Garigliano, which were mined and barbed-wired, are anything from five to ten feet high and the fifty-foot-wide river was in flood with an ice-cold current running at eight miles an hour. The approach was swamp. The field of fire of the German artillery was unimpeded and the whole sector was part of the Gustav Line defensive position where the formidable natural defences had been reinforced by concrete pillboxes built by the Todt Organization.

The American 36th Division attack on 20 January failed after three days with 1,681 casualties. General Clark then ordered the American 34th Division to attack north of Cassino and capture the monastery. The French were ordered to wheel south-west and capture Terelle, far closer to the monastery than Atina and not along the axis planned and desired by Juin.

General John Harding became Alexander's Chief of Staff at the time the Anzio landings took place; the immediate outcome did not affect the basic position at Cassino. Nevertheless, the salient established by X Corps was to prove of great value to Generals Alexander and Harding in planning the final assault. This bridgehead included Monte Ornito/Cerasola. Adjoining it was Monte Faito, the smaller neighbour of Monte Maio, 3,084 feet, the southern pillar of the great archway leading into the Liri Valley. From here Juin was able to launch his attack in May with four divisions of the French corps and capture Monte Maio, breaking through into the Liri Valley and achieving what he had always advocated − the outflanking of the Cassino massif. The Welsh Guards and Coldstream defence of this position contributed to this great victory.

On 24 January French casualties were 2,500 in this battle. They were ordered to make a new attack to the north of Cassino. A few hours later the American 34th Division launched an assault which nearly succeeded, despite the most appalling conditions; but instead of concentrating on Terelle, the French having already prepared the ground, the American II Corps Commander, General Keyes, veered south towards the Abbey and the most heavily and easily defended German positions. The US 34th Division lost 2,200 men. The monastery was a magnet.

Even so, in early February the monastery very nearly fell. An American platoon reached the walls of the building on 5 February and took seventeen prisoners. It needed, however, more than a platoon to capture the position. The attackers were exhausted and German reinforcements were arriving. Height 593, Mount Cavalry, the key to the monastery, exchanged hands more than once but finally remained in German hands after its recapture on 10 February. It was to be held by the Germans against attacks by Americans, British, Indians and Poles until they evacuated the position on 18 May.

On 12 February, in a driving snowstorm, General Freyberg assumed command of the Cassino front. His 2nd New Zealand Division had been brought over from the Adriatic and this, together with the 4th Indian Division, the British 78th Division and a combat group of 1st US Armoured Division, formed the 2nd New Zealand Corps.

His opposing generals were Colonel-General von Vietinghoff-Scheel, Commander-in-Chief German Tenth Army, and Lieutenant-General Frido von Senger und Etterlin who commanded the XIV Panzer Corps and whose front covered fifty miles from the mouth of the Garigliano to the Abruzzi mountains.

On 11 February General Freyberg was ordered to attack Monte Cassino, using 4th Indian Division. South of Cassino, the 2nd New Zealand Division was to cross the Rapido and establish a bridgehead. Snowdrifts caused the cancellation of these attacks, but at this moment the decision was taken to bomb the monastery. The monks and the refugees inside were warned to leave. The Indian troops nearest the monastery were not informed. The bombing had to take place a day earlier than was demanded − the attacking troops were not in position — as the planes were needed at Anzio and the meteorological forecasts indicated only a short spell of clear weather. Height 593, Mount Cavalry, the immediate objective, was not bombed. The Germans occupied the Abbey after the bombing. The main infantry attack which went in on 18 February, three days later, did not succeed.

The 2nd New Zealand Division attacked south of the town over flooded and mined land. The Maori Battalion of the New Zealand Division captured the railway station. The Germans brought up tanks and infantry and recaptured it. Three weeks of rain followed. General Baade's 90th Panzer Grenadiers were relieved by the 1st Parachute Division and on 26 February Lieutenant-General Richard Heidrich assumed command of the eight-mile Cassino sector.

15 March was the date of the third battle of Cassino and it was again, like the second, directed by General Freyberg. This time it was the town's turn to be obliterated. Nevertheless, only half the town was taken by the New Zealanders. This included the railway station and the castle. They lost one thousand men. Meanwhile, the Gurkhas captured but could not hold Point 435, Hangman's Hill, which was exposed, isolated and overlooked. They were pounded by incessant shelling and mortar fire. After five days of courageous resistance they were evacuated. The Indian division losses were 1,160.

The fourth battle of Cassino began on 11 May at 2300 with the great artillery barrage. It had four factors in its favour: the weather was no longer that of winter; the Monte Ornito/Cerasola feature provided the vital springboard for the French breakthrough; the lessons learnt in the first three encounters were firmly embedded; and, lastly, it gained surprise.

The German High Command were aware of the impending attack but were uncertain where its main thrust would fall. Field-Marshal Kesselring was unhappy about there being no intelligence concerning the whereabouts of Juin and his French Expeditionary Corps. He was even more unhappy when the intelligence reached him. Kesselring was also unaware of the transfer of Eighth Army and he later was to regard it as intolerable, vis-à-vis his Intelligence officers, that his information was so meagre. In the event, the French Corps on the Allied left wing broke through the German Tenth Army and laid open the advance to Rome.

Alexander had moved Juin to the mountain range earlier occupied by 1st Guards Brigade, including the 3rd Battalion Welsh Guards' positions on Cerasola and Purgatorio. The French were replaced in the mountains north of Cassino by the Polish II Corps. The American II Corps was near the coast.

On the right flank was the British X Corps, beyond the Poles. On the Polish left flank was the British XIII Corps with 4th British Division on the right, next to us in Cassino, and 8th Indian Division on their left, both divisions being poised to cross the Rapido. In reserve were British 6th Armoured Division and the British 78th Division.

The two British Corps, X and XIII, were under Eighth Army command with the Canadian I Corps (1st Infantry and 5th Armoured Division) plus the South African 6th Armoured Division as Army reserves. In all, twenty-one Allied divisions and eleven independent brigades faced fourteen German divisions and three brigades and the German forces were much understrength with little air support.

At daybreak on 11 May the German Tenth Army Headquarters in Avezzano near Frosinone and XIV Panzer Corps battle headquarters facing the French front were bombed and obliterated. General von Senger und Etterlin, XIV Panzer Corps Commander, was on leave. His return came too late to save the situation. The French took two days to capture and hold the objectives but the gallant Poles were in a reverse situation.

The Americans, meanwhile, had advanced, had been repulsed but advanced again and regained their objectives. British XIII Corps was not advancing with the speed intended: the plan of attack devised by General Kirkman was that his Corps cross the Rapido with 4th Infantry Division plus 1st Guards Brigade and 26th Armoured Brigade attached on the right flank with 8th Indian Division on the left reinforced by the Canadian 1st Armoured Brigade. They were to advance up the Liri Valley and link with the Poles in the area of Piedmonte.

Twenty-one artillery regiments put down a barrage on XIII Corps front, to the left of the town. This did not destroy the minefields, the wire or the heavily defended German infantry positions constructed by the Todt Organization, although to a large extent it neutralized the enemy artillery. A crossing was made by 4th Division but no bridges could be thrown across. One brigade was hurled back.

The 8th Indian Division had better luck. Two thirty-ton Bailey bridges were put up by the engineers across the river under intense enemy fire and by 0800 hours on the 12th forty tanks of the Canadian armoured brigade had crossed without the bridges collapsing or the loss of a tank − except one which had carried the second and fully constructed Bailey bridge on its hull, followed by a second tank which, by a connecting chain, kept it level. The first tank then drove slowly down the left bank towards midstream where it sank and its crew abandoned it. The second tank then pushed the Bailey across to the opposite right bank where it was embedded and made firm.

Forty tanks was a formidable firepower to have reached the enemy side of the river. On the 13th, the Royal Engineers in 4th Division had also thrown across a bridge during the night and shortly afterwards Sant Angelo, the bitter scene of an earlier American attack, was captured, four months after the initial attempt in January.

General Kirkman now poured his reserves across the river, including 78th Division under General Keightley, and the staff organization required to do so must not be underestimated. Meanwhile, the German Tenth Army under von Vietinghoff was also committing its reserves, but the battle was going against the Germans. Their artillery tried to take out the bridges and such Luftwaffe formations as were available tried likewise; both were neutralized by incessant air attacks and counter artillery barrages.

The 78th Division leapfrogged 4th Division on 15 May and the Indian 8th Infantry Division under General Russell also advanced. The British 4th Division was still meeting stiff resistance. Alexander, however, reinforced success by ordering General Burns' Canadian I Corps on 16 May through the 8th Indian Division lines to capture Pontecorvo in the light of Juin's rapid advance further west. Pontecorvo fell on 18 May and the von Senger Line was broken.

The Poles, meanwhile, took a terrible hammering; but if they received appalling punishment, they handed it out, too. There was also a feint attack by X Corps against Atina. The whole onslaught against this part of the German front was intended to draw off reserves.

There was to be no direct attack against the monastery but it was to be isolated by capturing the high ground to the north-west and then assaulted from there, while a simultaneous descent was to be made into the Liri Valley to join XIII Corps. In consequence, General Anders ordered the 3rd Carpathian Division to attack and hold Height 593, Mount Cavalry, which was, as always, the key to the monastery. They were also to take the Massa Albaneta beyond it. Anders' 5th Division was to capture Colle San Angelo, Height 575, to the right of Albaneta.

After desperate fighting, 5th Division was withdrawn from Albaneta. The 2nd Battalion of the 15th Carpathian Rifle Brigade had, with incredible bravery, captured Mount Cavalry and withstood no less than four German counterattacks with their numbers reduced to one officer and seven men. Then, at dusk on the 12th, reinforced by devastating artillery fire directed by Colonel Heilmann, whose headquarters had been nearly removed from the map by fighter bombers at daybreak, the fifth and final German counterattack succeeded and the position was held for six days by the Germans, wearing gas masks against the all-pervading smoke and stench of the dead in the heat of May, until they were ordered to leave by a direct command from, it is said, Field-Marshal Kesselring.

On 17 May, in the Liri Valley, 78th Division, supported by 6th Armoured Division, wheeled right towards the Cassino massif to link with the Poles. In thirty-six hours they had taken 400 prisoners, inflicted 400 casualties and destroyed some forty tanks as well as many self-propelled guns. On 18 May they made the link with the Poles. The Cassino bastion was at last outflanked. The route to Rome was open.

APPENDIX II

The Assault on the Gothic Line

It IS ACADEMIC TO ARGUE whether or not the decision taken by Alexander under the wing of a Dakota on 4 August, 1944, in the heat of summer near Orvieto in the presence of Generals Harding (his Chief of Staff) and Oliver Leese, Eighth Army Commander, was right or wrong: i.e. to switch the main thrust of attack from Fifth Army's front in the Apennines to that of Eighth Army on the Adriatic. The result either way was likely to have been the same when the difficulties facing Fifth Army are examined. The facts which faced him were that 96,000 men had been withdrawn to support the invasion of southern France (Anvil) which was a drop from 249,000. Air strength fell by two-thirds but it did not prevent the nineteen Po bridges between Piacenza and the Adriatic from being knocked out in July – a little too far ahead of time as it turned out – which it was hoped would block a German retreat and hinder reinforcements, the intention being to defeat Kesselring south of the Po before the winter.

The next objective was to cut off the oil, bauxite and copper of the Balkans from the German war machine, then advance via the Alps or through Yugoslavia into the Danube basin, thus saving part of central Europe from Russian occupation. Speed was paramount and the change of plan sacrificed speed.

Alexander wished initially to go for the jugular, the direct route to Bologna, and cut the Via Emilia, using both Fifth and Eighth Armies in the centre. A deception plan was inaugurated to make Kesselring think that there was to be an attack on the Adriatic. In fact he always thought that there would be an amphibious attack in the area of Venice and even a link-up from the west following the invasion of southern France on 15 August. Indeed, one of the better-kept secrets of the war was that there were not enough landing craft in Italy to launch such an attack.

In terms of the jugular option, Alexander was aware of both the strength and weakness of the Gothic Line (sometimes called the Green Line by the Germans). More than 15,000 Italian labourers and 2,000 Slovaks had been engaged under the supervision of the Todt Organization. Four Panther gun turrets had been sunk into steel and concrete bases, camouflaged and with excellent fields of fire, with further work on eighteen more. Around one hundred steel shelters had been constructed within the rocks and escarpments as cover for anything from six to fifty men. Embrasures had been created with enfilading fields of fire; 2,376 machine-gun posts had been set up; there were 47 anti-tank, mortar and assault gun positions; 75 miles of wire and 10 miles of anti-tank obstacles along the Futa Pass front (Route 65) had been built; and deep minefields had been laid throughout; further back was the artillery which the German commander of the Bologna front during the winter, von Senger und Etterlin, would concentrate with considerable effect, bringing the Allied slog through the mountains to a definitive halt.

The weakness − at any rate in the central mountainous part of the front − was that of any fixed line: once pierced, the whole line had to fall back and if it were forced to fall back far enough and fast enough, then the Allied Armies could debouch into the valley and destroy the enemy south of the Po. This was done, but in April, 1945, when Allied armour could be deployed to maximum advantage, Allied airforces had unimpeded vision and motorized infantry were able to manoeuvre as the rapidly changing situation demanded.

Speed and punch were therefore Alexander's intentions when he planned to launch both his Armies in early August at the central part of Kesselring's line. It was, however, the contention of General Oliver Leese that, having lost his best mountain troops, the French Expeditionary Force, it would be better to make full use of the combination which had provided Eighth Army with its past successes, namely its tanks and guns, which, certainly in terms of tanks, could not be used in the mountains. On the Adriatic coast, however, the mountains became ridges and beyond was the Po Valley.

In the event, Leese made his point, and the bulk of Eighth Army was transferred to the Adriatic less XIII British Corps, helped by a remarkable one-way, 120-mile tank route built by the Royal Engineers. The bluff of attacking on the Adriatic had to be made into a double bluff which, initially, was more or less successful, but not for long. The great attack was launched on 26 August with three corps − the Polish, Canadian and British V Corps, together with the New Zealanders − on a thirty-mile front, comprising ten divisions, 1,200 tanks and 1,000 guns.

On 30 August the Gothic Line was pierced. Seven days later, with the advance going well, the rain began to fall. Dust would soon be turned into mud, streams would become torrents, visibility would become restricted, thus handicapping the air forces and artillery, while the German defence was fighting furiously. Nevertheless, the advance continued and Rimini was the next objective. The enemy line, however, could not be broken until his defences on the Coriano Ridge inland, the 'little Cassino' of Gemmano, had been taken. These features were captured after heavy losses and heroic action on both sides on 14 September, and Rimini fell to the Canadians on 21 September. The German 1st Parachute Division under General Heidrich and Major-General Fritz Polack's 29th Panzer Grenadier Division, together with other enemy forces, withdrew to yet another line, leaving more rivers to cross and more ridges to climb and capture. The Eighth Army had advanced thirty miles in twenty-six days. It had suffered 14,000 casualties and lost 200 tanks. German losses were considered to be heavier, with 8,000 prisoners of war alone taken by Eighth Army.

On 10 September General Mark Clark launched his Fifth Army offensive. The objective was to break through these defences and cut the principal line of communication open to Kesselring, Route 9 or the Via Emilia, along which lay, in a diagonal direction from the south-east to north-west, the towns of Rimini, Forli, Faenza, Castel Bolognese, Imola and Bologna. All these towns were linked by mountain roads to positions held by both the Germans and the Allies. They ran through the Futa Pass in the west, then further east the Il Giogo Pass which led to Firenzuola and thence either to Bologna or Imola. Then also, there were roads to Forli and Faenza. Once Route 9 had been cut, Kesselring would not be able to move reinforcements from one front to another, and, in addition, his Tenth Army, facing Eighth Army, would be in dire difficulties.

There was no doubt that the Futa Pass, twenty-five miles north of Florence, was the most heavily defended position and for that reason Mark Clark chose to outflank it and advance on all fronts. His principal assault, however, was against the Il Giogo Pass, seven miles east of the Futa and at the extreme end of its fortified defences.

Clark had three Army corps, but these included three divisions of armour which could only play, as far as their armoured units were concerned, a limited role in mountain warfare. On the east of his line was XIII Corps under Lieutenant-General Sidney Kirkman, comprising 1st British Infantry Division (Major-General Loewen), 6th Armoured Division (Major-General Murray), including 1st Guards Brigade, 8th Indian Infantry Division (Major-General Russell) and 1st Canadian Armoured Brigade. The objectives of XIII Corps were Dicomana, Casaromana, Vicchio, the heights beyond, Borgo San Lorenzo, seventeen miles north-east of Florence, then to pierce the Gothic Line and thence cut Route 9 at Faenza and Castel Bolognese.

Further west was US II Corps (General Keyes) comprising four US infantry divisions. The objective of II Corps was the vital Il Giogo Pass, flanked by Monte Altuzzo and Monte Monticelli: then the Corps would push on to Firenzuola, branching to Bologna and Imola. Further to the west of the Futa Pass, one infantry division was to attack Monte La Dogana. The Corps were supported by three tank battalions.

On the left flank with US IV Corps (General Cuttenberger) were US 1st Armoured Division, 6th South African Armoured Division (General Poole) and a brigade group (regimental combat team) of the 92nd US Negro Infantry Division. Facing, on the enemy side, were the 16th SS Panzer Grenadier Division and the 65th Infantry Division in a weak part of the line but, nevertheless, easily defended in difficult and mountainous country.

The objectives of IV Corps were to push on up the coast and on the flank of II Corps whenever the opportunity presented itself against a comparatively weak front and also to keep an eye on the Brazilian Expeditionary Force commanded by General Mascarenas de Morais.

The Fourteenth German Army under General Joachim Lemelsen had five divisions facing Fifth Army and there were also two divisions on the east flank under Tenth Army (Colonel General von Vietinghoff-Scheel). The divisions in Fourteenth Army each had a front averaging ten miles and the 356th Infantry Division (as well as 29th Panzer Grenadier Division and the armoured reserve 26th Panzer Division) had been thrown into the battle on the Eighth Army front at the Coriano Ridge. The 4th Parachute Division on the east flank of Fourteenth Army and the 715th Infantry on the adjoining west flank of Tenth Army were ordered to thin out and fill the gap left by the 356th Division's departure for the Adriatic. However, Kesselring reinforced the Futa Pass by transferring 334th Infantry Division from Tenth Army reserve and which replaced 29th Panzer now on the Adriatic.

It fell to 4th Parachute Division to defend the Il Giogo Pass against an estimated Allied superiority of three to one. Four infantry divisions were concentrated within a front of two to three miles but the nature of the ground – gullies, defiles, peaks and ridges – meant that the success or failure of such an attack depended on the staying power and bravery of no more than a thousand men.

The battle of Il Giogo involved more than 500 medium bomber sorties and 1,300 by fighter-bombers. The artillery pumped thousands of shells into the enemy lines and as the infantry advanced the twin peaks of Monticelli and Altuzzo loomed up before them, each with altitudes of 3,000 feet. The approach was covered with enemy Spandau and mortar fire, supported by artillery. The ground was full of deep, dark gullies, rock-strewn and running down from knife-edged ridges. Over these features the assaulting American troops had to scramble and climb while they faced a murderous defence put down from fixed positions considered to be impregnable behind barbed wire and anti-personnel mines.

An initial assault had been made on 12 September by 91st Infantry Division, but after a night of attack and counterattack it was repulsed. At dawn, five days later, Altuzzo fell, as did 2,500 Americans of whom 500 were killed. German losses were equally heavy, including 200 prisoners.

In the meantime, General Mark Clark was quick to exploit the advance of British 1st Infantry Division along Arrow Route, the road which wound its way from Borgo San Lorenzo to Marradi, thence to Palazzuolo and down to Castel Bolognese on Route 9 between Imola and Faenza. The main fortifications of the Gothic Line on this front lay between Borgo San Lorenzo and Marradi. The first objective was Monte La Faggeta at 3,500 feet flanked by Poggio Prefetto and Poggio delle Travi. In the early hours of 15 September Prefetto fell. On the 17th the 337th Regimental Combat Team was pushed through to take Monte Pratone, two miles further north, one of the key positions in the Gothic Line.

At the same time, the 339th US Infantry took Monte Verruca. Monte Monticelli was to fall to the 91st Division and along the whole German front east of the Futa Pass the enemy was falling back and the great pass with its dug-in defences of minefields, barbed wire, tank turrets and machine-gun nests was outflanked and fell on 22 September.

The success in the centre of the line inevitably helped the flanks of Fifth Army: IV Corps on the left took Viareggio on 15 September and advanced to Forte dei Marmi, but the US 1st Division suffered losses of 500 men pushing up the Sechio Valley from Lucca. Indeed, the losses, overall, had been heavy and Mark Clark signalled on 6 October: 'Infantry replacement ... critical ... only sufficient to maintain divisions at authorized strength through 9 or 10 October. Losses in my four infantry divisions II Corps have averaged 550 per day per division over and above returns to units. Heavy fighting continues with enemy apparently rushing all available forces to halt our advance on Bologna. All divisions have been in heavy fighting twenty-three to twenty-six days under adverse weather conditions. Continuous supply of infantry replacements is imperative'. (*Calculated Risk*, Mark Clark).

This signal was sent the day after II Corps launched its attack against Bologna, along a seven-mile front on both sides of Route 65. On their right was the British 78th Division, fresh and newly joined within XIII Corps, and 1st Guards Brigade. On the German side, General Lemelsen was moving reinforcements from the western sector: the 16th SS Panzer Grenadier Division was facing the US 34th and the 65th Infantry Division was opposing the US 91st on Route 65 itself. Nevertheless, the 91st pushed on to Loiano in pouring rain and mist.

Loiano was only about ten miles from Bologna but gains on the flanks were not so spectacular and the advancing Americans came up against a formidable line of defence which the enemy called the Caesar Line, the main bastion of which was the precipitous Livergnano escarpment astride Route

65 and rising in parts to 1,500 feet. Initial, incredibly courageous assaults failed, but the weather cleared on 10 October and for three days the enemy suffered an intense bombardment from both artillery and air strikes. On 14 October the 91st Division occupied Livergnano. Casualties were heavy in US II Corps: 2,491 dead, wounded and missing in the attacks from 10 to 15 October. This made a total of 5,700 since 1 October. The power to repeat such assaults against the German positions was diminishing by the day. Also, on 15 October General von Senger und Etterlin took over temporary command of Fourteenth Army for five days and in that time assembled a formidable array of artillery in the Bologna sector which coincided not only with a dearth of reinforcements for Alexander's Armies but also of artillery shells. Eighth Army advanced to the shores of Lake Comacchio, while Fifth Army made some advances but not a break-through to the objective of Route 9. This goal had to wait until the spring and it was attained further to the north-west than had at first been considered practical.

Meanwhile, on the right of US II Corps the British 78th Division and 1st Guards Brigade continued pressure on the Imola axis, namely by holding Battaglia against two more coordinated German counterattacks, while the British 78th Division (Major-General R.K. Arbuthnott) which was on our left had been brought in between ourselves and US 88th Division. All three commands were using the same approach road which was barely wide enough for two vehicles to pass for it must never be forgotten that motor transport in 1944 was barely forty years old and the fact that there were roads at all through the Apennines, worthy of the name, was a tribute to the undoubted skill of Italian engineers and a certain political drive, if credit may be given where it is due. On this road I remember the experience of seeing the oncoming vehicles of the US Army, four-wheel-drive 3-tonners or whatever, driven at breakneck speed by negro drivers whose road discipline was diametrically opposite to our own; whereas we drove without lights at convoy speed with a red convoy light placed in the rear of each vehicle and well spaced out, our allies drove nose to tail with full headlights on. Their approach, signalled well in advance by their lighted path, was seen with resignation. None of them hit us, but quite a few of these drivers went over the edge.

In the meantime, surviving the dangers of the approach route, 78th Division attacked Monte Pieve on 13 October and after several days of heavy fighting captured it and then assaulted Monte Verro, Monte dell Acqua Salata and Monte Spoduro which fell on 23 October, while the American 88th Division took Monte Grande on 20 October only four and a half miles from Route 9; but the country between the two points was appallingly difficult to cross and Kesselring threw in reserves to block any further advance; for, as his lines of communication shortened, he was able to move units from one front to another with greater facility for the next six months, until he had no reserves or Armies to move.

Further west, Mark Clark could see Bologna from the American forward positions but in conditions where it took a thousand mules to lift supplies for a Brigade group — and the limits of a mule's endurance was eight miles there and back — where the mud even got the better of the superlative American motorized machinery, where even oxen were used as an alternative and where it sometimes took twelve hours to get one gun into position. The Fifth Army attack gradually faded into a holding operation. On 28 October General Keyes ordered US II Corps to dig in and stay where they were. Since 10 September his Corps had lost 15,716 men in killed and wounded. It was time for a pause, even though they were literally within sight of their objective.

The Germans, meanwhile, were under no illusions about the situation on the Adriatic front: 'It could be assumed,' wrote General von Senger und Etterlin, 'that the enemy would maintain the direction of his attack against the left [Adriatic] wing of the Fourteenth [German] Army. Movements across mountains were difficult and too time-consuming, because of the fresh deployment of artillery that they demanded; and so we were the sorrowful witnesses of the enemy's almost daily successes against our neighbours, 1st Parachute Corps. The incessant prodding against our front was like jabbing a thick cloth with a sharp spear. The cloth would give way like elastic, but under excessive strain, it would be penetrated by the spear.'

After the fall of Rimini on 21 September, the 2nd New Zealand Division passed through the 1st Canadian Division on 22 September and crossed the Marecchia River. The incessant prodding to which General von Senger referred was typified by the twenty-seven attacks which the New Zealanders made in battalion strength in thirty-six hours against General Heidrich's formidable 1st Parachute Division.

Further to the west was the 20th Luftwaffe Field Division and then the weakened 278th Division, backed, however, by the Austrian 100th Mountain Regiment, the gallant defenders of Gemmano; and even further west was the 114th Jaeger Division. In reserve, to cover Route 9, was the formidable General Baade and his equally formidable 90th Panzer Grenadier Division. In terms of being Alexander's *corps de chasse*, however, the New Zealand Division were compelled to use more the methods of a battering ram than the exhilarating chase of a cavalry pursuit.

Meanwhile, as the enemy stood and fought in front, the River Marecchia rose and flowed rapidly in the rear: a gentle summer stream became a twelve-foot torrent which presented bridging problems for the Royal Engineers and its muddy brown colour symbolized the problems relating to conditions which were becoming both difficult and different from those of even a day or two earlier. General Winter had seized the initiative: the rain poured down from 29 September until 2 October and provided no lucky dip for Eighth Army.

The German Tenth Army withdrew in good order and held its line on the River Uso, while Kesselring transferred units to meet threats on the Fifth Army front at Bologna and Battaglia. At this point Oliver Leese took up his command of Allied Land Forces in South-East Asia and was succeeded by General Sir Richard McCreery. The casualty list for Eighth Army was now 14,000. Eighth Army captured Ravenna on 5 December, despite ammunition shortage. Earlier (on the same day as he ordered the Partisans to reduce their activities during the winter) Alexander signalled Maitland-Wilson that Eighth Army had only enough shells for a fifteen-day attack in December, while Fifth Army had a reserve for ten. Nevertheless, Eighth Army made the slog to Lake Comacchio while the Germans entrenched themselves in a diagonal line running north-east and south-west on the banks of the Senio. The scene was now set for the great attacks of the spring, the fall of Bologna on 21 April and the surrender of the German Armies in Italy.

APPENDIX III

Repatriation Agreements

THE FUNDAMENTAL QUESTION which logically presents itself concerning events in Austria in 1945 is — why?

There are four potential premises. 1. It was a military necessity: 'clear the decks'. 2. It was not a military necessity. 3. It was a political priority. 4. It was not a political priority.

First, let us examine the facts about which everyone agrees.

The Yalta Repatriation Agreements of 11 February, 1945, signed (a) between the Soviet Government and the British Commonwealth, Great Britain acting as signatory for the latter, and (b) between the Soviets and the United States of America, covered the return of all citizens belonging to the signatory States to their respective countries at the end of hostilities. The United States said its interpretation of the agreement was that a Soviet citizen fighting in German uniform and/or in a unit of the German Army was to be regarded as German, in accordance with the 1929 Geneva Convention. The British did not interpret their agreement as such: a Soviet citizen in all circumstances remained a Soviet citizen. The British and the Americans made clear, nevertheless, that the populations of lands incorporated into the Soviet Union after 1939, such as parts of Poland and the Baltic States, were not Soviet citizens. British law did not run contrary to international law by declaring invalid foreign passports or Nansen League of Nations papers borne by those of Russian origin who had left their homeland after the revolution or had been born outside its boundaries, but these categories, despite their legal status, were not specifically mentioned in Foreign Office signals nor in any military communications. The presence of 'White Russians' was never raised except in an initial signal from Macmillan to the Foreign office who referred to 'men of Russian nationality who are not Soviet citizens'.

It was not possible under the Yalta agreements to restrict the number of Soviet nationals to be returned to an equivalent number of American and British Commonwealth citizens liberated from German captivity by the advancing Soviet Armies. The first figure was in millions. The second was in thousands. The object was to obtain the release of American and British Commonwealth prisoners of war and also to get rid of more than two million Soviet citizens.

Cabinet decisions, Foreign Office policy and signals made clear that the Government did not wish to retain any of the Soviet citizens and ordered their return by force. In expressing these sentiments the Foreign Office was consistent throughout, even after the return of the Cossacks had taken place.

Clear instructions were passed by the Foreign Office to both the Resident Minister, Harold Macmillan, and Field Marshal Alexander: Russians to be screened; all Yugoslavs to be evacuated. The latter signal was dated 29 April and passed on 2 May. No particular emphasis was placed in the military communications on screening nor on the presence of those of 'Russian origin who are not Soviet citizens'. Stress, however, was given to those of undoubted Soviet citizenship' being returned to the Soviet Union 'irrespective of their own wishes'. Thus, whether screening was mentioned or not, as no telepathic scanning machine existed or exists, it was paramountly clear that screening of each individual was a basic and just necessity, however long it took.

In practice, both Cossacks and Yugoslavs were dispatched, respectively, as military formations and as national groups in accordance with V Corps instructions during May and June 1945.

Military and political factors were complicated by Tito's intention to seize Carinthia, Venezia Giulia and Trieste. Whether his weakness or strength had been truly appreciated, estimated or overestimated, the fact remains that Higher Command and Governments took his threats seriously enough until 18/19 May when he ordered his troops out of Austria. Furthermore, the marauding incursions by partisan bands in Carinthia were in no way helpful to maintaining good order in V Corps area, particularly when preparations were being made simultaneously to clear them out by force and hand over their opposing compatriots by deception. To use Alexander's phrase: the decks were going to be cleared.

The date of 18 May was two days after Stalin had received the joint Anglo-American Note which reiterated previous agreements concerning boundaries and the determination of both Truman and Churchill to see it adhered to. It was also the date — 16 May — when Tito received Stalin's implicit withdrawal of any political backing he may have been offering up to that moment. Soviet military backing was never discounted, but there was no evidence of its ever materializing.

Three days before, on 13 May, Harold Macmillan flew to V Corps headquarters in Austria with his assistant Philip Broad and some members of Eighth Army staff. He gave his advice: hand over the Cossacks to the Soviet forces. He returned to Caserta and is cited by General Robertson as advising the return of the Croats. If this point were to be disputed, it would be a fine one as far as the Croats were concerned; they were returned after Robertson's signal of 14 May which ordered their expulsion and that of the Cossacks.

A further complication had been 15th Army Group's signal on 7 May, a week earlier, which ordered 'German forces in contact with Russians must surrender to Red Army. Those facing Tito must surrender to Tito.' The Croats wore the uniform of the independent State of Croatia. Like Slovenia, however, they were not recognized by the Allies. Neither they nor the Slovenians were Yugoslavs 'serving in the German armed forces'. Nor had they fought against the British Army. In terms of Churchill's orders of 29 April the Croats were Yugoslavs to be evacuated to Italy, pending further orders. According to 15th Army Group orders they were to be surrendered to Tito, but their surrender had been implicitly accepted by the British Army in their being offered asylum. Under the Geneva Convention, they were our prisoners. According to common sense and humanity, they and their 'camp followers' were likely to be annihilated if they were handed over to Tito. In terms of 'clearing the decks' they could be evacuated to Italy – or handed over. They were handed over.

The L of C (Lines of Communication) argument waxed and waned according to whim, as is shown by the signals. One side maintained that the roads and rail Italy/Austria could not support an exodus of Yugoslavs without clogging up the supply routes. Others differed. Food supplies were also a matter of discussion but thanks to Austrian agriculture, army supplies and organization, the Red Cross and Allied Military Government, no one starved.

On 19 May the L of C route for the evacuation of 109,000 Germans and 46,000 Cossacks to SHAEF was organized by General Morgan in conjunction with Twelfth and Fifteenth Army Groups. On the same date Macmillan flew to England and returned on the 22nd. Arrangements for the evacuation of the Cossacks remained in force. Except that now they were *all* classified as *Soviet citizens* by V Corps, which was heavily involved in organizing their expulsion to Soviet forces by designation as military formations – with the full knowledge of Eighth Army. Earlier Soviet sources had specifically asked for named Cossack leaders, by means of a typewritten list. Their likely fate, in consequence, was fully taken into account by Macmillan, according to his diary entry which also records a reference to the return of British prisoners of war. Stalin had cabled Churchill on 23 March, 1945, stating that all liberated British prisoners of war had been sent to Odessa for return to Great Britain and that none remained on Soviet soil.

Throughout this saga, AFHQ issued contradictory signals on several occasions, responding to pressure from Eighth Army on behalf of V Corps. The most significant was that of 14 May, Robertson's signal 'Cossacks to the

Soviets. Uniformed Croats to Tito'. The influx of 500,000 Germans and Croats culminating in the 15 May refusal to accept any of them was the high point of pressure and was fully backed by Alexander. On the 17th Robertson's signal was reversed; and then, after vacillating, AFHQ responded to pressure from Eighth Army and agreed that the Cossacks should be handed over on the *presumption* that they were Soviet citizens, but stipulated that force was not to be used. Then V Corps used persuasive practical arguments to obtain permission to use force, which had always been implied by Foreign Office signals. AFHQ signals, however, ordered NO force to be used.

Meanwhile the Yugoslavs were being handed over by the tens of thousands, during which time ad hoc definitions of who was or was not a citizen of Allied countries were posited in turn by V Corps and Eighth Army. 940 Germans were classified as Cossacks – and were handed over. Earlier, Alexander had tried to evacuate the Cossacks to SHAEF, but allowed his intentions to be subverted by other arguments. This initiative made military sense in terms of 'clearing the decks'. This being the case, it can only be concluded that he bowed to pressure, both military and political. It is, however, indisputable that in all post mortems Alexander supported his staff and his line of operational necessity at the time, adding that he could not deal with the Yugoslavs as he would have liked. It is likely that this thought of his could also be applied to the Cossacks. Macmillan, on the other hand, according to his biographer, expressed no regret for the advice he had given.

That said, before endeavouring to answer questions arising from the four premises concerning military necessity or not, political priority or not, in the broad concept of why the events took place, it is singularly relevant to remember that in the higher echelons of military and political command, neither the Cossacks nor the Yugoslavs had many friends at court, although those they had in their hour of need – Churchill, Eisenhower and Alexander – were highly placed. It is paramountly evident that their good intentions were thwarted. The phrase 'they fought for the Germans' was not the best character reference in the eyes of the British Government or the Higher Command and was no passport or visa to paradise for erstwhile Royalist allies.

On the higher levels of military command, however, hard-nosed decisions had to be taken, and from 8 May until 19 May there was always the possibility of a miscalculated Yugoslav attack. The fact that Tito was bluffing was the correct, if armchair, assessment of the British and American ambassadors in Belgrade. Field-Marshal Alexander was forced to call his bluff but in order to do so he required military force and military organization. Initially, for political reasons, he was uncertain which troops were available to him particularly American and those from New Zealand.

Then he was informed that all the troops under his command were at his disposal and this included land, sea and air forces. At the same time, any political or military backing for Tito's adventurism from Stalin disappeared when he received the joint Anglo-American note on 16 May. On 18 May Tito ordered his forces out of Austria, and as Macmillan had cabled Churchill five days earlier after his return from Austria on the 13th; 'President Truman's telegram to you radically changes position.'

However, before Macmillan arrived in Austria, the Russians had demanded the return of certain named Cossacks. Macmillan then advised that *all of them* – some 40,000 – be handed over during his visit to Klagenfurt; then on his return to Caserta Robertson followed this advice, as well as that concerning the Croats, and sent off his signal of 14 May. At this point, the first two premises – a military necessity or not – cease to be relevant: there was a military necessity, or presumed to be one, until 19 May. After that date it ceased to exist (a fact noted, with an incorrect date, by the State Department, which cited 23 May as the watershed.)

So why were the Yugoslav handovers launched, instead of the expellees being sent to Italy as ordered by the British Government? The answer is that what began as an expediency to mollify Tito and thus delay any aggression – if you cause trouble, you do not receive your enemies – and, at the same time, reduce congestion in the Corps area, was never cancelled because Eighth Army/V Corps did not wish that the agreement be abrogated or confused when everything was going so well. Handing over 33,000 people to Tito was no more a logistical challenge than transporting them to DISTONE in Italy, but abrogating a political agreement – although made by military men following local political advice – could well cause political belly-aching. In this case, the political or military backing initiated first at Klagenfurt then at Caserta on 14 May was essential to start the operation. Once started, despite superseding signals, it gathered its own momentum or as a brother officer of mine put it: 'V Corps got the bit between their teeth.'

AFHQ issued contradictory orders, Eighth Army emphasized undertakings already given, and on this basis all humanitarian issues were ignored until Alexander halted the operation on 4 June when he visited Austria 'on leave'.

The Cossack operation, on the other hand, was predominantly political, beginning with the Yalta agreement, continuing with the Soviet demand for certain Cossack officers to be handed over, followed by Macmillan's carte blanche advice and the culmination of 40,000 being transferred. Its only military aspect – Alexander's 16 May phrase 'clear the decks' – was the decongesting of V Corps area at the time of the approaching Tito crisis, which was resolved the following day. The intention was the planned and agreed evacuation to SHAEF which was backed by Churchill, Alexander and Eisenhower. Here Macmillan, by his own pen, comes forcefully into his own picture: he advised their being handed over and, contrary to his diary entry, they had somewhere to go, albeit he learnt this after his return to Caserta. Also, at no time did he mention screening. All Cossacks were equated as being Soviet citizens. Nevertheless, Alexander emphasized their military nature to Eisenhower, who responded similarly, thus placing them under the Geneva Convention as part of the German Army. So why were the Cossacks handed over? Superficially, because of another one of those local agreements to be honoured. More significantly, in pursuit of the Palmerstonian principle which maintained that the least risk for any country was always run by working closely with the power most feared. The prisoner-of-war factor came into it, of course: no one was sure whether all our POWs had left Russia. However, there is no doubt that Eden's brief to Macmillan in Athens after the Yalta conference was, among other matters: 'Do not upset the Russians.' It was the Resident Minister's duty to follow what he deemed to be Britain's national interests and the fate of the Cossacks was incidental.

It must also not be forgotten that Stalin had his own representative at AFHQ who was a member of the Supreme Allied Commander's advisory council: General Alexander Vasiliev. Did he do nothing? Did he receive or send no signals? It is far from improbable that the same message Stalin sent to Marshal Tolbukhin in Austria, 'I want the Cossacks!', was sent to Vasiliev. In which case it would have been conveyed to both the Resident Minister and the Supreme Commander, or their deputies. Whether this was the case, or not, two facts are incontrovertible: the Foreign office wished to return all Soviet citizens regardless of their will; and in Austria there was no attempt at serious screening. These two facts meant that military necessity or no — and there was none, or if initially there was, an evacuation to SHAEF had been agreed — the AFHQ instructions, of 14 May which were cancelled, then reinstated, fudged and reiterated, were effectively considered operative throughout, whether superseded or not, with the full support of Eighth Army and V Corps headquarters, whose local agreements were deemed to be binding; and they were determined to stand by their word with their Soviet opposite numbers.

As with the expulsions of the Yugoslavs, human factors did not enter into the matter of the Cossacks. Some were saved more by accident than design. Two formations were excluded en bloc, and were not handed over. The rest were transferred until the operation was stopped and screening introduced on Alexander's orders. Macmillan played a central role as the facts reveal. However, to imply that he represented metaphorically the dark side of Alexander's psyche — his MacMephistopheles, as it were — who padded around the corridors of Caserta or telephoned from his quarters giving sinister advice to Alexander, Robertson and whomever, is to create an unnecessary air of mystery. He advised the return of the Cossacks. He did not enlarge. He left it to the military — perhaps with a little prodding — to issue the right orders. Military action, on the Clausewitz principle, was being used as an extension of politics. If it was convenient to assume that all the Cossacks were Soviet citizens and to describe both them and the anti-communist Yugoslavs as 'Quislings' which was the case in many command communications, it was a description which reflected the state of mind of many at the time at that level. It is pointless to probe further as to who were or were not the high — or low — priests involved in the immolation of these victims on the sacrilegious altar of communism. 'Humanity' (to quote Nelson before Trafalgar) 'after victory' was not practised. Nor was the constabulary of the world in evidence. In other words, in one final phrase: if Ministers, whether Foreign or Resident, in the national interest as they perceived it, could (and can) 'advise' the Crown, they could certainly advise generals. It is evident, from the facts, they did. Compassion mistakenly has no place in real-politik.

APPENDIX IV

War Diary or Intelligence Summary

Month and Year May 1944 Unit H.Q. 1 Gds Bde

Place	Date	Hour	Summary of Events and Information
	24		Although the plan is laid on at maximum speed and 3 Gren Gds start moving at 1545 hrs, the congenstion of the tracks is too great to allow them to cover the necessary distance before nightfall. At 1800 hrs the town is clear but the bridge is not passable and 3 Gren Gds are ordered to harbour for the night with 16/5, about 4 miles short of the HITLER line. At 2200 hrs the Bde Comd holds a final conference at which orders are given for the adv of the whole Division tomorrow, with a view to breaking through beyond the MELFA RIVER with the same axis of adv through ARCE northwards to ISOLA.
	25		Bns are prepared to move from shortly after first light and Bde Tac H.Q. goes fwd at 0715 hrs to Div Tac H.Q. at 790185. 3 Gren Gds, closely followed by the other two bns start to move at 1300 hrs on the axis HEART ROUTE - SPADE ROUTE. Progress is extremely slow and it becomes evident during the afternoon that no part of the Division, except the Derby Yeomanry, which is already engaged on the MELFA RIVER, will be in time to intervene in the battle today. The 'O' Gps 3 Gren Gds are rushed fwd during the early part of the afternoon, and at 1600 hrs a conference is held at Tac Bde H.Q. 726206. The plan is for 3 Gren Gds to take over the R. MELFA in area 6925. From this point they are to patrol

fwd in order to prepare a way for a further adv of the Derby Yeo tomorrow. After recces have been completed this scheme is abandoned owing to shortage of time, and a bn of 11th Bde carry out the same function. Bns all concentrate during the afternoon in the area 7220 - 7219 with the armd regts close behind them. At 2115 hrs Bde Comd holds conference at which it is decided that after the patrolling by 5 Northants tonight it will be decided whether the Armd Bde or 1 Gds Bde lead in the adv towards ARCE tomorrow.

AQUINO
731217   25   (Cont) About 2100 hrs there is a sharp air raid over the Bde area. After dropping flares which showed up the concentration of vehicles the enemy dropped a score of bombs and many incendiaries. Casualties: 3 WG three killed, 20 wounded. Two 17 pdr A Tk guns under comd of the Bde were destroyed by the same enemy action.

R. MELFA   26
709251

During the morning the bridgehead over the river MELFA is slightly enlarged by units of the Derby Yeo, while 1 Gds Bde is brought up by the rough tracks to conc area a mile short of the river. At 1100 hrs 3 Gren Gds, mounted on the tanks of 16/5 L, move fwd and cross the river by the ford at 699259. The crossing is made without opposition, and the adv is at first rapid. By 1500 hrs 3 Gren Gds, now adv through very close country on foot, with the tks in close sp, report the line COLDRAGONE - CESE clear. They consolidate on this line for about an hr, and then push fwd behind the tks of 16/5 L, towards the pass at 6629. On approaching the highground on either side of the pass a few enemy M.G's open up and Route 6 which is the main axis of adv is heavily mortared and shelled. 3 Gren Gds lose about 20 casualties and it is decided to form a firm base on COLDRAGONE - CESE while the armour presd fwd. During the afternoon 3 WG, mounted on the tks of 2 L & B H move across the river MELFA and conc at 709255. The armour makes little headway in the very close country short of ARCE, and it becomes evident during the afternoon that the town will not fall today. The chief obstacles to the adv of 6 Armd Div is the absence of good rds leading to the MELFA river, and the closeness of the country limiting observation to about 100 yds. In the afternoon 3 Gren Gds remain fwd on the COLDRAGONE line with the other two bns uncommitted behind them. At 2130 hrs Bde Comd has conference at which it is announced that 3 WG will push fwd during the night ahead of 3 Gren Gds and make their way as far as possible towards ARCE. The night is very dark and the country scarcely allows them to move off Route 6, Intention to bring 3 Gren Gds into ARCE as soon as 3 WG report their arrival, and to pass 2 Coldm Gds with 17/21 L u/c through ARCE towards ISOLA when circumstances permit.

R. MELFA
709251   26   3 WG start to adv at 2300 hrs on the axis Route 6, towards ARCE.

27   By 0300 hrs 3 WG have reached the line PICCOLO - PROVIDERO. No opposition has been met up to this pt, but the bn is disorganised owing to the partial failure of wireless comns, and the Bde Comd gives permission for the bn to halt on the line they have reached. They halt on the low ground about 665290. The bn, with 2 Lothians under comd are then ordered to move up on to the heights either side of Route 6. When they began to adv the enemy shellfire harassed them considerably and on approaching the lower slopes of PICCOLO - PROVIDERO they came under intense mortar and machine gun fire. Owing to the closeness of the country the tanks are unable to leave the tracks and observation is restricted to about 100 yds, whereas the enemy on the heights themselves are comparatively better off. 3 WG attack on the two features is called off owing to the casualties suffered, and the extreme difficulty of cooperation with tanks. One coy is left at

679296, the remainder are withdrawn to area 672283. They remain here all day while the tks of 26 Armd Bde attempt unsuccessfully to make their way on to the two features, and to find a route behind them to approach ARCE from the S.W. 2 Coldm Gds remain concentrated area 690276 and 3 Gren Gds 692266. They suffered very slight casualties from enemy fire. In the afternoon a plan is evolved to attack PICCOLO and M. GRANDE by night. 3 Gren Gds to be directed on M. GRANDE and 2 Coldm Gds on PICCOLO. 3 WG make contact at 1830 hrs with R.F. of 8 Ind Div at ORIO, but no contact is made with 38 Bde advancing on the left of 6 Brit Armd Div.

712249   28   The attack by 3 Gren Gds reached pt 358 on M. GRANDE without much resistance, but owing to the difficulties of the country and stiffer opposition the north western end of the hill (639300) was never taken. 2 Coldm Gds est one coy on pt 321, 652295, and another on the eastern end of M. PICCOLO. Here too there was only slight enemy opposition. During the remainder of the night the enemy brought up his counterattack forces, and at 0800 hrs he assaulted our positions on pt 358. This enemy counterattack was put in in considerable strength, supported by intense mortar and arty fire, and 3 Gren Gds wre unable to hold their positions. Three coys were forced to withdraw down to the valley about 649285. The remaining coy remaining all day just beneath pt 358, unable to move owing to enemy fire. 2 enemy counterattacks were mounted against each of the two coys of 2 Coldm Gds. Pt 321 was held throughout the day. The enemy est small forces on the crest of the eastern end of M. PICCOLO, with our own tps just beneath the summit. During the day the enemy was harrassed by our fire, and it was decided, in view of the casualties suffered, that no attempt should be made to regain M. GRANDE, but that the whole of M. PICCOLO should be taken back from the enemy. In support of the bns were two armd regts of 26 Armd Bde, which though unable to move freely owing to the closeness of the country and the steepness of the hill, took up fire positions and successfully sniped at the enemy showing themselves on the crest. The only available counterattack force was 1 Coy 3 WG, which was passed through the right hand coy of 2 Coldm Gds at 1915 hrs to retake the eastern end of M. PICCOLO. This attack was successful. An enemy counterattack force formed up just before dark at 663295 was broken up by accurate arty bombardment. It was learnt by wireless intercept that the enemy intended to withdraw from the M. GRANDE and M. PICCOLO features during the night. Intense arty programme was laid on on their line of retreat towards ARCE, which was maintained during the whole of the night. At 0030 hrs a patrol from 3 Gren Gds reported that the summit of M. GRANDE was clear of enemy, a coy of 3 WG was prepared to follow up the retreating enemy u/c 2 L & B H at dawn. The three bns were very tired after 3 days continuous fighting.

29   At dawn the Lothian Force, with coy 3 WG under comd, advanced up Route Six towards ARCE, which was entered at 0845 hrs by the leading tks. On the capture of the town bns were withdrawn off M. PICCOLO to harbour areas just South of the feature, where they were put on 3 hrs notice to move. The coy 3 WG was withdrawn from u/c 2 Lothians at 1500 hrs. Bns spent the day in rest and in burying their dead. 10 prisoners were collected from the slopes of M. GRANDE and M. PICCOLO, who had remained behind in an exhausted or wounded condition, and over 90 German dead were counted on the southern slopes of M. PICCOLO alone. 6 Brit Armd Div has been promised a few days rest, handing over the pursuit of the enemy to 8 Ind Div.

660278   The remainder of 6 Brit Armd Div is withdrawn from the advance and concentrates between ARCE and CEPRANO. We are informed that we may expect 3 or 4 days out of battle to reorganise. Baths and Mobile Cinemas are laid on and reinforcements are brought up to Bns from the I.R.T.D. Lt. Col. E.J.B. Nelson takes over command of 3 Gren Gds from Lt. Col. G.A. Goschen. Major J.D. Buchanan, Gren Gds, arrives to take over appointment of Brigade Major from Major G.D. Chetwode, Coldm Gds, who goes to command a company in the 24th Guards Brigade.

668275   31   Bns are at 3 hrs notice to move but we are advised that 6 Brit Armd Div will probably not be needed until tomorrow, when they will be directed along a line parallel and North of Route Six. Major J.D. Buchanan takes over appointment of Brigade Major from Major G.D. Chetwode, and Captain F.P. Crowder Coldm Gds, leaves Bde HQ to take up appt of G 3(0) at Tac HQ Eighth Army.

[signed]   N. Nicolson, Capt. for
                                              Brigadier,
                            Commander 1st Guards Brigade

Cooper, Company Quartermaster Sergeant 'Duff', 78
Cori, 42
Coriano Ridge, 163, 164
Corps, British V, 96, 136, 138, 139, 140, 142-147, 162, 170-175
Corps, British X, 20, 126, 155, 157, 158, 159
Corps, British XIII, 57, 58, 66, 68, 96, 100, 101, 113, 119, 126, 139, 157, 158, 159, 162, 163, 165
Corps, Canadian I, 54-57, 60, 74, 96, 158, 159, 162, 163
Corps, French Expeditionary, 20, 45, 52, 53, 56, 74, 155-158, 162
Corps, German I Parachute, 133, 167
Corps, German XIV Panzer, 30, 54, 75, 87, 118, 126, 130, 133, 155, 156, 158
Corps, German LI Mountain, 29, 58, 69, 126, 130, 133
Corps, New Zealand II, 20, 28, 36, 87, 96, 156, 157, 162
Corps, Polish II, 2, 39, 45, 46, 49-54, 96, 107, 120, 126, 157-160, 162
Corps, U.S. II, 20, 53, 56, 101, 126, 155-158, 163-167
Corps, U.S. IV, 126, 164, 165
Corps, U.S. VI, 54, 56, 72
Cortona, 92
Cossacks, 135-141, 143-146, 152, 170-175
Cottom, Lieutenant D.G., 118
Cramm, Count von, 134
Croats, 138-142, 145, 171, 172, 173
Crowder, Captain F.P., 181
Cull, Major J.K., 92, 113, 114, 120-125, 127, 128, 129, 150
Cuttenberger, General, 164

Daniels, Lieutenant A.C., 17, 48
Danube, River, 161
Davidson, Company Quartermaster Sergeant, 121
Davies 08,. Company Sergeant Major W (later Drill Sergeant), 68
Davies, Drill Sergeant David, 23

Davies, Lieutenant J.H.G., 63, 67, 71, 151
Davies, Sergeant Emrys, 130
Davies-Scourfield, Lieutenant-Colonel D.G., 22, 24, 50, 59-63, 67, 71, 72, 75, 76
'D-Day' (see 'Overlord')
Denny, Lieutenant A.M., 66
Derbyshire Yeomanry, 56, 58, 130, 131, 140, 177
Desiderius, Abbot, 50
Devon Regiment, 91
Dicomano, 97, 163
'DISTONE' (District One), 173
Division, British Guards Armoured, 19
Division, British 1st Infantry, 101, 163, 165
Division, British 4th Infantry, 157, 158, 159
Division, British 4th Indian, 28, 36, 45, 52, 156
Division, British 6th Armoured, 19, 26, 56, 57, 59, 60, 65, 69, 79, 86, 87, 89, 96, 119, 120, 127, 128, 130, 142, 158, 159, 163
Division, British 8th Indian, 45, 53, 60, 66, 69, 96, 103, 105, 157, 158, 159
Division, British 56th, 119
Division, British 78th, 28, 101, 156, 157, 159, 165, 166
Division, Canadian 1st Infantry, 158, 167
Division, Canadian 5th Armoured, 56, 66, 68, 158
Division, German SS Mountain, 134
Division, German 1st Parachute, 29, 52, 157, 163
Division, German 4th Parachute, 164
Division, German 8th Mountain, 126
Division, German 16th SS Panzer Grenadier, 164, 165
Division, German 20th Luftwaffe Field, 167
Division, German 26th Panzer, 75, 164
Division, German 29th Panzer Grenadier, 163, 164
Division, German 44th Infantry, 101

Fonblanque, Major-General Edward de, 144

Fondouk, 114

Fontanalice, 107

Foreign Office, 137, 169, 170, 172, 174

Forli, 126, 163

Forlimpopoli, 127

Fornace, 75

Forsyth-Forrest, M.F., 5

Forte dei Marmi, 165

French Expeditionary Force (see Corps, French Expeditions)

Freyberg, General Sir B.C. (later Lord), 28, 29, 49, 156, 157

Frosinone, 58, 74, 158

Furlito, Monte, 20

Furse, Lieutenant G.R., 39

Futa Pass, 87, 94, 96, 162-165

Galantra River, 75

Garigliano River, 20, 30, 120, 155, 156

Gascoigne, Brigadier J. (later Major-General Sir Julian), 119

Gemmano, 163, 167

Geneva Convention, 140, 145, 169, 171, 174

George VI, King, 16, 89

Geviett, Lieutenant-Colonel, 145

Gestapo, 108

Ghedi (P.O.W. Camp), 134

Gibraltar, 2

Gibson-Watt, Major J.D. (later Lord), 23, 50, 67, 68, 88, 93, 97-100, 103, 105, 118, 130

Gibson-Watt, Lieutenant A.J., 107, 118, 131

Gilbey, Lieutenant M.N., 150

Goff, Major B.P.R., 25, 34, 39, 40, 48, 50, 54, 70, 78, 79, 80, 84, 86, 87, 88, 92, 93, 97, 114, 115

Goodwin, Sergeant Frank, 67

Gordonstoun, 153

Goschen, Lieutenant-Colonel G.A. (later Viscount), 66, 181

'Gothic Line', 87, 89, 90, 94, 97, 98, 152, 161-168

Gowrie, Colonel The Earl of, 150

Grande, Monte (Arce), 57, 58, 63, 66-69, 179, 180

Grande, Monte (Apennines), 166

Grant, Captain K.W., 40, 70

Graves, Robert, 61, 65, 74

Great Missenden, 151

Greece, 92

'Green Line', 161

Green, Major H.J.L. (later Brigadier), 21, 121

Greer, Captain B.R.T., 17, 24, 25, 26, 50, 62, 85, 113

Grenadier Guards, 5, 9, 14, 19, 23, 51, 58-62, 66, 67, 69, 75, 78, 79, 84, 87, 89, 90, 92, 101-106, 109, 119, 120, 123, 128, 130, 142

Gresham, Major J.F., 143

Greve, 107, 110, 113, 118

Grigg, Lieutenant J.E.P., 15

Grille, 90

Gröschke, Major, 57

Gruenther, General A.M., 119

Guards Chapel, 14, 17, 87, 88

Guards Club, 15, 150

Guards Depot, 6, 8, 76, 119, 150, 151

Gulland, Lieutenant H.M., 73

Gurkhas, 29, 52, 157

Gurney, Captain J.J., 25, 110, 113, 123

Gurney, Lieutenant-Colonel J.E., 75, 78, 87, 92, 93, 97, 99, 104, 106, 110, 114-117, 119, 123, 125, 127, 145

'Gustav Line', 20, 28, 52, 155

Hahn, Kurt, 153

Hall, Lieutenant S.A., 6, 10, 12, 17, 87, 89, 98

Hamlyn, Lieutenant G., 140

Hampshire Regiment, 21, 22, 23

'Hangman's Hill' (Point 435), 29, 31, 36, 157

Harding, Lieutenant-General Sir J. (later Field-Marshal Lord), 96, 119, 139, 155, 156, 161

Hardinge, Sir Alexander, 17

Hastings, Lieutenant P.R.H., 5

Haug, General, 133

Retallack, Lieutenant J.D.N. (later Lieutenant-Colonel), 61, 85
Rhys-Williams, Sir Rhys, Bt., 12
Rhys-Williams, Susan (later Lady Glyn), 12
Richards, Reverend T.M.H., 71, 113, 131, 132
Rifle Brigade, 128, 129
Rimini, 20, 87, 107, 162, 163, 167
Roberts 31, Guardsman J., 55
Robertson, Major-General (later General Sir Brian), 138, 139, 140, 170-173, 175
Robinson, Corporal, 129
Rocca d'Arce, 68
Rocca Janula (see Castle Hill)
Rollo, Captain D.I., 104
Romanov, Grand Duke Vladimir, 87
Rome, 20, 36, 42, 51, 53, 58, 72-78, 86, 87, 90, 97, 109, 110, 152, 157, 160
Romney, Lieutenant-Colonel the Earl of, 8
Roncesvalles, 59
Roosevelt, President Franklin, 73
Rose-Price, Lieutenant-Colonel R.C., 78, 127, 128, 130, 132, 140, 146, 150
Rosegg, 136
Rosenbach, 140, 141, 143
Rossi-Scotti, Count, 113
Route 4, 75
Route 6 (Via Casilina) 36, 41, 42, 53, 54, 56, 58, 59, 61, 62, 68
Route 9 (Via Emilia), 93, 96, 126, 161, 163, 165, 166, 167
Route 65 (Via Cassia), 94, 162, 165, 166
Route 6620 (Sette Valley), 120
Rowley, Captain J.F. (later Sir Joshua, Bt.), 79, 90, 109
Royal Air Force, 161
Royal Army Medical Corps, 91
Royal Army Service Corps, 74, 79, 139
Royal Artillery, 2, 43, 67
Royal Engineers, 53, 90, 108, 113, 130, 158, 162, 167
Royal Military College, 9
Royal Navy, 53
Rundstedt, Field-Marshal Gerd von, 153
'Rupee', 130

Russell, Major-General, 159, 163
Russian Imperial Cossack Bodyguard, 137
Rutzen, Major the Baron J.F.F. de, 107

Sacco, River, 42, 56
Saint Benedict, 55
Saint James's Palace, 14, 16, 39
Saint Philip Neri, 61
Salerno, 92, 119
Salivetti, Henrico, 109, 110
San Benedetto, 128, 130
San Marco ('Tulip'), 79, 80, 83, 84, 85, 87, 111, 117, 129, 152
San Martino Delfino, 79
Sandhurst, 6, 9, 10, 11, 82
Sandys, Major M.E.M., 66
Sant' Angelo, 158
Sant' Appollinare, 110
Santerno, River, 100, 107, 126
Sassoleone, 110
Schellowitz, Major-General von, 133
Schreiber, General Sir Edmund, 125
Schulenberg, Major Werner Graf von, 57
Schultz, Colonel Karl, 57
Schultz, General F., 132
Schuster, Lieutenant A.E.L, 22
Schweinitz, Lieutenant-Colonel von, 132
Schwerin, Colonel-General Graf von, 134
Scots, Guards, 6, 19, 66, 67, 92, 108, 119, 120, 121
Seager, Lieutenant G.E., 98
Secchio Valley, 165
Selkirk, 150, 151
Senger Barrier ('Adolf Hitler Line'), 54, 159, 176
Senger und Etterlin, Colonel-General Frido von, 30, 54, 62, 72, 78, 80, 87, 121, 130, 131, 133, 134, 153, 156, 158, 162, 166, 167
Senio Valley, 101, 108, 124, 126, 127, 168
Serbs (see Chetnicks)
Sette Valley, 120
S.D. (Sicherheitdienst/Intelligence Service), 121

193